The Child's Song

To Abigail,
Colleague and
friend.

Steve Orr

May, 1995

Also by Donald Capps
from Westminster John Knox Press

The Poet's Gift:
Toward the Renewal of Pastoral Care

The Child's Song

The Religious Abuse
of Children

Donald Capps

 Westminster John Knox Press
Louisville, Kentucky

Dedicated to James E. Dittes
Who Upholds by Letting Be

Book design by Drew Stevens
Cover design by Tanya R. Hahn

First edition

Published by Westminster John Knox Press
Louisville, Kentucky

This book is printed on acid-free paper that meets the
American National Standards Institute Z39.48 standard. ∞

PRINTED IN THE UNITED STATES OF AMERICA

95 96 97 98 99 00 01 02 03 04 — 10 9 8 7 6 5 4 3 2 1

Library of Congress Cataloging-in-Publication Data

Capps, Donald, date.
   The child's song : the religious abuse of children / Donald Capps. — 1st ed.
      p.   cm.
   Includes bibliographical references and index.
   ISBN 0-664-25554-X (alk. paper)
   1. Children—Religious life. 2. Family—Religious life. 3. Child abuse—Religious aspects—Christianity. 4. Parenting—Religious aspects—Christianity. 5. Shame—Religious aspects—Christianity. 6. Child rearing—Religious aspects—Christianity.   I. Title.
BV4571.2.C35   1995
261.8'32—dc20   94-27462

Contents

Acknowledgments

Grateful acknowledgment for permission to reprint copyrighted material is made to the following:

Ecco Press, for "Lost Love," "Animals," "A Fable," "Matins," and "Vespers" from *The Wild Iris* by Louise Glück, copyright © 1992 by Louise Glück.

HarperCollins Publishers, Inc., for "Mother's Day," "How It Is with Family," and "Scars" from *An Oregon Message* by William Stafford, copyright © 1987 by William Stafford; and "Young" from *Passwords* by William Stafford, copyright © 1991 by William Stafford.

Houghton Mifflin Company, for "The Old Moon" from *The Avenue Bearing the Initial of Christ into the New World* by Galway Kinnell, copyright 1953, 1954, © 1955, 1959, 1960, 1961, 1963, 1964, 1970, 1971, 1974 by Galway Kinnell, all rights reserved; and "The Still Time" and "Two Set Out on Their Journey" from *Mortal Acts, Mortal Words* by Galway Kinnell, copyright © 1980 by Galway Kinnell, all rights reserved.

Johns Hopkins University Press, for "Turning in Bed" and "Even the Weariest River" from *Fiddle Lane* by Thomas Carper, 1991.

Alfred A. Knopf, Inc., for "Now I Lay Me," "The Blue Dress," "After 37 Years My Mother Apologizes for My Childhood," and "Late Poem to My Father" from *The Gold Cell* by Sharon Olds, copyright © 1987 by Sharon Olds.

Liveright Publishing Corporation and W. W. Norton & Company Ltd., for "if there are any heavens my mother will (all by herself) have" from *Complete Poems, 1904–1962* by e. e. cummings, edited by George J. Firmage, copyright © 1931, 1959, 1991 by the Trustees for the e. e. cummings Trust.

Margaret Nemerov, for "Remorse for Time" from *The Collected Poems of Howard Nemerov* by Howard Nemerov, University of Chicago Press, 1977.

New Directions Publishing Corp., for " . . . That Passeth All Understanding" from *Oblique Prayers* by Denise Levertov, copyright © 1981 by Denise Levertov; "The Opportunity" from *Evening Train* by Denise Levertov, copyright © 1992 by Denise Levertov; and "True Confessional" by Lawrence Ferlinghetti from *Endless Life: Selected Poems*, copyright © 1981 by Lawrence Ferlinghetti.

W. W. Norton & Company, Inc., and the author, for "Collecting Future Lives" from *Between Angels*, Poems by Stephen Dunn, copyright © 1989 by Stephen Dunn; and "Regardless" from *Landscape at the End of the Century*, Poems by Stephen Dunn, copyright © 1991 by Stephen Dunn.

Princeton University Press, for quotation from *Fear and Trembling/Repetition*, 2 vols., by Søren Kierkegaard, edited and translated by V. and Edna H. Hong. Copyright © 1983 by Howard and Edna Hong.

Dorothy Stafford, for "Adults Only," "A Gesture toward an Unfound Renaissance," "Vacation Trip," "Vocation," "At the Grave of My Brother," and "Thinking for Berky," from *Stories That Could Be True* by William Stafford; "Learning to Like the New School," "Remembering Brother Bob," "One Time" from *A Glass Face in the Rain* by William Stafford.

My special thanks to John Capps for preparing the index with his usual competence and aplomb, and to Jeffries Hamilton and others at Westminster Press for seeing the book into print. *The Child's Song* is a small token of gratitude to James E. Dittes for his continuing support and friendship.

Introduction

In 1991 I gave the presidential address at the Society for the Scientific Study of Religion meeting in Pittsburgh on the topic "Religion and Child Abuse: Perfect Together." The phrase "Perfect Together" is well known to those of us who live in New Jersey. A former governor popularized the phrase through television commercials extolling the state's virtues—its beaches, its business opportunities, its standard of living, and so forth. At the conclusion of each of these commercials, he would say, "New Jersey and You: Perfect Together."

Given New Jersey's reputation for being somewhat less livable than, say, Oregon or Colorado, it isn't surprising that many New Jerseyans took offense at the idea that they and New Jersey made a perfect couple. Yet, a little self-examination also confronted these same protesters with the unhappy truth that, being who we are, we deserve this identification with New Jersey. In the same way, I suggested, the title of my address, "Religion and Child Abuse: Perfect Together," might offend, but this does not mean that it isn't so.

The substance of what I said in my address that night is incorporated in chapter 3 of this book, so I will not discuss here in these introductory comments what I had to say about religion and child abuse being "perfect together." Rather, I want to comment on the very mixed response my address evoked that evening, since I believe that this response reveals just how deep and threatening is the topic of religion and child abuse. As I got into the substance of my address, I was struck by how quiet the room became. I had never before experienced such quiet as this. This was no tribute to my skills as a public speaker, for I am not a trained public speaker, and, in fact, I have much respect for those seminary students who, like myself, somehow managed to avoid courses in speech communication. Rather, it was my topic of child abuse—and the suggestion that religion legitimates and promotes child abuse—that struck a chord with many who were gathered there, and, as I was later to learn, angered many others.

When I completed my address, I looked over at the person who had introduced me, a woman whom I have always admired as a tough-minded, no-nonsense type of scholar, and there were tears in her eyes. Then as I came down off the podium, some fifteen or twenty persons came up to me, and, one by one, began giving me brief accounts of how religious practices and ideas had caused them great suffering and anguish as children. Several thanked me for speaking that evening about a subject that touched them in a very personal way. As I had to remind myself later, they were established professors and scholars at a meeting of the society for "the scientific study of religion." There was nothing objective—coolly scientific—about their response to what I had said. They spoke from the heart, and I felt their pain as I listened.

I left the lecture hall feeling much as I imagine athletes feel when they have won an important but physically and emotionally draining game. The response I received from those who came up to congratulate me and to share their stories with me was almost overwhelming. It was all I could do to keep from crying too: tears born of sadness but of triumph too.

But then the bubble burst. I got on the hotel elevator to return to my room and the person who rode up with me said, "That was a pretty good lecture tonight, but I have to disagree with your interpretation of Jesus. You didn't get that out of the Bible." I answered, "Well, I know what I said about Jesus is controversial, but I relied on a very fine book by a first-rate biblical scholar. I didn't just make it all up." The next morning, I was accosted in the hotel lobby by an acquaintance of long-standing, a person who had bent my ear on many occasions. I liked him and believed that he liked me. This time, though, it was different between us: "You sounded angry last night, and some of the things you said were downright blasphemous." When I heard the word "angry," I thought immediately of how this word is often used against feminists. It took me by surprise, since I didn't feel angry the previous evening and could not recall feeling angry in the process of writing the address. A certain sadness for us as children was, I believe, rather prevalent in the writing process, but anger? I didn't really think so. His use of the word "angry" was mainly puzzling to me. But the word "blasphemous." That was a different story. Now I *was* angry. How could anyone say that what I had said the night before was blasphemous? Who or what had I blasphemed? And what a strange word to be used in reference to a lecture at a meeting of a society for the scientific study of religion. When I get angry, I usually find myself unable to say anything. In this case it didn't matter, because he stalked off before I had a chance to respond anyway.

Later that morning a journalist representing a denominational magazine asked me to mail her a copy of my address and to enclose a photo, because she would like to write a feature story on what I said. As it turned out, however, the article never appeared. The topic, I assume, was too controversial. Shortly after my address was published, I received a long appreciative letter from a sociologist who has been doing empirical studies of the relationship between religion and the abuse of children. He reported that whenever he fails to find a positive relationship between religion and child abuse (i.e., when his study fails to prove that religion contributes to child abuse), he has no difficulty publishing his results, but when a study does show that religion contributes directly to child abuse, the article is usually rejected for publication. In my case, my presidential address was published, for it is the custom of the Society for the Scientific Study of Religion to publish presidential addresses in its official journal. Although the editor did not at any time suggest he would not publish it—on the contrary, he published it immediately—I did wonder how it would have fared had it gone through the normal review process. Would it have been judged scientific enough? Would a reviewer have said that the article was too "angry" or too "blasphemous" for a scholarly journal that aims to be scientific, and thus objective and dispassionate?

What is going on here? Why does the suggestion of a connection between religion and child abuse evoke such disparate reactions, ranging from deeply felt stories of self-revelation to rude behavior toward those who note this connection, to reluctance on the part of magazine and journal editors to publish the work of those who have evidence that there is a fundamental, not just accidental, connection between the two? Published stories about priests and other clergy who sexually abuse children are becoming increasingly commonplace. Such stories, however, often include quotations from church officials who suggest that this is primarily an individual problem, as there are always a few "bad apples" in every profession. Occasionally, there will be an acknowledgment that the institutional church and its policies are partly to blame; in the case of priests who sexually molest children, the policy of having a celibate clergy is often cited. Yet in none of these articles on the priests' sexual abuse of children is there any discussion of the powerful association of religion itself and child abuse. Never is there mention of the possibility that religion qua religion is inherently, fundamentally disposed toward the abuse of children, that children are at risk not because someone has made a travesty of religion, but because religion has been faithfully adhered to. What if religion qua religion is inherently disposed toward the abuse of children? What if it is not just a matter of a few bad apples in every basket, or just a matter of institutional policies that might be blamed for contributing to the problem, but that religion qua religion places children at risk of being the subjects of abuse? This is the issue with which this book is fundamentally concerned.

I do not, however, view this book as a mere diatribe against religion, for I also believe, as I said in my address that night, that religion has been a protector of children as well. Furthermore, the purpose of this book is not merely to be critical of religion for what it does to children but also to be genuinely helpful to readers who have suffered abuse as children and now, as adults, are struggling to become whole again. While much of this book is concerned with exploring the problem of the relationship between religion and child abuse, it is also concerned with helping readers to experience an inner wholeness, or, if this is being too presumptuous on my part, it seeks to direct readers to those inner resources where the promise of wholeness lies.

In chapter 1, I provide a brief summary of the writings of Alice Miller on the theme of child abuse. Miller is certainly the most prolific author of our times on the problem of child abuse, and her views on the nature of the suffering that such abuse causes—primarily as threat to the innermost self of the child—is one with which I am deeply sympathetic.

In chapter 2, I focus on the beatings that Augustine suffered as a child, and explore his attempt, as an adult, to provide a theological rationale for these beatings. I also focus on his treatment of his own son, showing how he, as an adult, inflicted much the same shaming onto Adeodatus as he was subjected to as a child. Here, too, the rationale for his shaming of Adeodatus was theological.

In chapter 3, I focus on the religious roots of child abuse, noting that religion is abusive in two fundamental ways: It supports the abuse of children by providing theological legitimation for the physical punishment of children, and it more directly abuses children by promoting beliefs and ideas that are inherently tormenting to children. In support of the first point, I rely heavily on the work of Philip Greven, who, in his book *Spare the Child*, explores the theological legitimations for parents' and other adults' physical abuse of children. In support of the second point, I focus on certain Christian beliefs that directly torment children or that justify adults' adoption of a detached, emotionally distanced view of childhood traumas. It is this argument that evoked the charge of blasphemy.

In chapter 4, I focus on the effects of biblical literalism in the sanctioning of child abuse. Since the letter to the Hebrews provides the most frequently cited biblical support for such abuse, I discuss this letter as the work of an adult who was abused as a child and then provides a theological rationale for such abuse as an adult. In this chapter, I challenge the appeal that is made to the Bible in support of abusive treatment of children on the grounds that the author of Hebrews was unable to emancipate himself from the vicious cycle of child abuse.

In chapter 5, I continue my exploration of theological legitimations of child abuse, focusing specifically on the concept or doctrine of sacrifice. I use Alice Miller's own interpretation of the biblical story of Abraham and Isaac to explore this idea of sacrifice, supplementing her views on the story with a consideration of Søren Kierkegaard's theological defense of Abraham in *Fear and Trembling*. Thus, in this chapter, I challenge the idea that children are to be given up to God, an idea that influences parents (consciously or unconsciously) to mistreat their children, and that also leads children to believe that mistreatment at the hands of their parents is not to be resisted, but accepted as their due or fate in life.

In chapter 6, I continue the preceding chapter's exploration into the relationship of a son and a father in which the son assumes that it is his fate in life to be sacrificed, but I shift the focus to Jesus, and explore the reasons why Jesus viewed God as a father and why Christianity has understood Jesus' death as a sacrifice his heavenly Father required of him. I seek to differentiate these two beliefs, that is, Jesus' view of God as father and the view prevalent in Christianity that Jesus is the sacrificial victim. Thus, in this chapter, I continue my critique of the sacrificial concept as a theological rationale for the suffering of children at the hands of adults.

In sum, chapters 4–6 elaborate on my argument in chapter 3 that theological ideas are directly responsible for the unnecessary, gratuitous suffering of children. I do not want these chapters to be understood as an indictment of all theology, for I am convinced that, for every theological idea that is responsible for the suffering and torment of children, there is a theological idea that is the source of comfort, support, and empowerment of children. I believe that the Gospels, which focus on the life and teachings of Jesus, are the source of pain and suffering on the one hand, and comfort and support on the other. The problem is in learning to differentiate the one from the other. This task of differentiation is nothing new, however, for this is precisely the problem that Martin Luther sought to solve with his observation that the Bible both condemns and consoles, judges and reassures. His struggle, one that was lifelong, was to believe the words that consoled and reassured, and to use these words against those that condemned and judged. My project here is, in that sense, quite "Lutheran," as I am attempting, like Luther, to differentiate "gospel" from "law," to privilege those features of the Bible, wherever in the Bible they may be found, that offer reassurance and solace, and to downplay those features of the Bible, wherever *they* may be found, that judge and condemn. This means, necessarily, that some features of the Bible, including some aspects of the Gospels, need to be put in their place, circumscribed by those that envision a better, happier reality, that speak a higher and a deeper truth about life with others and life with the One whose love is unconditional.

Chapter 7 is my attempt to envision this new life—the life of grace, of reconciliation, of true happiness. For this envisioning, I use the image of the garden—an image first introduced in chapter 6—but elaborated here as the imaginative setting in which healing is most likely to have a chance to come about. I also use the image of the child's song, the song that so often turns into a cry and is then eventually extinguished. I use the child's song as a metaphor for that which was lost in childhood as we became troubled and tormented souls, and as we began to create, as a necessary reaction to our pain, this false, defensive, and defended self that we have carried with us ever since, and which has all too often displaced our God-given self. Our God-given self, the self of our true desires and the self that is the window to our innermost soul, is placed at risk by childhood abuse. Yet, it can come back to life again, as it is self-regenerative, if we are able to open ourselves to the gracefulness of the garden and to place ourselves in its loving hands, allowing it to nurture to life what has lain dormant these many years. To reawaken the child's song within us, I turn in this chapter to poets who have written about the hidden sufferings of children, about our resentments of our well-intentioned parents for the pain they inflicted on us, and about the complex fate that we have shared with our sisters and brothers, either as we stood helplessly by as they suffered or as we took our sufferings out on them. I am convinced that it is by confronting these sufferings, by allowing them to return to consciousness, that we will again find the song that was muffled so many years ago. Poets, in remembering their own childhoods, help us to remember ours.

In chapter 8, I address the problem of childrearing, offering a different theological frame for viewing the inevitable conflicts that arise between parents and children from the one that Philip Greven discusses so thoroughly in *Spare the Child*. He explores and exposes the abuses resulting from the theological view, predominant in the United States, and subscribed to by theological liberals and conservatives alike, that children are inherently rebellious and so it is incumbent upon parents (acting as instruments of God) to bend or even break the child's natural will so as to conform it to the will of God. In this view, sin is defined as rebellion. Against this view, I subscribe to the view that sin is best understood as alienation, both from others and within the self, and that such alienation is caused by shame more than it is caused by guilt. Shame, after all, is the lasting legacy of child abuse. My biblical text for this alternative theological frame is the familiar story of the Garden of Eden, which I interpret as a shame text. Thus, the book ends where alienation is said to have begun, in the Garden of Eden. Yet, unlike the story, I refuse to accept that the garden is irrevocably lost, for it continues to live in the inner landscape of our lives. It is here, now, and inviolable. If we can be taken out of it, no one can take it from us, for it lives in the innermost core of the self, in the soul, which is the very locus of life itself. Here grows the tree of life and beneath it flows the rivers of regeneration.

Alice Miller relates the following personal experience in *Banished Knowledge*:[1] One day in early December, while walking through a forest in Switzerland, she encountered a celebration. A number of families had come with their children to the edge of the forest where they lit candles in anticipation of an appearance of Saint Nicholas. By tradition, young mothers inform

Saint Nicholas prior to the celebration about the behavior of their children. So, when he appears, he carries with him a big book that lists precisely the vices and the virtues of each child. This enables him to speak to each of them as if he were all-knowing.

When Saint Nicholas appeared, there was a hush, and then he began to call on the children, one by one, chiding them for their misdeeds and praising them for their good deeds. Vera was called on first: "Where is little Vera?" Vera, a small girl, barely two years old, with a trusting, expectant look, came forward. She gazed with candid curiosity into the saint's face. He spoke to her:

> I must say, Vera, Saint Nicholas is not at all pleased that you don't always like to put away your toys by yourself. Mommy is too busy. You're old enough to understand that when you've finished playing you must put away your toys and also that you should share them like a good girl with your little brother and not keep everything for yourself. Let's hope next year will see an improvement. Saint Nicholas will be looking into your room to see whether you've improved. But he has also found out some good things: You help your mother to clear the table after meals, and you can play nicely by yourself and sometimes draw pictures too, without Mommy having to sit beside you. I like that very much, for Mommy is too busy to sit with you all the time; don't forget she also has your little brother and your daddy to care for, and she needs a Vera who can do things on her own. Well now, Vera, have you also learned a little song for Saint Nicholas? (14)

Vera stood there too scared to utter a sound, so her mother sang the song that Vera had prepared for Saint Nicholas. Vera was given a small package from his sack.

Next to be called on was little Stefan, who was about two and a half years old. As he came forward, Saint Nicholas addressed him:

> Well, well, Stefan, you're still using a pacifier; you're much too big for that, you know. If you brought along your pacifier you might as well give it to Saint Nicholas right away. (At this suggestion, the other children burst into laughter.) No, you haven't got it with you? Then tonight you will put it on your bedside table or give it to your little brother. You don't need a pacifier anymore, you're much too big for that. Saint Nicholas has also noticed that you're not always a good little boy at the table, always interrupting when the grown-ups are talking; but you must let the grown-ups talk, you're still much too small to be constantly interrupting the others. (15)

Miller noticed that little Stefan seemed on the verge of tears. He stood there looking thoroughly scared, shamed in front of all the others. So she intervened in his behalf. She said to Saint Nicholas, "A minute ago you were telling him he's too big for a pacifier, and now you say he's too small to speak up at table. Stefan himself will know very well when he no longer needs his pacifier." Immediately, some of the mothers interrupted her. One mother said, "Here it's up to Saint Nicholas to say what Stefan must do." So Miller held her peace, and the celebration continued as it had begun, leaving *her* to suffer in *her* quiet anguish. "No one," she writes, "noticed the cruelty, no one saw the stricken faces (although the fathers were constantly taking flash pictures). No one noticed that each of the reprimanded children ended up not being able to remember the words of the little poem or song; that they couldn't even find their voices, could hardly say thank you; that none of the children smiled spontaneously, that they all looked petrified with fear."

This episode beautifully illustrates the problem with which this book is concerned: the hidden suffering of children, and the role that religion, and especially theology, plays in legitimating the suffering. What these small children experienced was shame, and, as a consequence of the shaming, they were reduced to silence, unable to sing the songs or to recite the poems they had prepared for this occasion. This book is concerned, however, not only to illumine the problem of children's suffering—and the role of religion in it— but also to make a restorative contribution, enabling those who were si- lenced as children to recover their song, and thus to experience the re- evocation of the spirit and soul that were crushed so many years ago.

This book is concerned with reconciliation. As the Saint Nicholas cele- bration reveals, the hidden suffering of children is instigated by parents who intend no harm. The very fact that they mean no harm makes it that much more difficult for us, as adults, to get in touch with the hurt we experienced as children. As Miller has often pointed out in her writings, we tend to take our parents' side and to offer explanations for why they did what they did, and there is never any lack of explanations: They were only doing what their own parents had done, or they had heavy responsibilities at the time and were under great emotional stress, or they were concerned that their chil- dren grow up to be responsible, productive adults, or that some of us hap- pened to be unusually difficult to handle. Yet the fact that we can explain our parents' actions toward us cannot alter the fact that suffering occurred, and that they were its primary agents. The little Veras and Stefans of this world will grow up, and, if they are honest with themselves, will realize that they harbor resentments toward their parents for the times when they suffered unnecessarily. Explanations or rationalizations for their parents' behavior are not enough. Reconciliation is also needed, but, for many of us, reconciliation through honest confrontation is often impractical, either because our par- ents are deceased or because talking it out will only cause greater misunder- standing and hurt. Guided by the poets, I envision a different form of reconciliation with parents.

The Saint Nicholas celebration also points to the fact that brothers and sisters are often used as counterplayers in this "vicious power play at the expense of the children." Vera was asked to consider her mother's need to attend to her little brother's care, and Stefan was asked to give up his pacifier to his little brother. Both were told to subordinate their own desires in deference to the needs and interests of their siblings. The consequence of this appeal is likely that Vera and Stefan will come to resent their little brothers and may well carry such resentment into adulthood. Reconciliation will therefore need to extend to brothers and sisters, but, here again, while honest give-and-take is perhaps more practical than with parents, where this is not the case, the poets envision other ways for reconciliation to occur.

This, then, is a book about the hidden sufferings of children, the role that religion plays in the legitimation of these sufferings, and the things that we can do as adults to restore the spirit that was crushed so many years ago by well-intentioned adults. This is not a book that is concerned with counseling adult victims of child abuse nor is it primarily a book for adults whose parents were deliberately and systematically abusive. It is a book for the vast majority of us whose experience of childhood suffering is troubling because we were *not* the victims of systematic abuse, and yet, somehow, our spirits were crushed within us, crushed under the weight of what Miller calls the "poisonous pedagogies" that informed our parents' childrearing practices, pedagogies that they inherited from their own parents or were preached by the childrearing experts of their day. But neither am I primarily concerned to expose and critique such pedagogies, for this has already been done by Miller and others. My concern here is with the child who, for whatever reason, lost the ability to sing the song or recite the poem that he or she had prepared. I am concerned with an important nonevent—with what was supposed to happen at the edge of the woods that evening, but was preempted by another agenda.

This book is written from the conviction that what did not happen that evening may yet happen: The child's song will yet be sung, and, this time, it will be a song the children sing as with a single voice.

Listen! The forest is still. Saint Nicholas and the parents have gone away, receding into the darkness of the night. But the children remain. They take one another's hands. They look at one another. They begin to sing. At first hesitantly, their voices trembling, and then more confidently. Each a different song. But somehow their voices blend. Their melodies coalesce. The children are singing. Yes, the children are singing. Only, they are not children anymore. They are adults, like you and me, who have recovered the song of childhood, and are neither afraid nor ashamed to sing it.

I
The Loss of Innocence

1

Alice Miller on
"the Mutilated Soul"

In the Saint Nicholas ceremony described in the introduction, Alice Miller had the courage to speak out during the ceremony and to challenge what the adults were doing to the children. The adults, of course, viewed her speaking out as rude and interruptive, and told her that it was not her business to speak up, because in this context, Saint Nicholas is in charge.

For the past twenty-five years, Miller has been speaking out against child abuse. She is best known for her many books on the subject, but she has also appeared on television shows, been interviewed for magazine articles, and given lectures to many professional organizations and civic groups. Several of her books report on her public role as a champion of the child, as she will often refer in them to a public appearance in which she was challenged or criticized for her views. But she also includes positive testimonials from persons who have read her books and have written to her to tell her how profoundly helpful her books have been in helping them to realize that they were victims of child neglect or abuse, and to understand that these experiences had caused them to reject themselves as children. Only now, many years later, are they beginning to become reconciled to the child that they disowned, and they credit Miller with having initiated this process through her writings.

For many years of her life, Miller was a psychoanalyst who practiced in her native Switzerland. In her first three books, *The Drama of the Gifted Child*, *For Your Own Good*, and *Thou Shalt Not Be Aware*, which appeared in German in the late 1970s and early 1980s, she believed that her views on child abuse were not incompatible with psychoanalysis. By the time her more recent books, including *The Untouched Key*, *Banished Knowledge*, and *Breaking Down the Wall of Silence*, appeared in German in the late 1980s and early 1990s, her break with psychoanalysis had occurred, and in these books she sets forth her view that psychoanalysis and the recovery of childhood trauma are incompatible. In these books she asserts that psychoanalysis inhibited her from recognizing her own abuse as a child and from recognizing such abuse in the lives of her patients.

In this chapter I will discuss each of her major books, focusing on the book's key issues or themes, and identifying what distinguishes it from her previous writings on the subject of child abuse. Although some readers of Miller's work consider it repetitive, as it is always concerned with the same central theme, I do not agree with this criticism of her work. Each book is unique unto itself, and each book takes a fresh approach to the subject. I also believe that her steadfastness in writing about this topic, and *only* this, is a peculiar strength, not a liability of her work, as it illustrates the truth of the title of one of Søren Kierkegaard's works, *Purity of Heart Is to Will One Thing*.[1] Miller lives for the eradication of child abuse, and believes that it could in fact be eradicated if one generation of humans were enlightened enough not to do it, for child abuse is a learned behavior—one learned from our parents—and could therefore, in her view, become one of the many behaviors that humans, in the course of their evolution, have managed to unlearn. Admittedly, this viewpoint sounds very utopian, and Miller is not naïve about the fact that child abuse is so deeply entrenched. But she sees no necessary reason for its persistence and prevalence (there are other mammals that do not abuse their offspring) and it is her hopefulness, if not optimism, that is one of the impressive features of her work. This tone of hopefulness for humanity is one reason that individual readers of her books have been personally helped by them, for if she believes there is no reason in principle why child abuse could not be eradicated from human society, then surely the fact that *I* was neglected or abused as a child need not continue to have such a destructive influence on my life as an adult. There must be something that I can do about it.

The Drama of the Gifted Child

In her first book, *The Drama of the Gifted Child: The Search for the True Self* (originally published as *Prisoners of Childhood*),[2] Miller uses recent psychoanalytic theories of the narcissistic self as a perspective from which to address the matter of child abuse. She begins this book with the observation that "we live in a culture that encourages us not to take our own suffering seriously, but rather to make light of it or even to laugh about it. What is more, this attitude is regarded as a virtue, and many people—of whom I used to be one—are proud of their lack of sensitivity toward their own fate and particularly toward their fate as a child" (xi). Miller uses the psychoanalytic concept of narcissism to explain this disregard for one's own suffering, especially sufferings experienced during childhood. Noting that in popular usage narcissism means being "in love with oneself," or "always thinking of oneself," or "egocentrism," Miller shows that our very fear that a child may become narcissistic (as popularly understood) often has the effect of making a child narcissistic (in the psychoanalytic or clinical understanding of the term).

Parents are often convinced that they must teach their children not to be self-centered—always thinking of themselves—so they work hard to ensure that their child will not become spoiled, but will instead learn "very early to share, to give, to make sacrifices, and to be willing to 'do without' and forego gratification" (xviii). This, she argues, occurs long before the child is capable of a real willingness to "do without." In her view, a child who has been allowed to be egoistic, greedy, and asocial long enough (one who, in psychoanalytic language, has been permitted a "healthy narcissism") will develop a spontaneous pleasure in sharing and giving. But a child who is not allowed to have a "healthy narcissism" first may never experience the pleasure of sharing and giving, as such altruism is always felt to be at one's own expense. Requiring very small children to sacrifice for others not only makes them resentful toward those in whose behalf they are sacrificing their own desires, but also causes them to turn against the self that entertains such desires. As Miller points out:

> The usually accepted judgmental contrast between self-love and object-love, and their portrayal as opposites, springs from naive and uncritical usage in our everyday language. Yet, a little reflection soon shows how inconceivable it is really to love others (not merely to need them), if one cannot love oneself as one really is. And how could a person do that if, from the very beginning, he has had no chance to experience his true feelings and to learn to know himself? (xix–xx)

Ironically, narcissism of the unhealthy variety is borne of such self-denial, for, as recent psychoanalytic theory holds, the narcissist is one who has replaced the true self with a false, conforming self, and the conforming self is noteworthy for its lack of feeling both toward others and also toward self. Miller writes:

> The phenomenology of narcissistic disturbance is well known today. On the basis of my experience, I would think that its etiology is to be found in the infant's early emotional adaptation. . . . One serious consequence of this early adaptation is the impossibility of consciously experiencing certain feelings of his own (such as jealousy, envy, anger, loneliness, impotence, anxiety) either in childhood or later in adulthood. (9)

In this effort to be a "good child," the children developed the art of not experiencing feelings, for to reveal their true feelings risked the loss of their mother's love. They became especially adept at forgoing the expression of their own distress, because they learned very early that this only contributed to their mother's own distress, usually because she, too, had been narcissistically deprived as a child. Instead, this "good child" learned to accommodate herself to her mother's needs, an accommodation that usually leads to the formation of a false self. Expression of this false self meets her mother's need to view herself as a good mother, because a good child reflects favorably on her parents.

In *The Drama of the Gifted Child*, Miller is especially interested in the link between narcissism and depression. While some narcissists are able to deal with failure by availing themselves of grandiose defenses, most will become depressed when they are unable to live up to the demands and expectations placed on them by their false selves. For Miller, the true opposite of depression is not gaiety or absence of pain, but vitality, especially the freedom to experience spontaneous feelings, including not just "good" and "beautiful" feelings, but the whole range of human experience, including envy, jealousy, rage, disgust, greed, despair, and mourning. But such freedom cannot be achieved if the childhood roots are cut off, for this is where the capacity for feeling was originally stifled. Miller views psychoanalytic treatment as a process of aiding the patient to rediscover the "true, feeling self who has been hidden these many years behind the prison walls of illusion" (57). Noting that depressed persons are oversensitive, hyperconscious of their shame, and too much given to self-reproach, she points out that the more patients realize how unrealistic such feelings are and how inappropriate they are to present reality, "the more clearly they show that they are concerned with unremembered situations from the past that are still to be discovered" (58). It is the task of the psychoanalyst to help the patient discover what these unremembered situations were.

For Your Own Good

In her first book, Miller has little directly to say about child abuse. She is more concerned with accounting for the prevalence of narcissistic disorders among her patients, and with explaining how these can be traced to early childhood, where a false self was formed in place of the true self. In her second book, *For Your Own Good*,[3] subtitled "Hidden Cruelty in Child-Rearing and the Roots of Violence," she addresses the issue of child abuse in an explicit manner, focusing on the role of traditional childrearing practices in crushing the spontaneous feelings of children. She refers to these childrearing practices as "poisonous pedagogy," pointing out: "An enormous amount can be done to a child in the first two years: he or she can be molded, dominated, taught good habits, scolded, and punished—without any repercussions for the person raising the child and without the child taking revenge" (6–7). In her view, the child will overcome the serious consequences of the injustice suffered if she is able to defend against it, that is, by being allowed to express pain and anger. But, if prevented from reacting in her own way because her parents cannot tolerate these reactions (e.g., of crying, sadness, rage) and forbid these reactions by means of disapproving looks or other pedagogical methods, then the child will learn to be silent: "This silence is a sign of the effectiveness of the pedagogical principles applied, but at the same time it is a danger signal pointing to future pathological development" (7). If the child has no possibility of reacting appropriately to hurt, humiliation, and coercion, then these experiences cannot be integrated into the personality and the feelings evoked by them are repressed. The silencing of the child results in these experiences and the feelings associated with them being split off from the child's personality.

Miller is especially concerned in *For Your Own Good* with childrearing theories and methods that have proved effective in crushing the spontaneous feelings of children. These theories and methods address the fact that those concerned with raising children have often had difficulty dealing with the child's obstinacy, willfulness, and defiance and with the exuberant character of children's emotions. The poisonous pedagogies that Miller reviews in her book are largely concerned with advising parents on how to break the will of the child, and doing this without emotion (e.g., anger). By acting without emotion, the parent expects the child to react similarly. If the child persists in responding emotionally to a spanking or other reprimand, by getting angry or by crying, the parent threatens the child with another spanking as punishment for the child's emotional reaction to the original spanking. The goal is to eliminate feeling from the act of punishment and from the child's response to it.

Childrearing theorists also point out to parents that if they are successful in containing their own emotions, they thereby communicate to the child that they are not acting in their own interests, but in the interests of the child. They are punishing the child for the child's "own good." Thus, it is anticipated that the child, rather than being resentful of the punishment, will come to be grateful for it, and may even come to believe that the punishment is an expression of the parent's love for the child: "I would not hurt you if I did not love you." Children who learn to be grateful for the punishment they received as children will inflict the same punishment on their own children since not to do so would be an indication of their lack of interest, concern, and even love for the child. Children, in other words, learn to take their parents' point of view against themselves, and, as they themselves become adults, they praise their parents for the punishments they inflicted on them as children. Their own rejection of the "child" in themselves may even be stronger than that of their parents, for it was this "child" that caused them to suffer pain and humiliation.

Miller views this whole process as highly manipulative, and the result is an adult populace that is unquestioning, submissive, and deferential to authority. This submissiveness can easily be exploited by unscrupulous leaders. She quotes Adolf Hitler, who once said: "It also gives us a very special, secret pleasure to see how unaware the people around us are of what is really happening to them" (65). Hitler, who was himself a victim of child abuse, is also testimony to Miller's contention that we can all become future victims of the mistreatment inflicted on someone else's child (243).

Believing that there is no "pedagogy" that is nonmanipulative, even that of Jean Jacques Rousseau, who tried to raise his child according to the child's natural proclivities, and that all pedagogies actually serve the needs of adults, not of children, Miller argues for abandoning the term "pedagogy" in favor of the word "support." Children, she argues, need a large measure of emotional and physical support by the parent, support that includes respect for the child, respect for the child's rights, tolerance for the child's feelings, and a willingness to learn from the child's behavior (i.e., about the nature of this particular child, about the "child" in the parents themselves, and about the nature of emotional life) (100). In this way, the child is the "teacher" and the parent is the "learner." When we adults find ourselves tempted to subscribe to one or another childrearing theory promoted by so-called experts, we should remind ourselves that childrearing "is basically directed not toward the *child's* welfare but toward satisfying the parents' needs for power and revenge" (243), needs that are ultimately traceable to their own experience of being effectively silenced as children.

Thou Shalt Not Be Aware

In her third major book, *Thou Shalt Not Be Aware: Society's Betrayal of the Child*,[4] Miller moves from her primary focus in *For Their Own Good* on the sparing of parents' phenomenon (i.e., our disinclination to blame or condemn our parents for the hurt and pain they inflicted upon us) to an in-depth consideration of the phenomenon of repression (i.e., forgetting that such traumatic experiences ever occurred). In this book, there are distinct signs of her eventual decision to break away from psychoanalysis for, in the first chapter of the book, she identifies what she calls two psychoanalytic approaches, the traditional one that centers on finding out "what drive desires a person who enters my office for the first time is suppressing at the moment," and the one she favors that involves confronting "the person who enters my office with questions having to do with what befell him in childhood." In the latter approach, the psychoanalyst consciously identifies "with the child within him" even though the patient does not (11).

In Miller's view, there is a great difference between focusing, on the one hand, on drive conflicts, and, on the other hand, on the lost child. In focusing on drive conflicts, the psychoanalyst will be able "to absorb only that portion of [the patient's] early experiences which is made manifest in his drive conflicts" while the "reality of the patient's childhood, which has been inaccessible to him all these years, will be inaccessible to me as well. It remains part of the patient's 'fantasy world,' in which I can participate with my concepts and constructs without the traumas that really took place ever being revealed" (11). In contrast, the analyst who has been able to free herself from her "unconscious identification with the parents and their devious methods of upbringing" and who identifies instead with "the former child," will have "no trouble discovering the repetition of an earlier situation in the patient's *present* predicament" (12). For example, if

> the patient should describe with complete apathy a current partner relationship that strikes the analyst as extremely painful, the analyst will ask herself and the patient what painful experiences the latter must have had to undergo in early childhood, without being permitted to recognize them as such, in order to be able to speak now so impassively about his powerlessness, hopelessness, loneliness, and constant humiliation in the present-day relationship. (12)

Also, if the patient displays uncontrollable feelings directed toward other neutral people and speaks about his own parents either without any show of emotion or in an idealizing manner, the analyst will use these "as clues to the way his parents treated him as a child," whether "contemptuously, derisively, disapprovingly, seductively, or by making him feel guilty, ashamed, or frightened." In her experience, "all the features of a patient's early training can be detected in the very first session if the analyst is free to listen for them" (12).

Unfortunately, in Miller's judgment, traditional psychoanalytic practice is itself a well-intentioned pedagogy that does not challenge or subvert the analyst's unconscious identification with the parents against the "child" of the patient. The patient, having already been rendered docile and deferential, colludes in the analyst's identification with the parents' point of view, and accepts the analyst's explicit and implicit judgments against the "child" of the patient. After all, the point of the analysis is that the patient learn to grow up and face reality as a mature, responsible adult.

Thus Miller is especially concerned in this book with the tendency of psychoanalysis to minimize childhood traumas. Sigmund Freud's backpedaling on this issue is well known. In an addendum written in 1924 to his "Aetiology of Hysteria," originally published in 1896, Freud "confesses" that at the time he wrote this article on the sexual abuse of children, he had "not yet freed [himself] from [his] *overvaluation* of reality and [his] *low* valuation of phantasy" (41). In other words, he had accepted these accounts of sexual abuse as true. By backing away from his earlier view, Freud supports those poisonous pedagogies that blame the child and spare the parents (e.g., in this case, the child is blamed for "imagining" sexual episodes, and the "fact" that the child has such a vivid imagination is evidence that the child is devious). Miller is also critical of Melanie Klein's theory of the "cruel infant" and Otto Kernberg's theory of the child's "innate pathological narcissism," contending that both "pay insufficient heed to the fact that parents' unfulfilled needs and their attitudes toward the child are responsible for the forms taken by his aggressiveness, sexuality, and so-called narcissism" (42).

Thou Shalt Not Be Aware, then, is a book that stakes out Miller's position vis-à-vis psychoanalysis, charging it with being all-too-similar to the poisonous pedagogies that she attacked in *For Their Own Good*. It is also a book that goes further than her earlier books in exploring abuses of children that are not inflicted by "well-intentioned" adults (usually mothers) engaged in dubious childrearing practices, but by adults (usually fathers and other male relatives) who sexually abuse children (usually girls) for no other purpose than their own perverse pleasure. In the appendix to *Thou Shalt Not Be Aware*, Miller applauds the fact that "daughters are breaking their silence" and publicly revealing their experiences of being sexually abused by their fathers, grandfathers, uncles, and others. Why did they keep silent for so long, and why is it so difficult even now to speak? Because the abusive adult was usually one's own father and an object of sympathy. Moreover, "the child has scarcely any recourse but to hope that her emotionally ill father, who is causing her anguish, will someday, because of the daughter's docility, become the father she so desperately needs: someone she can trust, who will be affectionate toward her but not exploit her" (321). But to await this change in him while remaining silent is "soul murder," for she tries to appear "normal" and composed while "her true self and the whole range of her feelings (which include rage, indignation, disgust, shame, and a desire for revenge) remain stifled" (321).

We hope that, when she becomes an adult, she will meet a partner to whom she can express these feelings and experience acceptance. If this does not occur, she will express them in a destructive manner toward her own child, who "in his or her helplessness will be sure to accept the mother's outbursts and mistreatment and forgive everything" (321–22). Thus, the soul murder of one victim leads to the victimization of another, and the children are once again the ones who are placed in the position of exhibiting a "tragic tolerance" for the abusive behavior of adults against them.

The Untouched Key

Miller's next book, *The Untouched Key: Tracing Childhood Trauma in Creativity and Destructiveness*,[5] focuses on the lives of several well-known men and women who shared in common the fact that they were mistreated as children and went on to become highly creative adults. In effect, this book is a sequel to her earliest book on the drama of the "gifted child," as it is concerned with highly gifted individuals and is an elaboration on her point in *For Your Own Good* that the gifted child can "exhibit extraordinary acuity in criticizing the ideologies of his opponents" while, in other situations, displaying "a naive submissiveness and uncritical attitude that completely belie his brilliance in other situations."[6] She instances Martin Heidegger, "who had no trouble in breaking with traditional philosophy and leaving behind the teachers of his adolescence, but was unable to see contradictions in Hitler's ideology that should have been obvious to someone of his intelligence."[7]

The first section of *The Untouched Key* centers on repressed childhood experiences as expressed or revealed in art, and includes short essays on two painters, Pablo Picasso and Käthe Kollwitz, and the comedian Buster Keaton. The second section includes a long essay on the philosopher, Friedrich Nietzsche, and the third section centers on the biblical story of Abraham's sacrifice of Isaac and on Hans Christian Andersen's fairy tale, "The Emperor's New Clothes." The Picasso essay is about his experience of an earthquake in Málaga, Spain, when he was three years old, and his recollection of being snatched up in his father's arms as his parents ran to the hills where his father believed they would be safer. His sister was born three days later, and Miller guesses that labor may have been induced by the fright his mother experienced. Miller also believes that the following poem by Picasso, written when he was fifty-three, provides the verbal, whereas his painting *Guernica* offers the visual portrayal of this early traumatic experience:

> Children's screams screams of women bird screams flower screams screams of beams and stones screams of bricks screams of furniture of beds of chairs of curtains of frying pans of cats and of papers screams of smells that scrape at one another screams of smoke that burns in the throats of the screams cooking in the pot and screams of raining birds who flood the sea which gnaws the bone that breaks its teeth . . .

In *Guernica*, a scene that enables those who see it to experience their own feelings of horror, terror, and helplessness in the face of total destruction, Picasso painted himself over to the right as the bewildered child in the corner. Miller believes that Picasso was able to transform this harrowing experience into art because he experienced the love and support of his family.

Nietzsche is quite another story, as he did not experience a loving family and his philosophical writings, otherwise so brilliant, are deeply flawed because he was unable to confront the truth of his abuse as a child. Yet Miller suggests that Nietzsche's writings have been misunderstood precisely on this point: "Sentences from Nietzsche's writings could never have been misinterpreted in support of fascism and the annihilation of human beings if people had understood his words for what they were: the encoded language of the child who was forbidden to express his feelings," and young men "would never have been willing to march to war with his words in their pack if they had known that his ideology promoting the destruction of morality and traditional values such as charity and mercy stood for the raised fist of a child starved for truth who had suffered severely under the domination of hypocrisy."[8] Miller herself rails against the hypocrisy of adults. As a child, Nietzsche was severely punished—locked in dark closets—by a father who eventually lost his mind. As his father's illness progressed he became an embarrassment to the family for his "stupidity," but Friedrich himself continued to love his father in spite of—or probably because of—the abuse he had inflicted on his four-year-old son. When his father died, Nietzsche was raised by women—mother, grandmother, and aunts—who were intent on bringing him up correctly and used harsh childrearing techniques to achieve this end. To Miller, Nietzsche's later misogyny was his revenge for what he experienced as a child, a revenge displaced onto womanhood in general, as he continued to idealize his mother and his sister.

Writing about his great work, *Zarathustra*, Nietzsche observed that looking into the book one day prompted him to walk up and down in his room for half an hour, "unable to master an unbearable fit of sobbing." Commenting on this, Miller notes: "If Nietzsche had not been forced to learn as a child that one must master an 'unbearable fit of sobbing,' if he had simply been *allowed* to sob, then humanity would have been one philosopher poorer, but in return the life of a human being named Nietzsche would have been richer. And who knows what that *vital* Nietzsche would *then* have been able to give humanity?"[9]

In her briefer study of the painter Käthe Kollwitz, Miller centers on the "bent, lost-looking, depressive woman" to be seen in almost all her pictures. Was she Kollwitz herself, or was she Kollwitz's mother? Miller turned to Kollwitz's diaries, and found that she had grown up in a strict religious sect, founded by her maternal grandfather but under her own father's leadership when she was a child. She was raised to follow rules and orders to the letter and to suppress her feelings in the service of religious values, self-control chief among them. She herself attributes the physical problems she experienced as a child, her frequent and severe stomachaches, to the rigid childrearing practices of this religious sect. But Miller goes further in her search for the childhood roots of Kollwitz's art, and finds that three of her older siblings died at a very early age. Miller believes that these deaths made Käthe's mother unusually mindful of the dangers threatening her other children, and that Käthe, concerned to avoid causing her mother any unnecessary worry, became "a quiet, well-behaved, uncritical, psychically dead little girl."[10] Ironically and tragically, the consequence of her mother's concern that her daughter not experience physical death was that she experienced psychic death instead. As Miller puts it:

> When three dead siblings are held up as model children, serving as proof of the mother's supposed capacity for love, then the daughter will do everything in her power—will readily sacrifice all her own feelings—to show herself truly "worthy" of her mother's love. Thus, psychic death, whose

price is depression, gains double significance: it brings promise of the mother's unconditional, unlimited love, which the daughter has observed but has not experienced herself, and it satisfies the longing for death on the part of the mother, whose face looks transfigured, soft, almost happy only when she is standing by her children's graves.[11]

Especially in her essays on Nietzsche and on Buster Keaton (which I will discuss in chapter 3), *The Untouched Key* reflects Miller's concern with adults' abuse of children. But these essays are part of her larger concern to explain the whole range of childhood suffering, much of it due to circumstances beyond adults' control, and not directly related to their poisonous pedagogies. Rather, the theme that runs through these essays is the tragic effects that a child's loving concern for a suffering parent can have on the child. The child's empathic response to the parent causes the child to suffer too. This is true of Nietzsche and his father, and of Kollwitz and her mother. It is also true, as we will see in chapter 5, of Isaac and his father, Abraham. Their stories support Miller's argument that what children feel naturally toward their parents is love, and that this love is almost impossible to eradicate once formed. Parents who abuse their children know that they will not retaliate but will, if anything, love the parents even more. Parents who suffer are likewise assured of their children's love, a love expressed in the children's preference that they, rather than the parents, should be the ones who suffer.

Banished Knowledge

In *Banished Knowledge*, Miller elaborates on her point in *For Your Own Good* that children need support, not pedagogy. As she writes in *Banished Knowledge*: "A baby requires the certainty that he will be protected in every situation, that his arrival is desired, that his cries are heard, that the movements of his eyes are responded to and his fears calmed."[12] While the infant "can scream for help, he relies entirely on those around him to hear his cries, take them seriously, and satisfy the underlying needs. . . . The only possible recourse a baby has when his screams are ignored is to repress his distress, which is tantamount to mutilating his soul, for the result is an interference with his ability to feel, to be aware, and to remember" (2).

Banished Knowledge is a very personal book, for here Miller discusses the fact that she herself was an abused child, a fact that psychoanalysis never revealed to her but instead helped her to repress. It was only her spontaneous painting, begun in 1973, that gave her "the first unadulterated access to my early reality. In my paintings I came face to face with the terrorism exerted by my mother, at the mercy of which I had lived for so many years. For no one in my environment, not even my kind father, could ever notice or question the child abuse committed under the cloak of child-rearing" (7). A major chapter of the book focuses on her rediscovery of the self that had

been repressed in childhood, and another important chapter centers on our
need for "enlightened witnesses," persons who are able and willing to take
the side of the child unequivocally and protect her from the power abuse of
the parents. Had such a person been there for her, her life would have taken
a different course: "That person could have helped me to recognize the
cruelty and not tolerate it for decades as something normal and necessary, at
the expense of my own life" (7).

Miller is also critical of her efforts in earlier books to avoid blaming
parents, having done so because she felt she had no right to criticize someone else's parents "because it was not I whom they had raised, manipulated,
and hindered" (25). But now, viewing herself as a self-appointed "enlightened witness," she is "no longer afraid to entertain, and express, the thought
that parents are guilty of crimes against their children, *even though* they act
out of an inner compulsion and as an outcome of their tragic past" (26). She
does not expect parents to be perfect. What she asks is that they apologize to
their children when they have acted wrongfully against them so that confusion is thereby avoided:

> Love and cruelty are mutually exclusive. No one slaps a child out of love
> but rather because in similar situations, when one was defenseless, one was
> slapped and then compelled to interpret it as a sign of love. This inner
> confusion prevailed for thirty or forty years and is passed on to one's own
> child. That's all. To purvey this confusion to the child as truth leads to new
> confusions that, although examined in detail by experts, are still confu-
> sions. If, on the other hand, one can admit one's errors to the child and
> apologize for a lack of self-control, no confusions are created. If a mother
> can make it clear to a child that at that particular moment when she
> slapped him her love for him deserted her and she was dominated by other
> feelings that had nothing to do with the child, the child can keep a clear
> head, feel respected, and not be disoriented in his relationship to his
> mother. While it is true that love for a child cannot be commanded, each
> of us is free to decide to refrain from hypocrisy. (35)

In *Banished Knowledge*, Miller also returns to her earlier criticisms of psychoanalysis. Her chapter on the so-called "wicked child" takes Melanie
Klein to task, arguing that what Klein took to be an innate destructive drive
in the child is rather the effect of childrearing. A child's cruelty toward
smaller animals or children is not innate but learned, and this learned behavior is not acquired indirectly (e.g., by watching violence on television) but
directly as the victim of suffering and repression. Her chapter on theories
that serve as a "protective shield" against the discovery of child abuse once
again takes Freud to task for describing his patients' reports on sexual abuse
as fantasies attributable to their instinctual wishes. Here, she attributes his
reinterpretation of these reports to his having been shunned in psychiatric
circles after publicly asserting that all his patients had suffered child abuse.

He could not bear the professional isolation that his earlier pronouncement provoked. Thus, theories, even those that are presumably designed to get at the truth about our lives as children, are instead protective shields designed to keep us from discovering and accepting the real truth.

Miller argues, however, that we collude with these theories because we ourselves do not really want to know the truth. A woman who was abused by her father as a child may eventually arrive at a clinic suffering from schizophrenia and be treated by her psychiatrist with massive doses of medication, with the result that she will know even less than she did before, and never find out that it was her father's behavior that drove her into madness. She may in fact prefer this, for to salvage his image, to see at least something good in her childhood, she must not know the truth (63). She would rather lose her mind. Moreover, as Miller herself discovered, with every inner confrontation with her parents, the guilt feelings that were instilled in her reinforced her repression and barred her access to reality. Only when she could query her supposed guilt could her feelings of pain resurface (72). In her chapter on "pretending not to know," Miller discusses the difficulties she has experienced with editors and journalists who renege on their commitments to publish her writings or interviews for spurious reasons. This, she believes, reflects on the public's own desire not to want to know the truth about child abuse, and is an indication of how strong is the desire to protect and spare the parents, and to maintain our idealized image of our own childhood.

In virtually all of her writings, Miller is concerned with the intergenerational effects of child abuse, the fact that those who suffer child abuse are condemned to repeat the past with their own children. This is because whatever was repressed in their own childhood comes to overt expression in their behavior as adults. To illustrate this, she recounts (38ff.) a horrific story, first reported in *Newsday Magazine*, of the death of an eight-month-old infant: A young woman is alone at home with her three-year-old son and eight-month-old daughter. She has just had an unpleasant telephone conversation with her father and has phoned her sister to tell her about it, but the baby interferes with the conversation by continual screaming. Unable to hear her sister's voice, the mother becomes more and more desperate and suddenly begins hitting her daughter with the telephone receiver until the infant is silent: "Thus she becomes a child murderer, although she did not deliberately kill the baby. She merely wanted to get rid of the intolerable screaming" (38).

In her own childhood, her father was an alcoholic and would often run around the apartment brandishing a knife and threatening to kill his two young daughters. He beat them regularly and abused them sexually when they were small. Once he dragged her from her sleep and hung her by her nightgown from a nail on a closet wall, leaving her there for three hours. As she hung in the closet, her parents were having a quarrel, and her mother left the apartment, never to return.

Miller points out that in the magazine article the woman's childhood is mentioned at the beginning but then quickly forgotten. A whole series of circumstances from her adult life is put forward as cause for the murder: partners, men, poverty. Various experts are quoted, various theories advanced, various suggestions made, and research projects are called for: "What was so obvious at the beginning of the article has by its end been virtually obscured" (40). Miller proposes that we all try to imagine ourselves as this child, hanging from a nail in the closet for three hours by our nightgown, abandoned by our mother and totally at the mercy of a rampaging father. Then, let us go on to imagine what emotions this would arouse in us. What can a child do when she is left so utterly alone with her panic, her impotent fury, her despair and anguish?

> The child must not even cry, much less scream, if she doesn't want to be killed. The only way she can get rid of these emotions is to repress them. But repression is a perfidious fairy who will supply help at the moment but will eventually exact a price for this help. The impotent fury comes to life again when the girl's own child [daughter] is born, and at last the anger can be discharged—once again at the expense of a defenseless creature. (40)

Rounding out this interpretation is the fact that the woman had just had an unpleasant phone conversation with her father and had phoned her sister, also a victim of her father's abusiveness, seeking understanding and solace. The screaming child—a reminder of her terrible ordeal in the closet—cannot be tolerated. If only, says Miller, this woman could have consciously experienced her hatred for her father, she would then have known at whom her hatred was directed when she became so desperate on the phone, and she would not have made her own child pay the ultimate price for it. This story, then, provides a dramatic and sobering illustration of the price that is paid in human lives for "banished knowledge."

Breaking Down the Wall of Silence

Because it was written just after *Banished Knowledge*, the subtitle of Miller's *Breaking Down the Wall of Silence*—"The Liberating Experience of Facing Painful Truth"—is especially important, as it suggests that there is much to be gained by *overcoming* the desire not to know the events and experiences of childhood. It also suggests that if these experiences remain a mystery to us, this is not because they are inaccessible in principle, but because we have made a decision, usually unconscious, to keep them that way.

Miller points out that her own first experience of "the wall of silence" occurred in childhood, for this was her mother's method of demonstrating her total power over her little daughter. By ignoring Alice for days, refusing to talk to her, she reduced her daughter to subservience. She took no responsibility for her sadism because, as far as she was concerned, her behavior was justifiable punishment for her daughter's wrongdoings. Her "wall of silence" was her way of teaching her child a lesson she would never forget. For a child who at the time had no brothers and sisters and whose father, on the rare occasions he was at home, never offered his protection, this long, unremitting silence was a terrible agony. But, Miller notes, "even worse than the silence was the child's doomed but persistent attempt to discover its cause." The prolonged silence contained a message: "If you don't even know why you have earned this punishment, then it is clear that you are quite without conscience. Look within. Search. Try. Then your conscience will tell you what guilt you have brought on yourself."[13] Miller asks:

> Did I know that I had begun my life in a totalitarian state? How could I have? I didn't even realize that I was being hideously and sadistically treated, something I would never have dreamed of suggesting. So rather than question my mother's behavior, I cast doubt on the rightness of my own feeling that I was being unjustly treated. As I had no point of comparison of her behavior with that of other mothers, and as she constantly portrayed herself as the embodiment of duty and self-sacrifice, I had no choice but to believe her. And, anyway, I *had* to believe her. To have realized the truth would have killed me. Therefore, it had to be my wickedness that was to blame when Mother didn't speak to me, when she refused to answer my questions and ignored my pleas for clarification, when she avoided the slightest eye contact with me and returned my love with coldness. If Mother hates me, reasoned the child, then I must be hateful. (20)

The memory of the isolation of those times, the loneliness of the child as she desperately searched for explanations for the punishments she received, remained completely repressed in her for almost sixty years. As a result,

> I betrayed that little girl, who wanted above all to comprehend her mother's irrationality in order to finally be able to alter her fate by bringing her mother, the mother she needed, to speak. I had to betray her because there was no one to help me see the truth and live with it. There was no one to help me condemn cruelty. Instead, I continued the lonely search for my own guilt in the mazes of abstract thought, which didn't hurt so much as naked facts. It also held out to me the hope of an orientation that I had been denied. Because that little girl's feelings were so intense that they could have literally killed her, they were repressed before they could penetrate her consciousness. Only in recent years, with the help of therapy, which enabled me to lift the veil on this repression bit by bit, could I allow myself to experience the pain and desperation, the powerlessness and justified fury of that abused child. Only then did the dimensions of that crime against the child I once was become clear to me. (20–21)

Here Miller exposes what is arguably the most sadistic of all forms of child abuse, the silent treatment. It leaves the child in abject isolation, and initiates the process of the child's self-betrayal, and does so without the infliction of a single physical blow or a single word of parental anger. Miller uses the wall of silence image to describe what the victims of child abuse and their advocates constantly run up against in what is supposedly the enlightened society of our day. She again criticizes not only the psychiatric community for its complicity in the erection of this wall of silence but also the media for "pretending" to want to know the truth. But, in this book, these criticisms now also extend to reviewers of her books who have dismissed her most recent works (e.g., *Banished Knowledge*) because she is becoming, for them, tiresomely repetitive. As one reviewer suggested, one need not open her latest book because one already knows what it says. Miller asserts that such dismissive reactions to her work are not the experience of those readers who, wishing to deal with the experience of their own childhoods, rarely fail to find her books a great help to them. Rather, they are the experience of readers who, obliged to read her books because they have agreed to review them, find themselves "suddenly—and wholly unprepared—face to face with the sufferings of their own childhood, without any useful weapon at hand to fight off the old confusion and perplexity. Thus, they ensure in advance that such books have nothing to say to them, taking refuge in well-dug-in intellectual foxholes" (64).

Miller is therefore concerned with the role that denial plays in maintaining the wall of silence regarding child abuse. If child abuse is not the serious problem that Miller alleges it to be, then Miller is merely imagining that a wall of silence exists. She, and not Freud, has *overvalued* the fantasy life, in this case, her own. To combat this argument, she has tried, in all her writings, to explain why victims of child abuse would prefer *not* to know about their own victimization. These explanations include the desire to spare the parents, the desire to salvage a usable childhood, and the fact that the abuse itself has generated lasting negative feelings toward the child they once were.

In addition to her concern about the denial that is so strong at both the individual and societal level, Miller worries about the hypocrisy that is also so prevalent. If parents are hypocritical about the abuse itself—contending that they act out of love when in fact their behavior is cruelty pure and simple—there is also a great deal of hypocrisy at the societal level in regard to child abuse. Miller is most critical of opponents of abortion, who, in her judgment, substitute abstract conceptions of life for "lived life," and thereby divert society's attention away from the need to work toward the protection of the child's right to a life devoid of parental violence (by making child abuse a criminal offense). She also believes that those who oppose abortion are typically supporters of traditional childrearing practices (poisonous pedagogies) and therefore have no intention of seeing that the children they seek to have born into this world are subsequently protected from parental violence. To say that they "love" the unborn child without at the same time condemning traditional childrearing practices is to persist in the same confusion of love and cruelty that the childrearing practices themselves promote. To be sure,

> abortion can, indeed, be seen as the most powerful symbol of the psychic annihilation and mutilation practiced since time immemorial on children. But to combat this evil merely at the symbolic level deflects us from the reality we should not evade for a moment longer: the reality of the abused and humiliated child, which, as a result of its disavowed and unresolved injuries, will insidiously become, either openly or aided by hypocrisy, a danger to society. (147)

Miller also contends that a wall of silence is erected when a nation goes to war and hypocritically ignores or disguises the fact that children are war's inevitable victims. Moreover, the much-talked-about capacity of fighter pilots to carry out bombing missions without much emotion (unless it is the emotion of elation in performing a very dangerous and highly technical job with consummate skill) is related, in her view, to their childhood experiences of powerlessness and defenselessness, as though bombing raids offer the satisfaction of no longer being a helpless victim but of being able to threaten others instead.

Thus, Miller's latest book is at once one of her most personal, as she reveals that her mother's most potent weapon against her as a child was her silence, and one of her most prophetic, as she does not flinch from taking definite and controversial positions on the most divisive social issues of our times. While her criticisms of psychoanalysis and of traditional childrearing practices reappear here, she has entered a larger arena in this latest book of hers, addressing the life-and-death issues of modern civilization itself.

Saving Souls

Miller draws on religious and even biblical themes throughout her work. An essay on Abraham and Isaac appears in *The Untouched Key* and she interprets the book of Lamentations as the laments of a mistreated child in *Breaking Down the Wall of Silence*. But the key religious image in her work is that of the "soul," which she identifies as that which is lost, mutilated, or even murdered as a consequence of the suffering one endures in childhood. It is this soul that is found, restored, and regenerated when the feelings that were crushed in childhood are reexperienced, when the child that has existed in one's body for these many years is accepted as oneself and is no longer treated as a stranger, alien, or enemy, but as companion, friend, and beloved. To take the child's side unequivocally against the child's tormentors is to

regain one's soul, and to witness in behalf of the child in others is to participate in the reclamation of their souls as well. It is impossible to imagine a
more religious undertaking than this, for is not the saving of souls the very
essence of religion? However, in subsequent chapters, we will see how religion has been arrayed against the soul and has contributed to its mutilation.
As chapter 2 shows, this is partly due to the fact that religion has traditionally legitimated the childrearing practices that Miller terms "poisonous pedagogies." But it is also due to the fact that religious concepts and beliefs erect
a wall of silence around the pain and suffering of children, a wall that needs
to be breached if you and I are to have the liberating experience of facing
painful truths about ourselves and those we have always loved.

2

Augustine: The Vicious Cycle of Child Abuse

In the episode witnessed by Alice Miller, Saint Nicholas reduced the children to silence. When he was through declaring to them their faults and virtues, they were unable to sing the song or say the poem they had prepared just for him. In this chapter we focus our attention on another episode in which a child was also silenced by well-meaning adults. Only this time the child was prohibited from mourning the loss of his beloved grandmother.

Adults' efforts to prohibit children from openly grieving are common. What makes this particular episode stand out from many others is that the child was Adeodatus, the son of Saint Augustine, the man who—with the possible exception of Saint Paul—has done more than any other mortal to shape and define the Christian faith. His story has been told again and again. For many Christians, it is an inspiring story of a man who yielded to the power of the gospel and dedicated his life to the church of Christ. I want here to tell the story of his unsung son, the boy who tried to mourn his grandmother Monica's death and who himself died shortly thereafter. Unlike his father, who was seventy-five years old when he died, Adeodatus was only seventeen when he died, too young to make his mark in the world. I write of him because his story enables us to explore the subtle ways in which religion, including the Christian faith, crushes the spirit of a child.

To place his story in context, we need to go back in time to his father's childhood and lift up an episode that has direct bearing on what was eventually to become of Adeodatus.

"A Little One, but with No Little Feeling"

In his *Confessions*, Augustine relates how, as a child, he was severely beaten by his teachers at school. His account of these beatings reflects the fact that we adults, in looking back on our childhood sufferings, have very mixed reactions and responses to those persons who were implicated in these sufferings. That this account is addressed to God—with whom he, as an adult, is now on speaking terms—adds a further complexity.[1]

The interpretive frame that he chooses for his account of these beatings is deception and deceit: "O God, my God, great was the misery and great the deception that I met with when it was impressed upon me that, to behave properly as a boy, I must obey my teachers. This was all that I might succeed in this world and excel in those arts of speech which would serve to bring honor among men and to gain deceitful riches." The boy did not know that he was being prepared for an adult life based on the illusions of this world. He hadn't the slightest notion that what was occurring in school was for some unknown purpose in the very distant future: "I was sent to school to acquire learning, the utility of which, wretched child that I was, I did not know. Yet if I was slow at learning, I was beaten" (51).

The adult Augustine does not believe that his teachers acted from personal malice. After all, "this method was praised by our forebears, many of whom had passed through this life before us and had laid out the hard paths that we were forced to follow." But he cannot resist noting that all of this is the consequence of Adam's original sin: "Thus were both toil and sorrow multiplied for the sons of Adam" (51). As a son of Adam, the adult Augustine can accept the fact that he, and other children, were doomed to suffer, for suffering is a fact of life. Yet, if Adam is ultimately to blame for the fact of our suffering, there is the question of whether there is anything that God might do to alleviate the suffering, to soften the blows. As children, "we discovered, Lord, that certain men prayed to you and we learned from them, and imagined you, as far as we could, as some sort of mighty one who could hear us and help us, even though not appearing before our senses." Thus "while still a boy, I began to pray to you, my help and my refuge, and in praying to you I broke the knots that tied my tongue. A little one, but with no little feeling, I prayed to you that I would not be beaten at school" (51–52). So, two well-established traditions—the beating of children and the praying to God for deliverance—converged. As his teachers turned to the former, Augustine, the child, resorted to the latter.

But God did not heed his prayers. Nor did his parents. "When you [God] did not hear me—and it was 'not to be reputed folly in me'—my punishments, which were then a huge and heavy evil to me, were laughed at by older men, and even by my parents who wished no harm to befall me" (52). While we might have expected Augustine to ask why God did not respond to his entreaties—thus taking the side of the child—he centers instead on his parents' decision not to intervene in his behalf, and he offers a religious justification for this. Supposing, he says, that there is a person of "so great a soul, who clings to you with so mighty love," that he "so devoutly clings to you and is thus so deeply affected that he deems of little consequence the rack, the hook, and similar tools of torture." And supposing he deems these tools of torture insignificant in spite of the fact that he "loves those who dread such things most bitterly." Such love for God, that one would deem the sufferings of another as of little consequence, may explain why "our parents laughed at the torments we boys suffered from our teachers." Of course, "in no less measure did we fear our punishments, and no less did we beseech you to let us escape" (52).

By drawing this analogy between the beatings he suffered as a child and the torturing devices used against adults, the adult Augustine recognizes just how severe the children's sufferings were. Yet, in providing a legitimation for his parents' failure to intervene, and a religious one at that, he spares the parents and absolves them of any responsibility for what has occurred. Moreover, he goes on to acknowledge that the children brought their sufferings on themselves: "Yet we sinned by writing, reading, and thinking over our lessons less than was required of us." That we as children did not do as well as we should was not God's fault either, for "there was in us no lack of memory or intelligence, for you willed that we should have them in sufficient measure for our years" (52). If the children's behavior can be defended at all, it is only because they were doing what adults also do: "Yet we loved to play, and this was punished in us by men who did the same things themselves. However, the trivial concerns of adults are called business, while such things in children are punished by adults." So he returns to the issue of the delusion—the meaninglessness—of the whole scenario: "Perhaps some fine judge of things approves my beatings for I played ball as a child." Yet, in playing ball, all that he did was to resist "learning arts by which, as an adult, I would comport myself in still more unseemly fashion." By what right, then, did his teachers beat him? "Did the very man who beat me act different from me? If he was outdone by a fellow teacher in some trifling discussion, he was more tormented by anger and envy than I was when beaten by my playmate in a ball game" (52).

The bottom line, though, is that Augustine and the other boys sinned "by going against the commands of my parents and of those teachers." After all, he was able, later on, to "put to good use the learning that they wanted me to acquire, no matter with what purpose in my regard." And "I was disobedient, not out of a desire for better things, but out of a love for play. I loved to win proud victories in our contests" (53). As a child, he prayed for deliverance from the beatings inflicted by his teachers. Now, as an adult, he prays for deliverance from the love of trivial pursuits, including the same trivial pursuits to which his teachers were captive: "Lord, in your mercy look down upon these things and deliver us who now call upon you. Deliver also those who do not yet call upon you, so that they may call upon you and you may deliver them" (53). If God is a God of deliverance, it is not—as he thought as a child—that God delivers us from suffering, but that he delivers us from the illusions to which we were subject as children, and to which our teachers were also subject. If our teachers erred, it was not in the fact that they beat us, but that we were beaten for the wrong reasons. And if our parents refused to intervene, this was not because they were unfeeling—as we thought at the time—but because they clung to God with such a mighty love that they could resist their children's pleas, secure in the knowledge that the torments their children were suffering were for their own good.[2]

The Scourging God

The beatings that Augustine suffered as a boy have received little scholarly attention. Readers of this remarkable exercise in self-disclosure have paid far more attention to his account of his involvement in the stealing of a farmer's pears when he was a teenager. The boyhood beatings are passed over, as if they are of little significance. However, two scholars—E. R. Dodds and Leo Ferrari—have taken note of the fact that Augustine was beaten by his teachers, and both believe that the beatings left permanent scars on his psyche. In an essay published in 1927,[3] Dodds noted that Augustine "has none but painful memories" of his earliest schooling at the small country town of Thagaste. He resisted being compelled to acquire mechanically information whose value was not apparent to him, and "like other proud and sensitive children, he resented the cane still more. He tells us that he would pray to God with a passion disproportionate to his age that he might not be beaten in school; and he rightly blames his parents for laughing at his prayer, pointing out that the suffering which amuses the adults may be agony to the child." Also, "he never forgave the schoolmaster who beat him for faults which he habitually committed himself." These beatings had lasting effects, for "it is a fair inference from his language that these beatings produced what psychologists call a *trauma*, a permanent injury to his personality." Their lasting effects were reflected in his compensatory behavior: "For the humiliations of the classroom it seems that he sought compensation in dominating his fellows. Black jealousy tortured him if he so much as lost a game of ball. Puny, delicate and weak-voiced, he had not the physical qualities of a leader; but when he could not make friends otherwise, he bribed them with stolen sweetmeats, and when he could not win games otherwise, he won them by cheating" (462).

Note that Dodds claims that Augustine "blamed" his parents for laughing at his prayers, when, in fact, as we have seen, he offers a theological explanation for why his parents did not sympathize with him. It was not that they were callous or unfeeling, but that they were responding to a greater love than that they felt for their own beloved child. On the other hand, Dodds is quite right that the beatings Augustine suffered were traumatic and produced a "permanent injury to his personality," and the evidence that Dodds offers for this—a compensatory need to dominate others—is entirely plausible.

Leo Ferrari offers a much more extensive interpretation of the beatings and their impact on Augustine's personality.[4] He focuses on Augustine's tendency throughout his adult years to engage in excessive self-reproach, on his pervasive sense of sadness and hopelessness, and on his tendency to be mistrustful of others. Ferrari believes that all these traits can be attributed to the beatings he suffered as a child. As he points out, "There is ample evidence for the enduring influence of these early floggings, not only upon his most important formative years, but also upon his outlook as a mature man" (3).

Like Dodds, Ferrari believes that Augustine as a boy was of a uniquely sensitive nature, and "was thereby all the more susceptible to being profoundly disturbed by his first whippings." What neither he nor Dodds considers is the likelihood that it was the whippings that made Augustine so sensitive. Also, in stressing his sensitivity, both seem to imply that children, those who are less sensitive, might not be traumatized by beatings. On the other hand, Ferrari stresses the severity of the beatings, as suggested by the fact that the adult Augustine compared them to the worst devices of torture known to humankind.

For Ferrari, whether Augustine was thrashed at home prior to beginning school is an open question, since Augustine does not imply this in his *Confessions* or elsewhere. Yet he notes that Augustine's father Patricius was a man given to violent anger and that only the tact of his wife, Monica, saved her from the wife-beating that was traditional in the village. As a young married man, Augustine's father beat several servants who were the source of rumors injurious to his new wife: "Whether his frustrated anger could also have been released upon his children is not known. Certainly, the infant Augustine must have been at least the transfixed spectator to his father's rages, even if not the subject of his irate thrashings" (4).

In any case, Ferrari believes that Augustine's parents refused to intervene in his behalf because they were extremely ambitious for him from his earliest years, and they considered education to be the means whereby he would later make a name for himself in the world. But, "Considering the traumatic circumstances under which the sensitive infant was so early in life goaded on to seek worldly fame and wealth through his oratorical talents, it is the less surprising that he later so violently rejected all these worldly ambitions. Further, it would seem credible too that here in the first floggings administered by some grim tyrant of a schoolmaster, together with the mocking laughter of his very own parents at the painful stripes which he bore home, lay the first seeds of disenchantment with the adult world. Aided by other factors, this could later ripen into renunciation of the world and of worldly pursuits" (5–6).

In Ferrari's judgment, his parents' mocking laughter also had an enduring effect on Augustine's personality, especially in the fact that he was very sensitive to being the object of any kind of ridicule: "Humor there is in Augus-

tine, but it always seems to be directed at something other than himself. A
master of grinding irony when vanquishing some unfortunate opponent in
public debate, he is nevertheless consistently serious about himself and his
intentions" (6).

Thus, the beatings' long-term effects are reflected in his tendency toward
excessive self-reproach, his rather sorrowful temperament, his disenchantment with the world of adult pursuits, and the seriousness with which he
took himself. Especially concerned with the tendency toward excessive self-
reproach, Ferrari explains this in religious terms, noting that "cruel and
terrifying as were the beatings which the young Augustine suffered at school,
in his mature years through the light of his faith he was able to view these
scourgings as the work of God Himself. . . . Seen in the larger perspective of
eternal salvation, the scourgings of school days are merely an apprenticeship
to the sufferings of life, by which God calls wandering and wayward souls
back to Himself" (6–7).

Noting Augustine's many references in his *Confessions* to the scourges of
God, Ferrari suggests that "the irate schoolmaster of Augustine's infancy
therefore becomes the scourging God who purifies his soul through the
many punishments of life." There are some twenty references in the *Confessions* to the scourgings or floggings suffered at the hand of God, ranging
from the derision he endured when the Manichaeism to which he had devoted nearly a decade of his life was proven a sham; to God's redoubling of
lashes of fear and shame to bring him to conversion; to the grievous loss of
his mother in death. The flip side of this belief in the scourging God was his
conviction that he deserved these scourgings, for he was very much a sinner.
Moreover, the fact that he was the object of God's scourging was a hopeful
sign, for "just as the father loves a child when punishing it, so too God's
scourges are a sign of his love." Ferrari concludes, "There are grounds for
arguing that the traumatic terror of his first floggings as a very young
schoolboy contributed to an enduring sense of culpability and the formation
of a temperament disposed to self-reproach and suffering." Ferrari believes
that this led Augustine to overemphasize the stern Jehovah of the Old Testament at the expense of the merciful and loving God of the New, but he
thinks the end result was positive, for "just as the floggings of his first
schoolteachers drove him to the study of literature in which he was to excel
as a professional orator, so too in the school of life, the later scourges of God
impelled him to a profound study of the Bible upon which he became a
peerless authority and the principal interpreter for the western christian
tradition. Without the boyhood beatings which affected him so profoundly,
there may well have been no Saint Augustine" (14).

But I am not so sanguine. I share Alice Miller's view that nothing good
comes from the abuse of children, and that the cases of great historical
figures offer no grounds for suggesting otherwise. As she says of Nietzsche,

his greatness as a philosopher was not because, but in spite of the fact that he was abused, and the fact that he was a seriously flawed philosopher—however brilliant—is largely owing to the abuse he suffered as a child.[5] The same applies to Augustine. It is a tenuous argument to say that Augustine would not have become a peerless authority on the Bible had he not felt himself to be the object of the scourgings of God, and Ferrari himself suggests that his interpretation of the Bible was one-sided (and therefore flawed) precisely because he was the victim of beatings as a child.

Yet we are not here concerned with Augustine's contribution as a father of the church, but with what his childhood experience of being beaten meant for his relationship to his son, Adeodatus, and especially with how it happened that Augustine did to Adeodatus what his teachers had done to him. If Dodds and Ferrari are correct that the beatings he suffered as a child had a lasting effect on his personality, then we should want to explore these effects on his role not only as a father of the church but also as the father of Adeodatus. Key to these effects is the fact that the beatings prompted him to pray, and that in praying "I broke the knots that tied my tongue." Ferrari takes this statement to mean that the beatings happened when Augustine was so young that he "learned to talk by begging God not to allow him to be beaten at school." Rather, I take it to mean that, in being inflicted with beatings that he had no power to defend against, he began to speak to God, pleading with God to exercise his power to stop the beatings. Thus, the beatings caused him to pray, and from this time forth Augustine interpreted his sufferings within a religious frame of reference. The experience of being beaten and the impetus to pray are forever linked in his psyche. Furthermore, if he was unable to cry out during the beatings for fear that he would be beaten even more severely, prayer to God was a means of untying his tongue, of giving vent to his feelings of frustration and rage. In this way, God became more than his potential deliverer, for God also became the one on whom he could vent his rage, the scourging God to whom he could talk back, though always in a carefully modulated manner, lest he anger God and invite retaliation. Perhaps this explains the fact that his praise of God in the *Confessions* is often accompanied, and somewhat undermined, by an undertone of veiled criticism against God.[6] Even his decision to become a rhetorician may, in this sense, be related to his childhood beatings, for rhetoric is the skill of speaking on more than one level at once, of implying more than is literally spoken. All of this has direct bearing on the fate of Adeodatus, who was the indirect victim of the beatings Augustine suffered at the hands of his teachers.

"As She Breathed Her Last the Boy Began to Wail"

Adeodatus makes an important, if seldom noticed, appearance in Augustine's account of his own mother's death. The fact that Augustine concluded his account of his life not with his conversion to the Christian faith but with the death of his mother is significant, for with the account of her death his narrative comes full circle, back to its initial starting point in his account of being beaten by his teachers.

In recounting the event of his mother's death, he recalls that, as he closed her eyes, "a great wave of sorrow surged into my heart. It would have overflowed in tears if I had not made a strong effort of will and stemmed the flow, so that the tears dried in my eyes. What a terrible struggle it was to hold them back!" Then, as she breathed her last, "the boy Adeodatus began to wail aloud and only ceased his cries when we all checked him. I, too, felt that I wanted to cry like a child, but a more mature voice within me, the voice of my heart, bade me keep my sobs in check, and I remained silent. For we did not think it right to mark my mother's death with weeping and moaning, because such lamentations are the usual accompaniment of death when it is thought of as a state of misery or as total extinction. But she had not died in misery nor had she wholly died. Of this we were certain, both because we knew what a holy life she had led and also because our faith was real and we had sure reasons not to doubt it."[7]

When they had succeeded in quieting Adeodatus, Evodius, a friend of Augustine's, took up a psaltery and began to sing Psalm 100—"Of mercy and justice my song shall be; a psalm in thy honor, Lord"—and the whole house sang in response. As funeral preparations were being made, Augustine remained in another room, "conversing with friends on matters suitable to the occasion, for they did not think it right to leave me to myself." He continued to control his emotions, so much so that his friends "thought that I had no sense of grief." How little they knew, for throughout the day, "I fought against the wave of sorrow and for a while it receded, but then it swept upon me again with full force. It did not bring me to tears and no sign of it showed in my face, but I knew well enough what I was stifling in my heart. It was misery to feel myself so weak a victim of these human emotions, although we cannot escape them, since they are the natural lot of mankind, and so I had the added sorrow of being grieved by my own feelings, so that I was tormented by a twofold agony" (201).

During the day, he "found comfort in the memory that as I did what I could for my mother in the last stages of her illness, she had caressed me and said that I was a good son to her. With great emotion she told me that she could not remember ever having heard me speak a single hard or disrespectful word against her" (200). When her body was carried out later in the day for burial, he continued to keep control of his emotions: "I went and returned without a tear. I did not weep even during the prayers which we recited while the sacrifice of our redemption was offered for my mother and her body rested by the grave before it was laid in the earth, as is the custom there. Yet all that day I was secretly weighed down with grief. With all my heart I begged you to heal my sorrow, but you did not grant my prayer. I believe this was because you wished to impress upon my memory, if only by this one lesson, how firmly the mind is gripped in the bonds of habit, even when it is nourished on the word of truth" (201). At night, though, when he lay alone in bed, his feelings about his mother came back to him, little by little, and he began to cry. "The tears which I had been holding back streamed down, and I let them flow as freely as they would, making of them a pillow for my heart. On them it rested, for my weeping sounded in your ears alone, not in the ears of men who might have misconstrued it and despised it" (202).

In publicly admitting that he wept that night, he is aware that those who read his account will interpret it as they will. So be it: "Let him understand it as he will. And if he finds that I sinned by weeping for my mother, even if only for a fraction of an hour, let him not mock at me. For this was the mother, now dead and hidden awhile from my sight, who had wept over me for many years so that I might live in your sight. Let him not mock at me but weep himself, if his charity is great" (203). And so his account of his mother's death ends on a note of defiance: "You may say that I sinned in weeping for my mother, but do not mock me, for in mocking me, you mock the woman who shed so many tears for her good son, the son who never spoke a single hard or disrespectful word against her."

I suspect that many of us reading his *Confessions* today, if we were inclined to mock, would mock his herculean efforts to control his emotions, and would view with relief the fact that he was able to weep, finally, if only for a fraction of an hour. But his use of the word "mock" calls to our minds the episode with which he began the story of his life, and specifically the fact that his parents mocked him when he showed them the stripes on his back and sought their sympathy. Out of such mockery was born a son who was good to his mother, a son who never dared to speak a single hard or disrespectful word against her.

But what of Adeodatus? Once Augustine and his friends succeeded in silencing him—suppressing his cries of grief with the singing of a psalm—we hear nothing more of him. Father and friends repaired to a room where they conversed together on topics suitable for the day. If Adeodatus joined them, Augustine doesn't say. Later, when they took the body out for burial, Adeodatus was surely in the company of mourners, but again his father makes no mention of the fact. After he was silenced, he disappears from the text. He who had dared to weep openly is thenceforth stricken from the record.

Who was this Adeodatus? What do we know about him? Almost all our information about him comes from his father's *Confessions*. He was conceived when Augustine was nineteen years old and living as a university student in Carthage, the largest city in northern Africa,[8] and had found himself a mistress. Writing briefly about his son's birth in Book 4 of his *Confessions*, he mentions this illicit relationship, noting that he was ever faithful to this woman who was not his wife, and then adds: "With her I learned at first hand how great a distance lies between the restraint of a conjugal covenant, mutually made for the sake of begetting offspring, and the bargain of a lustful love, where a child is born against our will, although once born he forces himself upon our love."[9] He does not elaborate on the statement, "born against our will," but it is evident that, at least initially, Adeodatus was unwanted. In his biography of Augustine, Peter Brown suggests that the conception and birth of Adeodatus "may well have had the 'sobering' effect which Augustine would later recommend to young husbands."[10] But this is Augustine the older teacher, making a moral point about how a serious mistake may bring a young man to his senses. For the young man of nineteen years, the conception and birth of Adeodatus was a matter of deep, overwhelming shame: A young girl was pregnant, and he was the father. Hadn't his mother warned him, just a couple of years earlier, to "keep from fornicating," and hadn't he ignored her, for "such words seemed to be only a woman's warnings" (68)?

He had gone to Carthage and had sought love there, and indeed, he found it, in a woman's arms. But love had its costs, and God saw that he would suffer for it: "I plunged headlong into love, whose captive I desired to be. But my God, my mercy, with how much gall did you sprinkle all that sweetness of mine, and how good you were to do it! For I was loved, and I had gained love's bond of joy. But in my joy I was bound about with painful chains of iron, so that I might be scourged by burning rods of jealousy, and suspicion, and fear, and anger, and quarreling" (77). The young intellectual with a bright future before him was now possessed of a "wife" who was his social inferior and a son whom neither of them desired. They named the child Adeodatus, gift of God, as if to suggest that they could somehow make it right by giving credit (or blame) to God.

While Adeodatus managed to "force himself upon our love," to make them love him in spite of the circumstances of his conception, he was still, and always, associated in Augustine's mind with the shame he experienced as a nineteen-year-old youth who had sought the joys of love but discovered, too late, that these joys are accompanied with the scourgings of God. Moreover, while Augustine and this nameless woman remained together for nearly fifteen years, they never had another child.

Augustine also mentions Adeodatus in his brief account of his "wife's" return to Africa, though only in passing. She "returned to Africa, vowing that she would never know another man, and leaving me with our natural son" (153). Adeodatus was fifteen years old by now, and the three of them had been together all this time, having spent a year in Augustine's native Thagaste shortly after Adeodatus's birth, then seven years in Carthage, followed by a year in Rome and nearly two in Milan. She was now being sent back to northern Africa, perhaps to Carthage, because his mother, who had recently arrived in Milan, had arranged his engagement to marry into a wealthy Milanese family. (He would have to wait a year or so, however, because his fiancée was under age, i.e., not yet twelve years old.) His "wife's" vow never to know another man may suggest, as his biographers have assumed, that this was a selfless expression of religious piety; or, if not this, at least a willing acceptance of current social conventions regarding women in second-class marriages. Yet, her vow "never to know another man" and the act of "leaving me with our natural son" may also suggest her anger that she could be so callously dismissed after nearly fifteen years of life with Augustine and their son, Adeodatus, and for such dubious reasons. While Augustine speaks of his love for her and says her leaving "was a blow which crushed my heart to bleeding," he says nothing about the impact of all of this on Adeodatus, who was, after all, losing his mother.

Adeodatus is next mentioned in the account of their baptisms into the Christian faith on Easter Sunday a year later. Augustine notes that he and his close friend Alypius were joined in baptism by Adeodatus, who was "born of me in the flesh out of my sin. Well had you made him: he was almost fifteen years old, and in power of mind he surpassed many grave and learned men. O Lord my God, creator of all things most powerful to reform our deformities, to you do I confess your gifts. For in that boy I owned nothing but the sin. That he was brought up by us in your discipline, to that you and none other inspired us" (214). Augustine then goes on to describe the book that he and Adeodatus had produced together: "This is one of our books which is entitled *On the Teacher*, and in it he speaks with me. You know that his are all the ideas which are inserted there, as from the person of the one talking with me, when he was in his sixteenth year. I had experience of many still more wonderful things in him. To me his power of mind was a source of awe. Who except you is the worker of such marvels?" (214)

Here, in this passage, Augustine refers to his son in the past tense. This is because Adeodatus was no longer alive. After the death of Augustine's mother, Augustine and Adeodatus returned to Augustine's native town of Thagaste in northern Africa. Three years later Adeodatus died. Peter Brown notes that Augustine was, in fact, twice bereaved that year. Besides the death of Adeodatus, Augustine experienced the death of a longtime friend, Nebridius, who had returned with him to Africa and had gone to live with his mother in his country house near Carthage. Brown observes, "This double-blow is one of the most significant blanks in Augustine's life," for nothing is known about Augustine's reactions to these deaths.[11]

Just because the two deaths are a major "blank" in our knowledge of his life does not mean that they had identical effects. Augustine's refusal to travel to see his dying friend Nebridius would indicate that the two deaths were experienced very differently. We may assume that Augustine was physically

present when his son Adeodatus died, and we may further assume that Adeodatus's mother, the only woman whom Augustine had loved, was absent.
No doubt, Augustine's brother and sister were there to share his grief, and
undoubtedly there were several close and loving friends. But these could not
take the place of the mother of Adeodatus and of Augustine's own mother as
he grieved for his son.

A major blank in our knowledge about the death of Adeodatus is the
cause of death. We assume that he died of natural causes (there were certainly many such causes from which to die in northern Africa); and, given
the esteem in which Augustine held medical doctors,[12] we may assume that
he was greatly frustrated by their failure to save his son. But the cause and
circumstances of Adeodatus's death are inaccessible to us. All that we do
know is that Augustine viewed the death of his son as an unanticipated act
of God ("Quickly you took his life away from the earth") and that now,
writing his *Confessions* some seven years after his son's death, "I remember
him with a more peaceful mind, for I have no fear for anything in his
childhood or youth, and none at all for him as a man" (214). Nor is there
any mention of his having shed tears over the loss of his son on the day of
his death, for he concludes his remembrance of Adeodatus with this
statement:

> We made him our companion, in your grace no younger than ourselves.
> Together we were ready to begin our schooling in your ways. We were
> baptized, and all anxiety over the past melted away from us. The days were
> all too short, for I was lost in wonder and joy, meditating upon your far-
> reaching providence for the salvation of the human race. The tears flowed
> from me when I heard your hymns and canticles, for the sweet singing of
> your Church moved me deeply. The music surged in my ears, truth seeped
> into my heart, and my feelings of devotion overflowed, so that the tears
> streamed down. But they were tears of gladness. (214)

Again the psalms and canticles successfully blocked and contained the emotions of grief. Here, in this passage, his rhapsodic testimony to the "voices of
your sweet-singing Church" replaces any account that we might have expected of the death itself. If, on the occasion of Augustine's mother's death,
Adeodatus was silenced by Augustine and his friends, now, in his own death,
Adeodatus is textually silenced, as the day of his passing is neither described
nor commented on.

Of course, there is no reason in principle why Augustine should be expected to say more than he has in his *Confessions* about his son's death. He
has already written a very self-revealing book, and it may seem impertinent
for the modern reader to want or expect more. But the fact that we are left in
the dark about Adeodatus's death nevertheless frustrates our natural desire to
know how Augustine felt about himself as a father, and what light he could
have shed on Adeodatus's own feelings about his experiences as son of Au-

gustine. Can it be that the statement, "For in that boy I owned nothing but the sin," is a full and accurate summation of Augustine's fatherly role, and of the meaning that it finally had for him? Without an account of his son's death and its meaning for him, there is no way to tell.

Yet, the very fact that Adeodatus was born in shame, that he was an "unwanted" child, makes this an important question to ask, especially since his life was over almost before it began. Does Augustine suspect that the shameful circumstances of his son's conception are somehow responsible for his early death? Were his fears about his son's spiritual fate owing, in part, to concern that he himself would be to blame if Adeodatus were to suffer eternal torment? Is he relieved that his son did not live long enough to commit the sins and errors of his own youth, and that, as far as Adeodatus's "adulthood" was concerned, it was a clean and unblemished slate? that the whole course of events set in motion by the conception of Adeodatus has finally come to an end?

Augustine's comment, "For in that boy I owned nothing but the sin," is intended as praise for God, who was the author of everything good in Adeodatus. Yet it also suggests that he continues, even now, seven or more years after his son's death, to identify the boy with the circumstances of his birth, and therefore to associate him with his own personal shame. To be sure, their project together—the dialogue between student and teacher—communicates the father's delight in his son's intellectual prowess, and contrasts quite dramatically with Augustine's own sixteenth year, when *his* father admired his emerging sexuality. Yet, the dialogue itself, while occasionally spirited, conveys a father-son relationship in which the father is very firmly in control. When Adeodatus is offered the last word, he tells his father what he knows his father wants to hear ("I have learned by your warning words") and is appropriately submissive ("You have taken up and resolved all the difficulties I was prepared to urge against you; you omitted nothing at all that caused me to doubt").[13]

Thus, the child had been *born* in shame, but Augustine seems determined that the living child will not be the *source* or *cause* of shame, either to Augustine, or to himself. Brought up in God's discipline, Adeodatus would never be allowed to give his father cause for anxiety. He would be a son to whom Augustine could point with fatherly pride, even put on display, and the basis for this pride would be the son's "power of mind" in which "he surpassed many grave and learned men." What his son would not be allowed to exhibit is deep and genuine emotions: wailing over the death of his grandmother while his father and his father's friends succeed manfully in controlling their own emotions. How do we know that Adeodatus did not die the victim of such control? Bereft of his mother, and now of his grandmother too, he may well have died not of heartbreak—though surely this was present—but of the inability to express openly and freely how he felt. Is there not also a deep irony in the fact that the father's testimony to his son's acquired legitimacy centers on a book in which Augustine is the teacher, doing to his son in verbal form what his teachers did to him through physical beatings: controlling and exacting obedience and deference? The difference is in the fact that teacher and parent are one and the same person, so the boy in this case has no one to turn to for solace. Even God is inaccessible to him, for his father—unlike his father's teachers—is so clearly identified with God that there can be no hope or illusion that God would side with the son against his father. Adeodatus is utterly, painfully alone, and on his own. For him, there is no enlightened witness.

To Silence Is to Shame

And so, we come full circle. The story that began with the cries of a young boy in pain—from being beaten by teachers—ends with the cries of another boy who was experiencing another kind of pain, grief over the loss of his grandmother (and, no doubt, the reactivation of the grief he felt when his mother was taken from his side). In both instances, the adults turned a deaf ear and refused to hear the child's cries. Ironically, the first boy is numbered, at the end, among the adults who will not hear, apparently because he has learned to muffle the cries of the child within himself. As he heard the cries of his own son, he, too, "felt that I wanted to cry like a child, but a more mature voice within me, the voice of my heart, bade me keep my sobs in check, and I remained silent."[14] What is this but the silencing of children's emotions by adult codes of conduct? And what is this silencing but a subtle form of shaming? So the more things change, the more they remain the same, and the lessons that Augustine learned about shame as a child are forgotten by him, now an adult. If there is a moral to the story, it is that an otherwise praiseworthy act of self-revelation—the *Confessions*—has legitimized the shaming of defenseless children. And for this, it seems to me, no amount of self-reproach could possibly be excessive.

But Augustine has lived his life. There are no more lessons for him to learn from the silencing of Adeodatus. We, however, have much to learn from it if we will. Let us return to the room where Monica breathed her last breath: The mother dies, the grandson cries, the boy is rebuked, and the father and his friends sing a psalm. Does this scene somehow communicate or signify what our lives—yours and mine—are all about? Is this, the final episode in Augustine's narrative, the climax of the story, the event to which everything that went before is pointing, for which everything that precedes it was preparation? Our last image of Augustine, as the narrative comes to a close, is that of the father joining in the silencing of his son so that he and his friends may sing their praises to God. I suggest that the tragedy of human life is captured in this pathetic scene. Is this the dead woman's legacy, the faith for which she fought so hard? As the cries of Adeodatus are muffled, and the voice of Evodius gains strength and resonance, surely one feels that something is terribly wrong with this world, that the scene no doubt discloses some deep flaw in the universe itself. It should not have happened this way. Father and son, bereft of the women who were more to them than any other, should be joining in shared lamentation. Yes, the dying of Monica was sad and worthy of grief, but even more tragic was the rebuke and the silencing of Adeodatus.

Others, of course, may not react to this deathbed scene as I have reacted, and, since the silencing of Adeodatus has not been commented on by other interpreters of this scene, I am aware that my reaction may be totally idiosyncratic. The point, however, is that this is the episode in Augustine's narrative of his life where I experience a shift from reading his text to being read by it.[15] And, I find that, when this shift occurs, the episode depresses rather than inspires me, and causes me to take no pride in the fact that I, like Augustine, am a Christian. Rather, it fills me with a sense of the tragic limitations, not only of Augustine's life and his insights into his life, but of human life in general and of our capacity to understand ourselves. As I consider his struggle with the problem of whether to shed tears or to contain them, I feel shame for him, and I feel the undeniable truth of Helen Merrell Lynd's observation that "the import of shame for others may reach even deeper than shame for ourselves."[16] How trivial, and yet how tragic, that he would experience this dilemma—to cry or not to cry—as a reflection of who he is, as a person, and as a faithful Christian. And yet, wasn't this the very issue he confronted as a boy being beaten at school—to cry or not to cry— and didn't everything, including his very selfhood, depend on which course he took? Is it any wonder, then, that he should come to view his comportment in the death room of his mother as a test of who he is, both as a person and as a child of God?

Then the shame that I feel for him, I begin to feel for myself, as I sense that I am no less concerned to "do it right," not only or primarily in grieving, but in all areas of my life where I feel that others are observing me. As I reflect on past scenes, trivial by any objective standards, where I struggled so manfully to play my own part oh-so-correctly or demanded of my own son that he act so as not to embarrass me, I realize that I am no different from Augustine. The shame I feel for him comes back to me, and I am left feeling very much exposed and ashamed. In this shame there is a deep sense of loneliness, of being without God in the world, for my God—as for Augustine too—has been a God who discloses himself in the order and quiet dignity of our lives. I have known him, as did Augustine, in the psalms and canticles I have sung on occasions such as this. Although not without feeling, these songs have not much to do with primitive cries of pain and chaotic, unmanageable emotions, but with maintaining control. Surely I am not alone in feeling as I do, ashamed for my obvious skill in keeping emotions in check, but the weight of Christian tradition after Augustine is against those of us who feel this way, and this only increases our sense of loneliness.

The "Death" of Augustine

Now let us return to the schoolroom in Thagaste, where Augustine, the boy's father, was mercilessly beaten by his teachers. Tell me if I am not correct in asserting that the tragedy began there: A boy cried out to his Father in heaven for deliverance from the pain that was crushing his spirit, but his Father in heaven did not respond. What the boy learned from this nonresponse was that he must learn to control himself, to muffle his cries, to learn to hold his peace even—or especially—when in pain. Something died in that boy in that classroom in northern Africa, and this death, unlike that of his son, *is* recounted in his *Confessions*. Only it is not presented as a death, for it appears at the beginning of the narrative, and it would be absurd for an autobiography to presume to give an account of the death of its primary subject and author. Moreover, even if this had been a biography and not an autobiography, so that the primary subject's death could be related and described, we would not look for the account of his death in the first pages of the book, in a chapter on the childhood of a man who lived to his seventy-fifth year.

Still, I submit that a death did occur in that classroom, and no one mourned because no one realized that it happened. We, too, experienced a kind of death in similar settings in school, in church, at home, on the playing fields—wherever—as we, too, learned to muffle our cries, and, as we, too, allowed the adults to interpret our pain for us. Moreover, like Augustine, we have learned to take the adult's perspective on what occurred, and we have turned to religion to find therein the legitimations for adults' assault against the spirit of the child. In so doing, we have allowed ourselves to be deceived, as when Augustine claims that it was the "more mature voice within me" that was "the voice of my heart," when, in truth, it was his desire to "cry like a child" that voiced his heart, now crushed and broken.

It is time to resurrect the child's perspective, whether or not it is able to command religious support and respect. If the psalms composed by others communicate our feelings too, then, by all means, let us sing the psalms. But, if not, let the psalms go unsung, and let us hear instead the cries that come truly from the heart.

3

Religious Sources
of Childhood Trauma

Augustine was not the first child to suffer a beating at the hands of an adult who felt he was acting in the child's best—future—interests. Nor is he the first adult to have written about his experience of being beaten as a child. But he was enormously influential, as Christianity's greatest theologian since Paul, in providing a theological legitimation for these beatings. To be sure, he questioned his teachers' grounds for inflicting punishment on the children, believing that the educational objectives these beatings served supported trivial social and cultural aspirations and values. Yet he interpreted the beatings as the work of God himself, and viewed his parents' failure to intervene as evidence of their love for God.

One wonders what life in the Christian world would have been like had Augustine instead offered a powerful theological indictment of the beating of children by adults. Perhaps he would have been ignored or dismissed as too soft, too permissive, and unrealistically oblivious to the inherent wickedness of children.[1] But it is more likely that a man of his great influence would have been heard and respected, and that hundreds of thousands of children of Christian parents would have been spared unnecessary suffering.

In this chapter we will continue our exploration into the role played by religion, especially the Christian faith, in the physical and emotional suffering of children. This is not a pleasant subject, especially for those of us who have deep personal attachments to the Christian faith. But we dare not avoid the subject, for the abuse of children in the name of religion may well be the most significant reason for why they leave the faith when they are old enough to do so. We must ask ourselves: Who can blame them? Why should they not abandon the scene of their silent torment?

The association of the Christian religion and child abuse is the subject of an important book by Philip Greven, a Rutgers University historian. In *Spare the Child: The Religious Roots of Punishment and the Psychological Impact of Physical Abuse*,[2] Greven explores the religious legitimations that support parents' and other adults' physical abuse of children, focusing especially on the widely held conviction that children enter this world with a distorted or wayward will. It is therefore the responsibility of parents to break, or at least, so successfully to challenge and frustrate children's natural will that they will then be able to respond to parental guidance and live in conformity with the superior will of God. Weak or permissive parents who fail to carry out this responsibility are abdicating their God-given obligations and are cheating their children of the deep personal satisfactions that come from knowing that God loves them and is proud to be their heavenly Father.

However, Greven shows through quotations from biographies and auto-biographies of well-known religious personalities, as well as from religious books on child discipline, that the very idea of "breaking the child's will" is an instance of what Alice Miller has called "poisonous pedagogy."[3] Parents have taken this injunction to break the child's will as a mandate to inflict severe physical punishment, usually with a leather belt or a hickory stick, and sometimes before the child is even able to crawl. Here is a typical quotation taken from Marshall Frady's biography of Billy Graham:

> His father would sometimes withdraw a wide leather belt to apply to him, once when he was discovered with a plug of chewing tobacco in his cheek, another time snatching him up from a church pew where Billy had been fretfully squirming, shoving him on out into the vestibule and there strap-ping him thoroughly. Over all the years since then, Billy maintains, what he still remembers most about his father is the feel of his hands against him: "They were like rawhide, bony, rough. He had such hard hands." In one instance, after Billy had gained some size, his father stood over him flailing away with the belt as Billy was lying on his back, and "I broke two of his ribs, kicking with my legs."[4]

Note that, in one of these instances, little Billy was punished for "fretfully squirming" in church, indicating that religion was as much the cause as it was the putative cure for his sinful temperament.

Unlike his physical struggles against his father, Graham recalls that, while he was "occasionally whistled with a long hickory stick by his mother . . . 'I never fought back with her.'" In turn, she reflects back on the whippings she and Mr. Graham inflicted on Billy and the other children:

> Mr. Graham was right stern, I suppose. Perhaps we were both a little too strict, perhaps we whipped them more than we should have. But it was just that we had to work so hard then, we had little time for anything else, we had too little patience. We thought that little disobediences, you know, were terrible things.[5]

As Greven points out, a central part of parents' infliction of physical punishment is the belief that they are doing it for the child's own good and are not acting out of personal malice or vindictiveness, or even on the basis of their own personal emotions or response to the child's misbehavior. The crucial thing is that the parent is unemotional, acting in a detached, objective manner. Greven cites the following statement by J. Richard Fugate, author of *What the Bible Says About . . . Child Training*:

> Chastisement is the *controlled* use of force. It should never be administered by an angry or emotional parent. If a parent cannot control himself, he should send the child to his room to wait for his whipping. This action provides the parent time to "cool down," and it allows the child time to anticipate the coming consequences of his action.[6]

On the other hand, the same authors who advocate the avoidance of negative emotions by the parents stress that after the punishment is inflicted there typically occurs a moment in which parent and child affirm their love for one another. As James Dobson writes in a section of his book *Dare to Discipline* titled "The Best Opportunity to Communicate Often Occurs after Punishment":

> Nothing brings a parent and child closer together than for the mother or father to win decisively after being defiantly challenged. This is particularly true if the child "was asking for it," knowing full well that he deserved what he got. The parent's demonstration of his authority builds respect like no other process, and the child will often reveal his affection when the emotion has passed. For this reason, the parent should not dread or shrink back from these confrontations with the child. These occasions should be anticipated as important events, because they provide the opportunity to say something to the child that cannot be said at other times. It is not necessary to beat the child into submission; a little bit of pain goes a long way for a young child. However, the spanking should be of sufficient magnitude to cause the child to cry genuinely. After the emotional ventilation, the child will often want to crumple to the breast of his parent, and he should be welcomed with open, warm, loving arms. At that moment you can talk heart to heart. You can tell him how much you love him, and how important he is to you. You can explain why he was punished and how he can avoid the difficulty next time. This kind of communication is not made possible by other disciplinary measures, including standing the child in the corner or taking away his fire truck.[7]

A noteworthy feature of these punishment scenarios is that parents believe they are acting in God's behalf, while the child—as we saw in the case of Augustine—appeals to God for deliverance. The evangelist Aimee McPherson tells how she prayed to God that the anticipated punishment would somehow be averted:

> Like all other restless youngsters, I was constantly getting into dilemmas and difficulties. After similar outrages to the dignity of my household, I would be banished to my room and told that in exactly one-half an hour I would be spanked. I was thoroughly familiar with those whippings. They were not gentle love pats, and my parents never stopped till I was a thor-

oughly chastised girl. The time of waiting for the footsteps on the stair, the opening of the door, and the descending palm was the worst of all. On one such occasion I stood looking wildly about for a way out of the dilemma. No earthly recourse was nigh. Taught as I was about heavenly intervention, I thought of prayer. Dropping to my knees on the side of my bed, I began to pray, loudly, earnestly. "Oh, God, don't let mama whip me! Oh, God, dear, kind, sweet God, don't let mama spank me!"[8]

Thus many children who pray to God to spare them from physical punishment do not view the punishment scenario as parents intend. Instead of viewing their parents as the legitimate agents of God's discipline, they see God as a potential savior, as the one who could stop the whole process if God wanted to. That God does not intervene in the child's behalf may, of course, confirm the parents' view of the matter, although neither McPherson nor Augustine, writing in later years, was wholly convinced that this was true. Instead, as we saw in the case of Augustine, there is a distinction made between what his parents believed (i.e., that the beatings would enable Augustine to become more successful in a competitive world) and what he came to believe (i.e., that they, no less than his teachers, were deceived into thinking that the adult world for which he was being prepared was any more real or true than the world of children's natural pursuits, for engaging in which they were being punished).

Whereas some children seek protection through direct divine intervention, for David Wilkerson, the evangelist, the attempt to escape punishment took the form of physical flight. When he was in trouble and needed a refuge, he would go to the top of a small mountain near his home:

> From Old Baldy, I could look down on our house and watch Mother and Dad and the other children running around the neighborhood trying to find me. Sometimes I would stay up there for the better part of a day, thinking through the problems a boy has to conquer. When I got back, I always got a licking, but Dad's switch never kept me from making my journey again, because up there I found an aloofness and a detachment that I needed.[9]

According to Ruth Harris, David's sister, after punishment the children would be subjected to the even greater "humbling" of being expected to put their arms around their father's neck and to say, "I love you, Daddy. Forgive me for disobeying." Then Daddy would respond, "I love you too, but now we must ask God to help you overcome your stubbornness."[10] Greven comments, "Love and pain, rebellion and submission, disobedience, punishment, and forgiveness thus were intertwined in a powerful mixture of opposing feelings and experiences."[11] Thus through the experience of physical punishment, children learn to associate religion and love; in being reconciled to the punishing parent, the child learns what it means to be a loved child of God.

In their recent article on parents' use of the threat that God will punish their misbehaving child, Hart M. Nelsen and Alice Kroliczak explored the relationship between parents' use of this threat and children's images of God.[12] They found, as did Clyde Nunn before them,[13] that children who believe God punishes them are more likely to believe in a personal than an impersonal God. For some children, God is apparently personalized through the threat, voiced by parents, that God will punish them for misbehavior. The Nelsen and Kroliczak study does not address the physical punishment of children but only parents' use of the verbal threat that God will inflict punishment. Still, if the verbal threat of God's punishment is significantly related to identification of God as personal, we may assume that parents' actual use of physical punishment, especially when accompanied by an explicitly theological rationale for doing so ("God wants me to do this because God loves and cares for you"), would be at least as effective in establishing the child's view of God as personally concerned for the child. This means that proponents of the physical punishment of children might well be correct, if through such punishment God is both personalized and, in a very real (if perverted) sense, experienced as loving.

However, these same proponents of physical punishment are wrong when they assure parents that such punishment will effect positive changes in the child's behavior. This is not borne out by the biographical and autobiographical accounts that Greven cites, and the reasons are not difficult to see. Since it is through physical punishment that children experience whatever parental and divine love they are likely to receive, it is not at all surprising that they would continue to commit the offenses that force reenactment of the punishment scenario. How else will they fulfill their desire to love and be loved? Commenting on the fact that such abusive scenarios are instances of what Freud called the "compulsion to repeat," Leonard Shengold, in *Soul Murder: The Effects of Childhood Abuse and Deprivation*,[14] has pointed out that children will provoke their own beatings to fulfill the imperative need for some parental attention, and they serve the largely delusive expectation that this time they will be unconditionally loved. As David Wilkerson put it, "When I got back, I always got a licking, but Dad's switch never kept me from making my journey again." *He* believed this was because of what he experienced on Old Baldy, the "aloofness" and "detachment" it afforded him. I agree. Yet it could also be because, after the switching had stopped, parent and child would declare their love for each other.

James Dobson's experience of being physically punished is also illustrative of this compulsion to repeat. He reports that he persisted in the very behavior that caused his mother to attack him:

> My own mother . . . was very tolerant of my childishness, and I found her reasonable on most issues. . . . But there was one matter on which she was absolutely rigid: she did not tolerate "sassiness." She knew that backtalk

and "lip" are the child's most potent weapons of defiance and they must be discouraged. I learned very early that if I was going to launch a flippant attack on her, I had better be standing at least ten or twelve feet away. This distance was necessary to avoid being hit with whatever she should get in her hands. On one occasion she cracked me with a shoe; at other times she used a handy belt. The day I learned the importance of staying out of reach shines like a neon light in my head. I made the costly mistake of "sassing" her when I was about four feet away. She wheeled around to grab something with which to hit me, and her hand landed on a girdle. She drew back and swung that abominable garment in my direction, and I can still hear it whistling through the air. The intended blow caught me across the chest, followed by a multitude of straps and buckles, wrapping them-selves around my midsection. She gave me an entire thrashing with one massive blow. From that day forward, I cautiously retreated a few steps before popping off.[15]

Here Dobson indicates that he knew full well what kind of misbehavior would stimulate an angry response from his mother, and that being punished for it did not cause him to stop. Perhaps the reason this particular episode shines in his mind like a neon light is not that it was physically more painful, but because, in throwing her own undergarment at him, his mother injected a sexual element into the punishment scenario, one both stimulating and threatening, arousing and repulsive. As an adult, he writes about the incident in terms of tactics—how much physical distance to maintain between him-self and his mother—but, as a child, the deeper issue was surely that his flippant talk precipitated the transgression of previously safe emotional boundaries between mother and son. As Greven says, the punishment sce-nario creates "a powerful mixture of opposing feelings," and Dobson makes clear that he had every intention of repeating the act for which he knew he would be punished.

Exploiting the Child's Natural Fears

A major theme in Greven's work is the relationship between the physical abuse of children and an apocalyptic religious worldview. As he points out, for the last few centuries, "the apocalyptic impulse has continually been present in this land, waxing and waning in intensity, taking various forms, but often anticipating the imminent end of this world and the inauguration of the millennium, the thousand years of peace promised in the book of Revelation to those who survive the horrors of the tribulation marking the end of humanity and history. Only 'true' Christians, obedient and submissive children of God, are expected to survive the ultimate holocaust and the Last Judgment and to become the eternal inhabitants of the New Jerusalem on this earth and elsewhere."[16]

Greven asks: What are the roots of this apocalyptic thinking? Why are so many people enthralled by the imagery and the fantasies of punishment, devastation, destruction, and doom set forth in the book of Revelation and other New Testament texts? And why are so many individuals and groups captivated by the fantasies of rescue implicit in the doctrine of the rapture (i.e., when twice-born Christians will be spared the horrors of the tribulation on earth by being lifted bodily up from the earth)? Greven believes it is "surely no accident that so many of the Protestant Christians who are ardent advocates of corporal punishment for children are also intensely apocalyptic."[17] Herein lies the connection: "The painful punishment of children creates the nuclear core of rage, resentment, and aggression that fuels fantasies of the apocalyptic end of the world. This has been true at least from the early seventeenth century to the present. The most consistent thread connecting apocalyptics generation after generation has been the experience of pain, assault, and physical coercion resulting from harsh corporal punishments in childhood."[18]

Greven points out that David Wilkerson, who postponed his father's beatings by escaping to Old Baldy, has a fantasy of the end time that recapitulates the dynamics of the childhood punishment scenario. Wilkerson himself describes it:

> These are exciting days for true Christians. God, in His love and mercy, is allowing disasters to strike the earth to warn all who will hear that Jesus is coming back, and that it's time to get ready. He loves His children too much to bring His new kingdom to pass without warning. . . . These disasters are a kind of countdown, too painful to ignore, choreographed by God to set the stage for the final moments of time.[19]

Yet, unlike his earthly father, the heavenly Father intends "to deliver His true children from His final fury that will be outpoured on the earth. He will deliver His children from the most gruesome hour of disaster that the Bible predicts will fall upon the earth."[20] In other words, the impulse to escape will, in this alternative scenario, be honored, and the true children of the heavenly Father will be spared the punishment that God will inflict on all the others.

Part of the appeal of Wilkerson's message is his emphasis on the true believer's ability to live above fear. If children who are about to be punished experience an overwhelming sense of fear, leading them to seek desperately for some means of escape or to pray for God's deliverance, the message that Wilkerson and other evangelists preach is that, for the believer, fear will not be a constituent part of the holocaust that is to come: "When you have God's glory, you can rejoice in God's doom. You and I may live to see the wreck of matter and the crash of worlds—nevertheless, we will not fear."[21]

Greven notes that a strong theme in the apocalyptic literature is God's wrath, that "rage and retribution by the Divine Father against his sinful and disobedient children on earth are the primary reasons for God's long-planned punishments and destruction of life on earth."[22] We might also note that, like the childhood punishment scenario, God increases the tension by refusing to disclose when the dreaded event will occur. Observing that Hal Lindsey, the most widely read apocalypticist of our times, once informed his readers that his own father "gave me my share of lickings, too, and I know now that it was really for my good, though at the time I didn't think so," Greven suggests that apocalyptic thought involves a projection of the earthly father onto God, the difference between them being the sheer scope of God's punishments, as God, "the ultimate authoritarian," intends "to destroy the entire world and nearly every person living on his planet."[23] Another crucial difference, however, is that in the religious scenario, there is deliverance: "Fundamentalist Protestant forms of apocalyptic Christianity mirror theologically the violence and abuse that so many once experienced in childhood, transforming their earlier pain and fear and terror into fantasies of rescue and triumph."[24]

The Case of Little Albert

Greven draws our attention to the relationship between the physical abuse of children and apocalyptic thought. What he does not explore is the attraction that behavioristic theories have long held for Protestant fundamentalists, especially in legitimating harsh methods of child discipline in home and school. In an ingenious study of John Watson, the founder of American behaviorism, Paul Creelan connects Watson's behaviorism to the fundamentalist cultural milieu in which Watson himself was raised, arguing that behaviorism is a "secularized" form of American apocalypticism, one in which Watson adopts the "role of the Covenant God of dispensational millenarianism, 'promising' and 'threatening' his people according to precise numerological formulae, in order to accomplish social transformations of millennial proportions."[25]

Born in 1878 in the tiny village of Travelers Rest, near Greenville, South Carolina, Watson grew up under the tutelage of an intensely devout Southern Baptist mother who gained a local and statewide reputation as a leader in the Women's Missionary Union, one of the offshoots of the millenarian effort to convert the world in preparation for the second coming. When his father, a dissolute ne'er-do-well, abandoned the family, Watson embarked on an adolescent phase of delinquency and insubordination, including mocking his teachers, fighting in the classroom, and even being arrested in Greenville for "nigger fighting" and firing a gun. His mother wanted him to go into the ministry, and while he gave some consideration to her desire, her death left him free to embark instead on graduate studies in psychology at the University of Chicago.

Creelan believes that Watson's moral revulsion at what he saw and experienced in Chicago inspired him to create in his laboratory a symbolic version of the "mystical Babylon" depicted in the book of Revelation. The elaborate "city" that he created—comprised of rats whose behavior he could manipulate at will—bore a striking resemblance to the Babylon whose destruction had been prophesied by the author of Revelation. Creelan concludes that "Watson's recreation of the 'mystical Babylon' thus suggests that his childhood religious training remained a powerful force in his character, keeping him at a considerable distance from the sensual freedom offered in the urban environment to which he had journeyed. However much he was fascinated by the image of 'mystical Babylon' that he had created in his laboratory, his ultimate attitude of distantiated observation reveals a moral judgment of puritanical condemnation and negation toward the horrible evil that he observed. Ultimately, he would recommend behavioristic technique as a means of predicting and controlling the external world, not of becoming more sympathetically and personally involved with it. The moral basis of the behavioristic attitude therefore appears to be the judgmental condemnation hurled against the evils of 'mystical Babylon' by the Covenant God of millenarian Protestantism."[26]

Readers interested in the precise symbolic correlations between the book of Revelation and Watson's experiments with rats may consult Creelan's article. What interests me here, given our concern with the religious legitimation of child abuse, is Creelan's discussion of Watson's experiment with a human infant, whom he named "Little Albert." (Watson, whose full name was John Broadus Watson, was named after John *Albert* Broadus, professor of preaching at the Southern Baptist Theological Seminary in Greenville.) The purpose of the "Little Albert" experiment was to determine whether fear can be made a conditioned response. Little Albert, an eleven-month-old infant, would be placed in a room with small furry animals (black cats, white rats, rabbits, and dogs). Albert exhibited no natural fear of these animals. Nor did Watson succeed in eliciting the slightest reaction from Albert to reptiles, frogs, turtles, and snakes. Even a bonfire failed to elicit the fear reaction whether it was lit in an open room or a dark room. The only stimuli that would call forth the fear response were "loud noises" and "loss of support." However, by placing a white rat before Albert while simultaneously striking a metal bar behind his ears with a hammer, Watson was able to condition the infant to express fear of furry animals whenever they were presented without the accompanying loud noise. He was also able to condition Albert to express fear of fire by setting a small bonfire before him and subsequently pulling the blanket out from under him, causing him to topple over, to cry, and to crawl away.

While Creelan is mainly interested in establishing the symbolic connections between the Little Albert experiment and the book of Revelation, what is striking to me about this experiment is that it is designed to condition the child to fear. Watson was surprised to learn that children have so few natural fears (only loud noises and loss of support). Other fears exhibited by children are learned. Yet these two fears are precisely those that are evoked by the physical punishment of children, as the parent confronts the child in a raised voice and, by pushing, shoving, or hitting, throws the child off balance. Thus, what Watson did to Little Albert was analogous to the physical punishment of a child inflicted by an abusive parent. Watson also demonstrated that it is possible to condition a child to exhibit fear by producing an object at the same time (e.g., a fuzzy animal) so that eventually the object itself is sufficient to instill fear. In child beatings, the belt or the stick serves this function. (In Dobson's case, it was the dreaded women's undergarment.) In this way, the parent can appear to be detached and unemotional, neither loud nor physically threatening, because the belt or stick is enough to strike fear in the child. Or, if the parents choose to use their own hands in punishing the child, these hands become, as it were, disembodied objects and the child, as in the case of Billy Graham, never forgets the "hardness" of the parent's hands. Thus, the point that Watson's abusive experiment on Little Albert enables us to make is that fear is at the core of the relationship between religion and the physical abuse of children.

It is therefore not surprising that Greven identifies paranoia as one of the main psychological consequences of child abuse. As he points out in *Spare the Child*, "The anticipation of pain often is as hard to bear as pain itself, and the sense of vigilance rooted in that anticipation—captured in the familiar words 'Go to your room and wait until your father comes home'—lays the groundwork for subsequent anticipations of harm, of injury, and of pain, as well as the persistent sense of threats and dangers to life, spirit, and limb as characteristic of paranoid forms of being and behavior."[27] Greven notes that paranoia comes in many guises and degrees, but common to all forms "is a pervasive sense of being endangered. The anticipation of harm from outside is the core of paranoia. . . . Paranoia arises from the keen and persistent sense that the body, the will, and the self are at risk" (168–69).

Greven contends that children whose wills are assaulted and broken often become paranoid as adults, that the seedbeds for subsequent paranoia are the coercion and threats to the autonomy of the self inherent in the breaking of children's wills. Also, the pervasive suspiciousness and fear of subversion and of conspiracies that are so characteristic of paranoia reflect the earlier battles over the child's willfulness and autonomy (173). Greven believes that paranoia arises later in life, and may not appear in childhood itself, because children are forbidden to react appropriately and effectively to adults' aggression, so that expressions of rage and of counteraggression that arise from self-defense are suppressed by both the adults and the children themselves. Later, these feelings, long suppressed, can be displaced, attributed to others, and projected onto persons and situations entirely removed from the earlier scenes of aggressive assaults and threatening encounters with discipline. Augustine's view of God as one who scourges is illustrative of this projection. Also, the situations in which Augustine perceives God to be acting in this fashion are often far removed from the context of the original childhood beatings, as they have to do with adult sexuality, intellectual ambition, and even the death of loved ones. Yet, as Greven points out, the very fact that paranoid thoughts and feelings are associated with persons and situations that are unrelated to the original scene of punishment should not deter us from seeing a dynamic connection between the one and the other. Common to all is the pervasive sense of being an endangered self, fearful and afraid.

The Strategy of Detachment

Another prominent psychological effect of the physical abuse of children is dissociation. As Greven points out, the ability to disconnect feelings from their contexts and to disconnect one's sense of self from the external world are at the heart of the process of dissociation. It is one of the most basic means of survival for many children, as they learn early in life to distance themselves, or parts of themselves, from experiences too painful or frightening to bear: "Traumas, both physical and emotional, are often coped with by denial and repression of the feelings they generate" (148).

Greven notes that, like paranoia, dissociation takes many shapes in subsequent life. Hysterical, borderline, and multiple personality disorders are expressive of dissociation: "Since pain felt and experienced takes many forms and comes in many degrees, from mild to severe to unbearable, children often discover ways to survive their pain through disconnecting and splitting, in the most extreme cases creating alternate selves and personalities, which bear and express feelings that otherwise would have been overwhelming to a small child" (148). He also notes that, while these traumatic experiences are split off, they nonetheless survive in the unconscious, and are "encoded in our memories, permanently, in visual, tactile, and verbal forms." We too often fail to realize that these memories persist throughout our lives, for most of them are buried and inaccessible to us despite our utmost efforts at recovery. Moreover, "the ability to *appear* to forget, through repression or amnesia, is crucial to the dissociative process, for inability to connect parts with the whole underlies the protective measures that sustain so many varied responses to early traumas and pain" (150). But these experiences are not forgotten, only repressed. Through hypnosis and other therapeutic interventions, they can be recovered down to the minutest detail.

What also concerns Greven is that such repressed experiences can be reenacted in adult life, with the child victim now taking the role of the parent abuser. Recall Alice Miller's harrowing tale of the young girl whose father thrust her into a closet and hung her by her nightgown; of how she dared not scream out from fear that he would return to kill her; and of how, years later, she impulsively struck her daughter's head with the phone receiver and accidentally killed her. As we have seen, this, in Miller's view, is an instance of the repressed experience being reenacted. What the woman could not endure was the fact that her daughter had the temerity to scream—in response to a minor frustration—when she, a truly endangered child, had been forced to control herself and not allow herself to scream in spite of her pain and terror.[28]

In his discussion of the devastating consequences of dissociation and splitting, Greven makes much use of the last paper written by Freud's disciple, Sandor Ferenczi, entitled "Confusion of Tongues between Adults and the Child." In this paper, Ferenczi noted that "trauma, specifically sexual trauma, cannot be stressed enough as a pathogenic agent," and then proceeded to discuss the dissociative effects of such trauma, especially the dissociation where children identify with the adult who is abusing them: "The overwhelming power and authority of the adult renders them silent. Often they are deprived of their senses. Yet that very fear, when it reaches its zenith, forces them automatically to surrender to the will of the aggressor, to anticipate each of his wishes and to submit to them, forgetting themselves entirely, to identify totally with the aggressor."[29] Ferenczi described this identification with the adult as a "dreamlike state" or "traumatic trance," and noted that "when the child recovers from such an attack, he feels extremely confused, in fact already split, innocent and guilty at the same time; indeed his confidence in the testimony of his own senses has been destroyed."[30]

Greven cites an instance of this identification with the aggressor and dissociation from the self in the diary of Cotton Mather. In describing his experience of being chastized by God, Mather says that "I fly away from even my very self into Him, and I take part with Him against myself: and it pleases me, that He is pleased, tho' I myself am dreadfully torn to Peeces in what is done unto me."[31] According to Ferenczi, "there can be no shock, no fright, without traces of a personality split," and "if traumatic events accumulate during the life of the growing person, the number and variety of personality splits increase, and soon it will be rather difficult to maintain contact without confusion with all the fragments, which all act as separate personalities but mostly do not know each other."[32] Ferenczi also recognized that such splitting can result not only from sexual traumas but from traumas of all kinds, including those arising from the pain of corporal punishments: "We have known for the longest time that not only forced love but also unbearable punishments can have a fixating effect."[33]

Greven discusses other psychological consequences of childhood abuse, including sadomasochism, aggression and delinquency, and authoritarianism, but paranoia and dissociation would appear to be the most direct and immediate psychological effects of physical punishment. Paranoid thoughts and feelings are produced by the assault itself (as the children experience themselves to be in mortal danger), and dissociation is their only defense against such endangerment. Tragically, the response of dissociation allows the very outcome that the child sought to defend against, as its effect is the fragmentation of the self.

The Case of Buster Keaton

Alice Miller's brief chapter on the comedian Buster Keaton, in *The Untouched Key*, provides a particularly bizarre example of dissociation as it focuses on Keaton's ability to keep a straight face while the audience was laughing at his antics.[34] Miller recalls being bothered by this discrepancy as a child, and adds, "I wasn't able to find his antics funny when I had to look at that sad face."[35]

Keaton began appearing on stage with his parents when he was only three, and he helped make them famous by taking severe abuse in front of an audience without batting an eyelash. The audience would squeal with delight, and by the time the authorities (alerted to the abuse by social workers) were ready to intervene because of the physical injuries he sustained, the family would already have moved its act to another city. In his autobiography, *My Wonderful World of Slapstick*, Keaton describes the "knockabout act" that he and his father performed: "In this knockabout act, my father and I used to hit each other with brooms, occasioning for me strange flops and falls." Note here the same experience of the child being thrown off balance that we saw in our discussion of Little Albert. Keaton continues:

> If I should chance to smile, the next hit would be a good deal harder. All the parental correction I ever received was with an audience looking on. I could not even whimper. When I grew older, I readily figured out for myself that I was not one of those comedians who could jest with an audience and laugh with it. My audience must laugh *at* me.[36]

Keaton also noticed that whenever he smiled or let the audience "suspect how much I was enjoying myself," they didn't seem to laugh as much as usual. If he happened to begin to grin, "the old man would hiss, 'Face! Face!' That meant freeze the puss. The longer I held it, why, if we got a laugh the blank pan or the puzzled puss would double it. He kept after me, never let up, and in a few years it was automatic. Now when I step onstage or in front of a camera, I *couldn't* smile. Still can't."[37]

Miller believes that Keaton "completely missed the *significance* of these scenes for his whole later life and for his art" because, in spite of remembering what had happened to him, he "undoubtedly repressed the trauma of being abused and degraded. This is why he had to repeat the trauma

countless times without ever feeling it, for the early lesson that his feelings were forbidden and were to be ignored retained its hold on him."[38]
Here Miller describes the phenomenon of dissociation: Keaton learned
to dissociate the feelings he had from the traumatic event (the beating)
itself.

Yet what is curious about his experience is that the feelings he had were
initially pleasurable, for the fact that the knockabout act made people laugh
made him want to smile too. I think this can be understood as an example of
identification with the aggressor, including not only his father but also the
audience, and of the confusion and splitting of the self that results from the
trauma of abuse itself. Keaton wanted to participate in the audience's enjoyment of the experience—to identify with the aggressors against himself—but
was forbidden by his father from doing so, as this would reduce the audience's enjoyment. (There is a striking similarity here between the audience
in Keaton's case and Augustine's parents' laughter on being shown the effects
of the beatings he had sustained at the hands of his teachers.) The confusion
he experiences is due to the fact that it was in and through the infliction of
pain that he won his father's approval. This juxtaposition of punishment and
love creates a powerful emotional bonding of child to parent. Keaton's biog-
rapher tells about the numerous instances when Keaton's father inflicted
severe physical injury on Buster and then talked about it boastfully, "proud
that the boy put up with such treatment without complaining." Clearly,
Keaton learned to dissociate not only from the pleasure he experienced in
making audiences laugh but also from the pain he felt as his father inflicted
severe physical injury. Such dissociation is reflected in his impersonal references to his own body—"the pan" or "the puss." It is also reflected in the
title of his autobiography—*My Wonderful World of Slapstick*—for this is a
fictive world, a fantasized world, split off from the actual world in which he
lived, systematically beaten by his father day after day and instructed not to
show an iota of emotion.

Since Keaton was a popular comedian, it might be argued that this case of
dissociation, unlike that of Cotton Mather, has nothing to do with religion.
Yet, as we will explore in chapter 5, a central dynamic in religion is the
scapegoating of an innocent individual—often a child—who is punished so
that the others may go free. A major appeal of Keaton's vaudeville act for
audiences was that they could *witness* the physical abuse of a child from a
position of safety, that is, in a highly ritualized context in which they were
not themselves threatened or endangered. This may explain why they were
less disposed to laugh when Keaton appeared to be enjoying himself, as this
would break the spell both of the scapegoating ritual itself and of the reenactment of the original trauma—the childhood beatings—to which members
of the audience had themselves been subjected, turning it instead into a mere
"act." It was necessary for the audience, in other words, to be convinced that

Keaton was truly experiencing pain, pain that hurt him not only physically but psychologically too.

Religious Ideas and the Tormenting of Children

Thus far, we have been concerned with the *physical* punishment of children. However, if we were to limit our attention to physical abuse, as Greven does, there is a danger that adults who do not physically abuse their children will merely take comfort in this fact. Greven himself points out that religious moderates and liberals alike have traditionally advocated some form of physical punishment, but his book has generally been viewed as a critique particularly of Christian conservatives and fundamentalists, both because religious legitimation of the physical punishment of children is widely known to be a centerpiece of certain conservative and fundamentalist theologies, and because he argues for the connection between physical abuse and apocalypticism.

Thus, in the interests of making all Christians, including moderates and liberals, uncomfortable, I want to shift focus from Greven's concern with the religious roots of the physical abuse of children to the more direct role of religious ideas and beliefs in the traumatizing of children. If, as Greven has shown, a religious idea (i.e., the idea that children have a natural will that is opposed to the will of God) can legitimate the physical abuse of children, what about religious ideas that have a more direct, unmediated effect on children, ideas that children experience as inherently traumatizing?

I believe that many religious ideas that children are taught cause them emotional torment and are therefore inherently abusive. I further suggest that one reason children will internalize God via physical punishment is that they simultaneously experience religious ideas as inherently tormenting. Webster's *New World Dictionary* says that the word "torment" "implies harassment or persecution by the continued or repeated infliction of suffering or annoyance." Torment differs from torture in that torture "implies the infliction of acute physical or mental pain, such as to cause agony."[39] In the light of these distinctions, it is appropriate to claim that religious ideas are more tormenting than torturing, since they are unlikely to cause acute emotional pain of the sort that occurs as the child awaits physical punishment, but are fully capable of harassment and persecution through repeated infliction of suffering or annoyance.

To test this theory, I asked the persons with whom I often have lunch to recall any experiences they might have had as children when a religious idea caused them such torment. Recollections of such experiences did not always come easily, but all were able to recall instances in which a religious idea, taught by a well-intentioned adult, caused unnecessary, even gratuitous suffering. One reported that, as a child, she believed that she had committed the unpardonable sin, but wasn't sure that she had, because she didn't know exactly what it was. Assurance that "if you are worried about having committed it, you haven't committed it" was ineffectual, because it is equally plausible that she wouldn't be thinking about having committed it unless she had actually done so. Another had a similar experience with the familiar injunction not to drink of Christ's blood or eat of his body "unworthily." What constituted "'unworthiness" in this instance was unclear to him. What these and many other examples had in common was the fact that the idea itself was inherently tormenting. It was not the manner in which the ideas were presented that caused confusion or fear. Rather, the ideas themselves were inherently confusing and frightening. When I asked my lunch mates whether they could recall similar experiences with tormenting ideas in their classes at school, none of them could recall a single idea that was threatening in this same fashion.

Of course, it could be argued that these recollections give a very skewed picture, that many of the religious ideas that children are taught are quite benign, if not positively reassuring. Yet our conversations elicited few recollections of this nature, since even religious ideas that are meant to be reassuring were not experienced as such. One individual recalled being assured by a church school teacher that if he had enough faith, his prayers would surely be answered. When he prayed for the recovery of his aunt who was afflicted with cancer, and she subsequently died, he was devastated, because he was certain that he had prayed with all the faith he had. As he put it, "The life went out of my faith at that point, and it has taken all these years to get this much of it back." In concert with Carl Goldberg's argument that shame always involves a sense of incompetence,[40] I believe his inability to save his aunt through prayer was a shaming experience, the proof of his incompetence, and that shame, along with fear, are the most common experiences of torment caused by religious ideas.

These experiences suggest that religious ideas may be as abusive as the physical punishment of children in the name of religion. There is compelling evidence for this in the fact that adults relate to religious ideas in much the same dissociative manner as adults who were subjected to physical abuse as children. Among the various forms that dissociation may take, I would suggest that those that have particular relevance for the traumatizing effects of religious ideas are (1) repression or amnesia regarding the experiences that were so traumatizing; (2) splitting, where the threatening experience is cut off from the rest of one's thinking processes and not incorporated into them; (3) withdrawal of feeling or affect, a blandness or roteness in thought processes associated with the threatening experience; and (4) the loss of confidence in the testimony of one's own perceptions and senses regarding these and similar experiences—that is, when the subject is discussed, one tends to defer to others and to their perceptions and judgments.

In my conversations around the lunch table, I found a great deal of evidence for repression or amnesia from childhood experiences with traumatizing religious ideas. All my companions had partially or totally forgotten about these experiences. However, as more and more details emerged, they discovered that they had powerful feelings about the torment they had suffered, feelings of deep sorrow and pity for the child each once was, and rage at the person or persons who had promulgated the religious idea in question, even though these persons had not been intentionally abusive.

These conversations offered no direct evidence of the other forms of dissociation, but it would not be difficult to demonstrate that, for many persons, religious ideas are split off from the rest of their thought processes and are not incorporated into them. Furthermore, the same person who engages in complex and energized thinking about science, technology, or politics thinks in clichés, or in bland fashion, where religion is concerned. There is also a tendency for persons who are generally able to think independently, and to trust the testimony of their own perceptions in other areas, to become very deferential to other authorities where religious ideas are concerned, even in instances where they themselves have direct personal experience bearing on the issue in question.

In an article on cognitive styles in religious thinking, Russell Allen and Bernard Spilka identified a phenomenon they called a "detached-neutralized" cognitive perspective. For those with this cognitive orientation, "religion is considered thoroughly important, but is mainly severed from substantial individual experience or emotional commitment. Ideals remain abstracted from specific behavior and rarely realistically influence daily activities. . . . Religion is primarily an emotional 'clinging' or over-dependence. [There is] a magical or encapsulated feeling tone which is not meaningfully related to daily activities. . . . The importance of religion is neutralized, reduced, or rendered ineffectual by other concerns or by lack of positive affect and identification. There may be an unrestrained admiration for religious ideals or ideas which are selectively neutralized or attenuated by use of exceptions or diffusions."[41]

I am suggesting that many adults for whom religion is detached and neutralized in this fashion experienced religious ideas in childhood as traumatic. Apparently, subjects of Allen and Spilka who took a "detached-neutralized" approach to religion were not so detached and neutralized about other cognitive domains, indicating that dissociation was occurring only where religious ideas were at issue. Such dissociation could be caused by other experiences, including physical punishment inflicted for explicitly religious reasons. However, I would guess that it might also have a more direct cause, that is, that religious ideas in childhood are intrinsically traumatic, and therefore, among adults, religious ideas continue to be accompanied by such dissociative features as repression, compartmentalization, withdrawal of affect, and lack of confidence in one's own perceptions and judgments.

Religious Legitimation for Adult Detachment from the Traumas of Childhood

In addition to religious ideas that cause dissociation similar to that caused by physical punishment, certain religious ideas have the effect of legitimating or normalizing the dissociative process. These are ideas that contribute directly to the tendency of adults to view childhood traumas as detached and neutralized observers. I suggest that one such idea is the doctrine of the virginal conception of Jesus, an idea that is not only subscribed to by the vast majority of Christians, but also, and more important, is a basic feature of the religious ethos of Christian churches. The possibility that it might not be true, and that Jesus might have had a human father, is rarely mentioned or discussed among Christian adults. While this idea might also be one that is inherently tormenting for children because it may produce fear or confusion, I would rather draw attention to the fact that this idea legitimates adults' emotional detachment from the pain and distress that children experience; it encourages them to treat their own experiences of childhood trauma as insignificant or as never having happened.

Specifically, the idea of the virginal conception of Jesus stretches a veil of secrecy or denial over the actual circumstances of Jesus' conception, thus denying the childhood traumas that Jesus himself experienced, and therefore creating a religious ethos in which the traumas of children are not taken seriously. Also, because this concept insists that Jesus' conception was unique, fundamentally different from all other conceptions, it invites the compartmentalization of religion from other cognitive domains; not only those that, on biological grounds, question the physical possibility of a virginal conception, but also, and more important, those that, on psychological grounds, view such a story as an instance of the suppression of childhood trauma. This concept also contributes to the undermining of confidence in the testimony of our own perceptions and senses, as this is an "event" for which we have no corroborating personal experience. Typically, when we encounter religious ideas that find no support in our own experiences and perceptions, we invoke the word "faith," with faith meaning to accept the truth of an idea precisely because no such support exists. Thus the idea of the virginal conception of Jesus invites various forms of dissociation.

In her book *The Illegitimacy of Jesus: A Feminist Theological Interpretation of the Infancy Narratives,* Jane Schaberg has argued that there are strong historical grounds for believing that Jesus was illegitimately conceived, that Mary's pregnancy was by a man other than Joseph, and that, as Mary was probably only twelve years old, she was the victim of rape (and not a consenting participant in the sex act).[42] Since I will be discussing her grounds for making these assertions in chapter 6, I will not elaborate on her admittedly controversial position here, but will simply note that, if she is right, then the idea of the virginal conception of Jesus places a veil of secrecy over these traumatic events—both for Mary, who was a mere child when they occurred, and for her son Jesus, who was condemned by the circumstances of his birth to live out his life as one who was deeply stigmatized, having what Erving Goffman terms a "spoiled identity."[43] For children who are the victims of abuse, and adults who were abused as children, this idea of the virginal conception of Jesus effectively eliminates Mary and Jesus as sympathetic figures, sufferers in common, since the fact of their own victimization is swept aside and categorically denied. Thus, in much the same way that Alice Miller, in *Banished Knowledge*, has argued that Freud's oedipal theory throws a protective shield over abusive or negligent parents by viewing the child as the instigator of aggression and sexual perversity,[44] so does the virginal conception of Jesus spare adults from even having to consider the possibility that the child Jesus (and the child Mary) suffered greatly due to the irresponsible actions of an adult.

The vast majority of New Testament scholars reject the theory that Mary was the victim of rape and that Jesus was therefore illegitimate. Only a handful have had the courage to put in writing what they say in private, that, in their view, Joseph was Jesus' natural father, for the concept of the virginal conception of Jesus is a later tradition. By taking issue with Schaberg's view without explicitly stating their alternative view, they give implicit support to the virginal conception idea and thus participate in the church's longstanding tradition of supporting adult detachment from the traumas of childhood. The concept of the virginal conception of Jesus makes it difficult for adults to think of him as a child who could have experienced any form of child abuse whatsoever, for it carries with it the corollary notion that adults held the child Jesus in reverence and awe. The concept thus places a halo around the childhood of Jesus, and desensitizes adults to the realities of childhood, so that they fail to hear the cries of children in their own midst, and the crying child within. If one chooses to believe this concept, one should at least be aware that the child Jesus—and the child Mary—surely did not. But it would be a sign of our maturity as Christian adults if we relinquished it, for this would indicate that we intend to take seriously the fact that children are being abused and tormented, and that the Christian religion has done more to support than to counter it.

Religion and Love

I realize that in singling out the idea of the virginal conception of Jesus, I have gone farther than Greven in my critique of the Christian faith, for he has been content to attack only the apocalyptic thinking of Christian fundamentalists, whereas I have focused on what is a central affirmation of Christians of all persuasions, and one that was central to the teachings of Saint Augustine himself.[45] My intent is not, however, to debunk or condemn Christianity, for there is much that it has done and continues to do in behalf of children.

I first read Gordon Allport's brief essay "'Religion and Prejudice" when I was a graduate student.[46] The very simplicity of his argument left a deep impression. His point was that religion has historically been a major *cause* of bigotry, but it has also been instrumental in *condemning* bigotry in all its forms. The same simple point can be made regarding the relationship of religion and the abuse and tormenting of children. I have presented evidence in this chapter that religion is often at the root of such abuse, providing a legitimation for it. However, there is another side to the matter, namely, that religion has often been society's most vocal advocate for children against their adult abusers, and religion has often provided legitimation and motivation for some adults' active condemnation of child abuse. For them, child abuse cries out to heaven as an outrage that neither they nor their God can tolerate. The social workers who tried to put a stop to the public abuse of Buster Keaton were undoubtedly motivated by their religious convictions.

In his book *Molech: A God of Human Sacrifice in the Old Testament*, John Day tells an absorbing and distressing story about how children were sacrificed to Molech, one of the gods of the Canaanites. He quotes the following passage from a commentary on Leviticus 20 by a nineteenth-century Jewish scholar, in which the ritual sacrifice was described:

> The children, as they expired, cried out loudly owing to the intensity of the fire. In order not to arouse the compassion of father and mother at the wailing and crying of their sons, the pagan priests sounded [their trumpets] to confuse the listeners and prevent the screams of the children from being heard.[47]

Day points out, however, that there was a great outrage among the prophets of Israel concerning the ritual sacrifice of children, and that this was a major reason for their opposition to Baal worship.[48] So children were tormented and abused in the name of religion, but their victimization was also decried in the name of religion.

The Gospels tell us that Jesus, too, took a protective approach to children, thus, in his own adult life, breaking the vicious cycle of child victimization. When parents brought their children to him he instructed his disciples to let them do so, and he stretched out his hand—the same hand that other adults have used to strike their children—and blessed them instead (Matt. 19:13–15). Also, according to Matthew, he charged his disciples: "See that you do not despise one of these little ones; for I tell you that in heaven their angels always behold the face of my Father who is in heaven" (Matt. 18:10). As one who knew what it meant to be a "despised" little one, Jesus' charge to his followers here is more than a moral injunction. It is a powerful act of *personal* self-affirmation, one that was the basis for his affirmation of the self-affirmations of others, self-affirmations that he called their "'faith" (e.g., Luke 7:50), a very different understanding of faith from the idea that it is acceptance of a claim that has no corroborating evidence or support in our own personal experience.

My lunch mate who recalled that his teacher had said his prayers would be answered if he had sufficient faith told another story. It was about a teacher who read the children stories, and would allow them to take turns sitting on her lap as she read. As he told this story, his eyes filled with tears, because he knew that, in recalling this incident after these many years, something deep within him had been touched by her. If only we could forgo the lofty pretensions of religion, those that cause us to torture and torment the children, and instead tell simple stories of human goodness, courage, resourcefulness, cooperation, compassion, and, above all, of loving and being loved.

In *God Bless You, Mr. Rosewater*, Kurt Vonnegut's "hero," Eliot Rosewater, has agreed to baptize Mary Moody's twins because no one else would do it. When challenged about his qualifications to perform this religious act, he totally agrees with his questioner. After all, he had already told Mary herself "that I wasn't a religious person by any stretch of the imagination. I told her nothing I did would count in Heaven, but she insisted just the same." "Then," asked his questioner, "What will you say? What will you do?"

> "Oh—I don't know." Eliot's sorrow and exhaustion dropped away for a moment as he became enchanted by the problem. A little smile played over his lips. "Go over to her shack, I guess. Sprinkle some water on the babies, say, 'Hello, babies. Welcome to earth. It's hot in the summer and cold in the winter. It's round and wet and crowded. At the outside, babies, you've got about a hundred years here. There's only one rule that I know of, babies—':
> "God damn it, you've got to be kind."[49]

One could, I suppose, point out the Eliot was addressing the wrong audience, since it is not children, but adults, who need this lesson in kindness. However, I assume his point is that it is never too early, nor, presumably, too late, to learn to be kind. As Billy Graham's mother confessed, "We had too little patience," and "We thought that little disobediences, you know, were terrible things." If religion and the abuse of children go together, so, too, do religion and love, and sometimes it takes an Eliot Rosewater, who is convinced that nothing he does could possibly count in heaven, to remind us of this, and to make it so. And, if I find myself preferring the gospel of Eliot Rosewater to that of James Dobson and other professed Christian spokespersons, it is because he does not allow abuse to masquerade as love.

4

Letter to the Hebrews:
The Lasting Effects of Childhood Trauma

A few days before Christmas, the other pastors and I in my synod received our bishop's annual Christmas letter. In the letter he notes the fact that just a few days after we celebrate "the serenity of a nativity scene" in Bethlehem we will be memorializing the children (the Holy Innocents) whom Herod murdered in his search for the Christ child. He goes on to comment on the slaughter of innocents that occurs on our city streets for no apparent reason, and inspires no special memorial, "except perhaps if we remember them in connection with Herod's victims."

The same day that I received this letter from our bishop, I received a copy of a professional journal to which I regularly subscribe. The lead article, by Christopher G. Ellison and Darren E. Sherkat, is titled "Obedience and Authority: Religion and Parental Values Reconsidered."[1] In it the authors provide compelling evidence that parents' support for authoritarian parenting orientations is positively linked with three theological positions: biblical literalism, belief that human nature is sinful, and punitive attitudes toward sinners. As the authors note, this evidence is very much in line with previous studies of the influence of religious beliefs on methods of parenting. However, contrary to expectations, they also found that, when asked whether they favored *intellectual heteronomy* (or the obedience of children to the dictates of authority figures) to *intellectual autonomy* (or the inclination of youngsters to think and reason independently), many Conservative Protestant parents came down on the side of intellectual autonomy. This finding was a surprise to the researchers, who assumed that Conservative Protestant parents would oppose intellectual autonomy in their children. (They found that Catholic parents did oppose such autonomy.) On the other hand, they also found that Conservative Protestant parents who did oppose intellectual autonomy in their children strongly supported two of the three theological positions noted above. These were biblical literalism and punitive attitudes toward sinners.

This study suggests that theology plays a significant role not only in legitimating authoritarian parenting practices (the issue with which we were concerned in chapter 3), but also in discouraging children from learning to think and reason for themselves. Apparently belief that human nature is sinful is not a significant contributor to the latter, but biblical literalism and a punitive attitude toward sinners are.

In reading our bishop's letter, I found myself anguishing with him over the fate of children in our world today. But I also felt the predictable frustration that letters of this nature tend to evoke in those to whom they are written, the frustration of feeling rather helpless to do much about this senseless slaughter of the innocents (and some not so innocent). Then, however, I noticed a sentence or two in the letter that I had passed over in my initial reading, having done so, I believe, because the letter writer had invited me to do so. He wrote:

> At the present rate we will be hardpressed to create a peaceful space wherein the celebration of Christ's birth can take place. It's not just a matter of all the restless young children who on Christmas Eve will kick the pew in front of them with hard leather shoes they are wearing for the second time this year, or chatter and squirm incessantly to the chagrin of older members who came hoping for *stille nacht*. The peace is far more broken than that.

From here he went on to write about the senseless killings of innocents on our city streets.

I agree. It's not just a matter of all the restless young children who chatter and squirm through the Christmas Eve service. Yet these restless young children are important too, and there is something we can do about them, and, specifically, about the fact that in many of our churches these children are being taught that to be a Christian means to favor intellectual heteronomy over intellectual autonomy. What is at stake here is the freedom of children to think for themselves and to feel secure in the knowledge that adults will not hold their expressions of intellectual autonomy against them. Especially where biblical literalism is taught and practiced, and where punitive attitudes toward sinners are voiced and countenanced, children are unlikely to experience such freedom to think and reason for themselves. Rather, they are likely to feel that it is wrong for them to think for themselves and that, if they do, they are likely to incur the disapproval, if not the wrath, of precisely those adults who have power over them. Fearing the negative consequences of their exercise of intellectual autonomy, they are likely to overreact, to place even greater strictures on their own freedom of thought than these adults may have required of them.

Of the two theological views—biblical literalism and punitive attitudes toward sinners—the one that apparently has the most damaging effect on intellectual autonomy is biblical literalism. As Ellison and Sherkat conclude:

"While members of Conservative Protestant denominations are no less enthusiastic about autonomy than other persons, certain theological views commonly espoused within these conservative groups—especially biblical literalism—are negatively related to valuation of [intellectual] autonomy."[2]

Ellison and Sherkat are quick to acknowledge that "biblical literalism" is a value-laden term. In the national survey on which their study was based, the biblical literalism item was worded thus: "The Bible is the actual word of God and is to be taken literally, word for word." While this statement may seem straightforward enough, the authors point out that there is enormous ideological freight behind it:

> The term "literalism" evokes heated debate. . . . We [the authors] understand contemporary notions of biblical literalism to denote an interpretive strategy, implying both a common set of "ground rules" for reading the scriptural text and a set of a priori assumptions about the text. Specifically, self-proclaimed literalists tend to argue that the Bible is *unitary* and *inerrant*—containing no error (and thus no contradiction), and leading to no error. . . . Indeed, for literalists the "soundness" of a particular scriptural interpretation often depends upon the degree to which the interpreter both accepts and preserves these core claims. . . . As many observers recognize, "literal" readings of scripture are social products, generated and disseminated within communities of conservative evangelical theologians, pastors, and influential laity, with recourse to a select number of extrabiblical commentaries and reference materials. . . . What is most important for the present study is that the ideological foci and social structure of literalist interpretive communities operate to constrain the "legitimate" interpretive options and practices of many contemporary Conservative Protestants.[3]

Thus we cannot conclude that those who responded affirmatively to the biblical literalism item in the survey read the Bible without prejudgments whereas those who did not respond affirmatively have such prejudgments. Moreover, such prejudgments are not derived from or even supported by the biblical text itself, but derive from a theory about the biblical text (i.e., its alleged unitariness and inerrancy, which are claims that the biblical text itself does not explicitly make). We must also assume that this theory about the biblical text derives from its proponents' social and cultural locatedness, and that these may bear very little relationship to the social and cultural locatedness of the biblical authors.

Of course, those who take the view that the Bible is "the actual word of God" reject the very notion that the biblical writings are themselves socially and culturally situated, and therefore see no need to discriminate between the cultural or social biases of the author, on the one hand, and the purposes and intentions of God for the world, on the other. Yet, the very capacity to make such discriminations, and to develop rationales for doing so, requires the exercise of intellectual autonomy that "biblical literalists" (as defined by the survey) vigorously oppose. As the Ellison and Sherkat study demonstrates, those who responded affirmatively to the biblical literalism item in the survey were also disposed to devalue intellectual autonomy.

In the introduction to this book, I alluded to Luther's own principle for discriminating between biblical passages, which was to believe the biblical words that consoled and reassured him and to disbelieve those that condemned him, doing so on the grounds that these condemnatory words no longer applied to him, as he was now living in a state of grace and no longer under the law. This principle is essentially personal (even psychological), and differs from the principle that would differentiate biblical passages on the grounds of whether they reflect only the cultural and social biases of the author (and therefore present a false or inadequate understanding of the purposes and intentions of God for the world). But these two principles— the personal and the sociocultural—can be compatible, especially when the biblical texts at issue are those that concern adults' treatment of children. A biblical passage that advocates the abuse of children can be attributed both to the cultural and social milieu in which it was written and to a law (or legalistic and moralistic) orientation on the part of the biblical author. This orientation is always superseded and called into question by the orientation of grace, which is not only the predominant message of the Bible but also the fundamental reason why we continue to read the Bible and find therein the strength and courage we require to see us through the difficulties and problems and complexities of daily living. It is not that the Bible, as James Dobson claims, fortifies parents to "dare to discipline," but rather that it "dares" parents to relate to their children within the framework of grace, and thus to dare to accord their children dignity and respect, even when they seem undeserving of it. As all who have been parents can readily attest, the latter requires far more courage, far more inner strength, than the approach that Dobson advocates. After all, it requires great inner strength for parents to have respect for a child when the child is out of control, and there is enormous courage involved in hearing the desire or need that underlies the child's acting out.

In his *Table Talk*, Luther contrasts his experience as a child who was beaten by his mother for stealing a nut (noting that the punishment was excessive for the crime committed) with a scene he had witnessed earlier that day where his children resolved a controversy between them without adult intervention. This, he told his listeners, is how it is with God, who encourages us to use our own skills at reconciliation to resolve our differences and conflicts. It is noteworthy that the children did not settle their argument by beating one another. Instead, they spoke to one another, face to face, and then returned to their common play. Here, the children themselves model a nonpunitive approach to conflict resolution. If the children can talk out their differences, why is it necessary for adults to inflict pain on children? If children can use language to overcome misunderstanding, why must adults use physical blandishments?[4]

In another episode recounted in Luther's *Table Talk*, Luther was describing to the group assembled around the supper table the interpretive principle alluded to above, that is, his distinction between biblical passages that made him experience condemnation versus those that confirmed his sense of being enveloped by God's grace. This insight that biblical passages could be so discriminated had a profound influence on him, for he could now read the Bible without becoming demoralized and despairing. Whereupon John Bugenhagen, a friend who often frequented Luther's evening table, related a similar experience when it had occurred to him that the love of God was the central theme in the Bible, and he could therefore take hold of those passages in which the love of God was clearly expressed and was felt by him, and dispense with those passages in which God's love was compromised, obscured, or even obliterated.[5] This conversation not only supports the idea that the Bible need not be read as a unitary whole and that some biblical texts ought to be privileged above others. It also encourages the intellectual autonomy of each individual reader, as it shows that these two men could experience the Bible as profoundly transformative when they no longer treated it with undue reverence.

It is not the case, therefore, that only biblical literalists take the Bible seriously. Indeed, those who challenge the biblical literalists' assumption of the unitary and inerrant nature of the Bible read it more discriminantly (i.e., making discriminations between those biblical passages that evoke the transforming power of God from those that drive another nail in the coffin of our personal and collective lives). And so there *is* something that we can do for the children in our midst, the children who sit in church on Christmas Eve and kick the pews in front of them. We can create an environment in our churches in which the biblical literalism of which Ellison and Sherkat speak is not tolerated, and we can do this not because we have a personal ax to grind against those persons in our congregations who are biblical literalists, or because we are theological or ideological liberals, but simply and solely because we truly care for the children in our midst. Where biblical literalism of the kind Ellison and Sherkat identify prevails, a punitive attitude toward sinners (e.g., children who are judged to be anything but "innocents") also prevails, and there is parental disapproval of intellectual autonomy in their children. Significantly, the Ellison and Sherkat study also shows that it is not a belief in human sinfulness as such that supports either a punitive attitude toward sinners or parental disapproval of intellectual autonomy in their children. Thus it is not necessary for us to abandon the belief in human sinfulness in our contestation with the biblical literalists in our congregations. What we do reject is a punitive attitude toward sinners and the biblical literalists' inhospitable attitude toward children's exercise of intellectual autonomy.

In *Banished Knowledge*, Alice Miller makes an impassioned plea for the importance of children being allowed and encouraged to think for themselves, to exercise what we have been calling intellectual autonomy. This plea occurs in the context of her discussion of the enlightened witness, her term for those adults who treated children with kindness and respect, and "who thus enabled them to become aware of their own parents' cruelty."[6] Such adults provided a "supporting and thus corrective witness." Yet Miller also notes that for adults to acknowledge that they were abused as children, they may need something more than an enlightened witness who affirms the likelihood of their having been abused as children. They also need the capacity to think for themselves. How an adult makes use of the enlightened witness's supportive perspective "will depend mainly on whether in their childhood they were sufficiently at liberty to query their parents' behavior and opinions or whether this was totally forbidden because the parents had to be regarded as infallible, blameless persons" (170). If the latter, "the doors to any later questioning of the parents and of instilled opinions sometimes remain closed forever, and the learning capacity of such people is severely handicapped. As a result, they pass on to their own children their parents' pernicious ideas of disciplining and childrearing, without the slightest misgivings" (170). Thus, the fact that biblical literalism discourages the exercise of intellectual autonomy among children may explain why the inability to recognize that one *was* the victim of child abuse is more prevalent among Christians, especially Conservative Protestants, for biblical literalism and the discouraging of children's capacity to think for themselves go hand in hand.

Thus, a key factor in breaking the vicious cycle of child abuse is precisely the intellectual autonomy of which Ellison and Sherkat speak. Without it, the adult will be unable to take advantage of the efforts of enlightened witnesses. Since Alice Miller's own books are the effort of such a witness to testify to what typically happens in childhood, children who were unable to think for themselves will, as adults, refuse to read books by Miller and others like her. Or, alternatively, they will be disinclined to understand such books, because, if they did, they would have to feel the tragedy of their childhoods and the pain of having been misled at such an early age (170–71). Biblical literalism is pernicious because it both encourages a punitive attitude toward children by adults and discourages intellectual autonomy—the capacity to think for oneself. This is a very dangerous combination, one that invites parental abuse of children from generation to generation.

Biblical literalism is therefore not something to be tolerated for the sake of keeping peace within a congregation, for it is a direct and powerful threat to the formation of intellectual autonomy in children, the very autonomy that is required so that the abuse they suffered as children can be recognized when they become adults, and, in recognizing it, make a self-conscious (autonomous) decision not to inflict the same abuse on their own children. If we fear that our intolerance of biblical literalism will disrupt the peace of our congregation or other context of ministry, then the words of the bishop in his pastoral letter are instructive. As he goes on to say:

> The peace that we invent for ourselves is not the peace which God gives. We don't really understand much about the wondrous gift that peace can be, preferring to measure peace only in terms of our own quiet and contentment. That is a peace into which we can escape, an invention of our own making. The peace which God gives is a peace unlike that which the world may try to offer. It is a peace that does not require escape, a peace sure and certain that even the worst terror cannot fold the welcoming arms of God's love and mercy.

He concludes by quoting Jesus' words of assurance: "Peace I leave with you; my peace I give to you; not as the world gives do I give to you. Let not your hearts be troubled, neither let them be afraid." The role of the enlightened witness is not to be a peace lover but a peacemaker, and this means challenging those who would use the Bible to curtail and undermine the intellectual autonomy of our children. The freedom of our children to live in peace, to sleep at night knowing they are secure, is the peace that Jesus gives. This is far more important than maintaining congregational peace when that peace is bought at the expense of the children.

The Letter to the Hebrews:
A Bundle of Weeds?

The Ellison and Sherkat study notes the negative relationship between biblical literalism and intellectual autonomy but does not explain why this negative relationship occurs. I believe the explanation is that biblical literalism supports authoritarian parental orientations, since it is the Bible that is invariably invoked when authoritarian parenting orientations (or poisonous pedagogies) are advocated or defended. Furthermore, the texts that are used to support these authoritarian parenting orientations are prominent examples of those biblical texts that support intellectual heteronomy against intellectual autonomy. In my view, the major offender in this regard is the letter to the Hebrews.

In one of his parables about the activity of God in the world, Jesus tells about a man who sowed good seed in his field, but while he was sleeping, his enemy came and sowed weeds among the wheat. When the plants began to spring up and bare grain, the weeds also began to appear. Noting the weeds, his servants came to him and pointed out what had happened. He immediately suspected his enemy of trying to sabotage his crop. When his servants asked if he wanted them to gather the weeds, he said no, lest in gathering the weeds they root up the wheat along with them: "Let both grow together until the harvest; and at harvest time I will tell the reapers, Gather the weeds first and bind them in bundles to be burned, but gather the wheat into my barn" (Matt. 13:30).

I am reminded of this parable when I hear the oft-repeated claim that Martin Luther viewed the letter of James as a bundle of straw, on the grounds that its author was confused about the relationship between faith and works. As he is quoted as saying of James in his *Table Talk*:

> There's no order or method in the epistle. Now he discusses clothing and then he writes about wrath and is constantly shifting from one to the other. He presents a comparison: "As the body apart from the spirit is dead, so faith apart from works is dead." O Mary, mother of God! What a terrible comparison that is! James compares faith with the body when he should rather have compared faith with the soul![7]

Obviously, Luther, whose profound reverence for the Bible is beyond question, was nonetheless able to exhibit considerable intellectual autonomy with respect to the letter of James. Luther, of course, was especially sensitive to what he perceived to be the inferiority of this particular letter to much of the rest of the Bible because it dealt with his central theological issue: the relationship of faith and works. I, too, have difficulties with the letter of James, because the author, in making his case that faith without works is barren, cites Abraham's threatened sacrifice of Isaac as an example of one whose faith was not barren: "Was not Abraham our father justified by works, when he offered his son Isaac upon the altar? You see that faith was active along with his works, and faith was completed by works" (James 2:21–22). The analogy between body and faith and spirit and works of which Luther is so critical follows this illustration (v. 26).

However, I am more concerned about the letter to the Hebrews than that of James, for it provides a theological rationale for the abuse of children. As Philip Greven points out:

> The key text in the New Testament cited in favor of harsh physical discipline of children is Hebrews 12:5–11, which many Christians assume to have been written by the Apostle Paul, who converted to Christianity after Jesus had been crucified. Modern scholars, however, have concluded that Paul was not the author of this book, which thus remains anonymous. Although no one actually knows who wrote Hebrews, this unknown author has had, and continues to have, an incalculable impact upon the lives of children.[8]

Greven notes that "the justification of corporeal punishment by the author of Hebrews . . . drew upon an ancient history filled with instances of divine chastisements and pains, while he himself supplied memories of the personal anguish that once felt 'grievous' to him and to others."[9] Thus, in Hebrews 12:5–6, the author asks his readers: "Have you forgotten the exhortation which addresses you as sons?" and then proceeds to quote Proverbs 3:11–12: "My son, do not regard lightly the discipline of the Lord, nor lose courage when you are punished by him. For the Lord disciplines him whom he loves, and chastises every son whom he receives."

The author next compares divine chastisement to the discipline that sons receive from their earthly fathers: "It is for discipline that you have to endure. God is treating you as sons; for what son is there whom his father does not discipline? If you are left without discipline, in which all have participated, then you are illegitimate children and not sons" (12:7–8). In the light of Schaberg's argument that Jesus was illegitimate, this statement that the only children who are not adequately disciplined are the illegitimate ones is deeply ironic, especially because it occurs in the midst of the author's discussion of Jesus' death on the cross as the full and complete sacrifice for the sins of all humankind. He even alleges that Jesus' own attack on the sacrificial system in Jerusalem was not for the purpose of ending sacrifice, once and for all, but rather in order to abolish this system in order to establish another one, this one based on "the offering of the body of Jesus Christ once for all" (10:5–10).

Having advanced his analogy between the discipline that he and other legitimate sons received from their fathers and the discipline that they, now adults, are enduring from God, he continues: "We have had earthly fathers to discipline us and we respected them. Shall we not much more be subject to the Father of spirits and live? For they disciplined us for a short time at their pleasure, but he disciplines us for our good, that we may share his holiness. For the moment all discipline seems painful rather than pleasant; later it yields the peaceful fruit of righteousness to those who have been trained by it" (12:9–11). Here, the author claims that God's discipline is "for your own good," and then distinguishes between earthly fathers who beat their sons for the pleasure it affords them and God who does so only so that we may become more like him.

Greven notes that nowhere in the letter to the Hebrews does the author "cite words spoken by Jesus to confirm his beliefs about the necessity for scourging sons. If any such text existed in his own time and place, the anonymous writer does not make use of it."[10] I would add that such a text would conflict with the Gospels, as they represent Jesus as an advocate of mercy toward errant sons (cf. the story of the prodigal son in Luke 15:11–32). But even more to the point is the fact that the Gospels have nothing to say about Jesus' death being a sacrifice. As René Girard points out in *Things Hidden since the Foundation of the World*:

It must be admitted that nothing in what the Gospels tell us directly about God justifies the inevitable conclusion of a sacrificial reading of the Epistle to the Hebrews. . . . If we keep to the passages [in the Gospels] that relate specifically to the Father of Jesus, we can easily see that they contain nothing which would justify attributing the least amount of violence to the deity. On the contrary, we are confronted with a God who is foreign to all forms of violence. The most important of these passages in the synoptic Gospels formally repudiate the conception of a vengeful God, a conception of whose traces can be found right up to the end of the Old Testament. Even if we discount all the explicit and implicit identifications of God with love that we find in the Gospel of John and in the Epistles attributed to the same author, we can confidently assert that in respect of the rejection of violence, the Gospels are fulfilling the work of the Old Testament.[11]

Girard then suggests that, in his opinion, the basic text that shows us a God who is alien to all violence and who wishes to see humanity abandon violence is Matthew 5:43–45: "You have heard that it was said, 'You shall love your neighbor and hate your enemy.' But I say to you, 'Love your enemies and pray for those who persecute you, so that you may be [children] of your Father who is in heaven; for he makes his sun rise on the evil and on the good, and sends rain on the just and on the unjust." He adds, "Beside this text we can put all the texts denying that God is responsible for the infirmities, illnesses and catastrophes by which innocent victims perish—in particular, of course, for conflict. No god can be blamed for this; the immemorial and unconscious practice of making the deity responsible for all the evils that can afflict humanity is thus explicitly repudiated" (183). Then, against the contention that this seems to make God into a sort of distant or indifferent deity, for, after all, at least the old Yahweh was interested enough in humans to be roused to anger by their iniquities, Girard counters:

In fact, we do not meet an indifferent God in the Gospels. The God presented there wishes to make himself known, and can only make himself known if he secures from men what Jesus offers them. This is the essential theme, repeated time and time again, of Jesus' preaching: reconciliation with God can take place unreservedly and with no sacrificial intermediary through the rules of the kingdom. This reconciliation allows God to reveal himself as he is, for the first time in human history. Thus mankind no longer has to base harmonious relationships on bloody sacrifices, ridiculous fables of a violent deity, and the whole range of mythological cultural formations. (183)

Also, against the argument that the Garden of Gethsemane story implies that God the Father was making a sacrifice of his son, Jesus, Girard argues that this is not the case at all. It *was* necessary for Jesus to die, not, however, "to satisfy a deity's need to revenge his honor, which has been tainted by the sins of humanity, and who therefore requires a new victim, one who is very precious and dear to him, his very own son" (182). Rather,

> when Jesus says: "your will be done and not mine," it is really a question of dying. But it is not a question of showing obedience to an incomprehensible demand for sacrifice. Jesus has to die because continuing to live would mean a compromise with violence. I will be told that "it comes to the same thing." But it does not at all come to the same thing. In the usual writings on the subject, the death of Jesus derives, in the final analysis, from God and not from men—which is why the enemies of Christianity can use the argument that it belongs within the same schema as all the other primitive religions. Here we have the difference between the religions that remain subordinated to the powers and [a religion that centers on] the act of destroying those powers through a form of transcendence that never acts by means of violence, is never responsible for any violence, and remains radically opposed to violence. (213–14)

The problem, then, is that the letter to the Hebrews introduces the logic of sacrifice (which will be discussed in greater detail in chapter 5), using it as a theological rationale for the punishment of children, even as it uses the punishment of children to support its view of God as requiring Jesus' death, as Girard puts it, "to revenge his honor, which has been tainted by the sins of humanity." In addition, the author of Hebrews links the love of God not to mercy, as the Gospel writers do, but rather to chastisement. Even with the sacrificial logic, he might have made a case for God's mercy on the grounds that God can now be merciful because Jesus' life has been sacrificed in our behalf, and therefore, there will be no more divine chastisements. But, according to the author of Hebrews, the sacrifice of Jesus does not put an end to all divine chastisements, for God now chastises because, through the sacrifice of Jesus, he views us through the eyes of love. The sign of God's love is not in his mercy, as Jesus taught, but in his chastisements.

The author also asserts that by means of these divine chastisements we become more like God (holy as God is holy). This means, in effect, that we become godlike in the degree to which we discipline our own children, and do so "for their own good" rather than for our own perverse pleasure. Of course, this distinction between beating for pleasure and beating for the good of the child may be totally lost on the child, for it hurts just the same. Chastisement "for the good of the child" is experienced as even more ruthless, since it is represented as an entirely rational act.

The author also warns that if we sin after receiving knowledge of the truth, then Jesus' sacrifice is no longer in effect, and we face "'a fearful prospect of judgment, and a fury of fire which will consume the adversaries" of God (10:26–27). He continues:

> A man who has violated the law of Moses dies without mercy at the testimony of two or three witnesses. How much worse punishment do you

think will be deserved by the man who has spurned the Son of God, and profaned the blood of the covenant by which he was sanctified, and outraged the Spirit of grace? For we know him who said, "Vengeance is mine, I will repay." And again, "The Lord will judge his people." It is a fearful thing to fall into the hands of the living God. (Heb. 10:28–31)

Thus the letter to the Hebrews offers a view of God that is diametrically opposite to that affirmed by the Gospels, where God is presented as one whose mercy knows no bounds and as one who is unalterably opposed to violence, including sacrificial violence, of any kind. This view is already prefigured in the Hebrew prophets. Micah says it well:

"With what shall I come before the Lord,
   and bow myself before God on high?
Shall I come before him with burnt offerings,
   with calves a year old?
Will the Lord be pleased with thousands of rams,
   with ten thousands of rivers of oil?
Shall I give my first-born for my transgression,
   the fruit of my body for the sin of my soul?"
He has showed you, O man, what is good;
   and what does the Lord require of you
but to do justice, and to love kindness,
   and to walk humbly with your God?
                   (Micah 6:6–8)

The Letter to the Hebrews as Teaching Text

Does this mean that we should discard the letter to the Hebrews as a bundle of weeds? In raising this possibility, I am reminded of Thomas Jefferson's famous effort to pare down the Gospels to their essentials, eliminating all "supernatural" elements, including the miracles and the resurrection narratives. As he wrote in a letter to John Adams, the basic story and teachings of Jesus "are easily distinguished as diamonds in a dung-hill."[12] But the parable of the wheat and weeds gives me pause, and prompts me to ask if there is something important for us to learn from the letter to the Hebrews, something that the author surely did not intend for us to learn, but that we can learn by reading his text in a way that he did not, could not, envision.

It is very significant that this is the one biblical text where the author alludes to having been abused as a child. Alice Miller suggests reading the book of Lamentations as the words of a mistreated child.[13] But, by the author's own self-attestation, the letter to the Hebrews *is* the work of an adult who was the victim of child abuse (beaten by his father for his father's pleasure). We can learn a great deal from reading this text as the work of a victim of child abuse, and, more specifically, as the work of an adult who now identifies with those who inflicted abuse on him as a child. Thus, his text provides insight for us into the thought world of a person who remains trapped, emotionally and cognitively, in the abusive structure. To read the letter to the Hebrews is to allow oneself to experience the continuing effects of child abuse on the adult psyche, and to see how the abuse is transmitted to the next generation (i.e., as poisonous pedagogy). The letter to the Hebrews is a teaching text from which we can learn a great deal about the long-term effects of child abuse.

In our discussion in chapter 3 of the consequences of child abuse, we noted that two of the most common long-term effects of child abuse are paranoia and dissociation. Paranoia, as Greven noted, "is a pervasive sense of being endangered. The anticipation of harm from outside is the core of paranoia. . . . Paranoia arises from the keen and persistent sense that the body, the will, and the self are at risk."[14] Dissociation, as Greven pointed out, takes many forms in later life, but a characteristic of all forms is the tendency toward self-splitting, in which one identifies with one's aggressor and surrenders one's will to him. Also, confused, disjointed, and disconnected thought sequences, especially involving the inability to connect the parts with the whole, are quite common.[15]

It isn't difficult to discern in the letter to the Hebrews a similar paranoia, as the author is convinced that those to whom he is writing are in danger because they are provoking God's anger and wrath. Nor is it hard to perceive that his thought processes are often disjointed and disconnected, due mainly to the fact that he feels obliged to conform his own thoughts to those of the authors whom he considers authoritative, and to whom he defers. In other words, the disconnectedness of his discourse (e.g., its irrationalities, its tendency to shift from one topic to another without appropriate transitions, its strained analogies) is not due to any obvious cognitive deficiencies on the author's part, but to his need to subordinate intellectual autonomy to intellectual heteronomy. The letter reads like a student's term paper that is held together, more or less, by frequent quoting of sources, exhibiting a rather strained effort to make the quotations say what the author needs them to say. Moreover, the authoritative texts that he chooses are ones that support his paranoia, his pervasive sense of being endangered.

The warning that runs through the letter to the Hebrews is that those to whom the author is writing are in mortal danger, because they have provoked God through their rebellious attitude. Thus, in chapter 3, he cites the rebellion of the people of Israel in the wilderness and the psalmist's claim that God was greatly provoked with their generation and vowed that none of them would ever enter his rest (Ps. 95:7–11). He then cautions his readers: "Take care, brethren, lest there be in any of you an evil, unbelieving heart, leading you to fall away from the living God. But exhort one another every day, as long as it is called 'today,' that none of you may be hardened by the

deceitfulness of sin" (3:12–13). Continuing, he asserts that a rebellious attitude is reflected in acts of disobedience, and disobedience is certain proof
that one has an evil, unbelieving heart:

> Who were they that heard and yet were rebellious? Was it not all those
> who left Egypt under the leadership of Moses? And with whom was he
> provoked forty years? Was it not with those who sinned, whose bodies fell
> in the wilderness? And to whom did he swear that they should never enter
> his rest, but to those who were disobedient? So we see that they were
> unable to enter because of unbelief. (Heb. 3:16–19)

Thus rebellion, disobedience, and unbelief are intimately linked, and therefore the attitude of rebellion and the actions that flow from it are deserving
of God's wrath.

In chapter 4, the writer begins, "Therefore, while the promise of entering
his rest remains, let us fear lest any of you be judged to have failed to reach
it" (4:1). Repeating his point that those who received the good news were
unable to enter his rest because of disobedience (v. 6), he challenges his
readers:

> Let us therefore strive to enter that rest, that no one fall by the same sort
> of disobedience. For the word of God is living and active, sharper than any
> two-edged sword, piercing to the division of soul and spirit, of joints and
> marrow, and discerning the thoughts and intentions of the heart. And
> before him no creature is hidden, but all are open and laid bare to the eyes
> of him with whom we have to do. (Heb. 4:11–13)

Thus, there is no point in trying to deceive God, for God sees all the way
through us, and cannot be fooled. This capacity of the one who has absolute
power over us to discern our inner thoughts, especially our hostile thoughts
toward him, is what strikes the greatest terror in the heart of the child.
Punishment for inner thoughts ("I know what you are thinking and I don't
like it") is typically more vicious than punishment for wrongful deeds precisely because inner thoughts are less subject to the abuser's control.

In chapter 5, the author introduces the idea that Jesus is our high priest,
standing before God in our behalf, because he was obedient even unto death
(5:1–10). He tells his readers that he will have more to say about Jesus as the
high priest whose obedience is counted as righteousness in our behalf, but
admits that this idea

> is hard to explain, since you have become dull of hearing. For though by
> this time you ought to be teachers, you need some one to teach you again
> the first principles of God's word. You need milk, not solid food; for every
> one who lives on milk is unskilled in the word of righteousness, for he is a
> child. But solid food is for the mature, for those who have their faculties
> trained by practice to distinguish good from evil. (Heb. 5:11–14)

Here the author's tone reflects his identification with the aggressor, as he puts down his readers because, in spiritual matters they are like children when they should be more like adults. And what is the basic difference between children and adults? Well, children don't listen to their parents (they are "dull of hearing") and adults "have their faculties trained by practice to distinguish good from evil." The implication here is that children are unable to distinguish between the two, which is why they need to be punished, for otherwise, how will they learn? Also, we must physically punish them because they are dull of hearing, that is, they do not listen to their parents' and teachers' voices, so the only way to get through to them is by striking their bodies and inflicting physical pain.

In chapter 6, the author assures his readers that, while he has warned them about their immaturity, he is certain that God will not abandon them, "for God is not so unjust as to overlook your work and the love which you showed for his sake in serving the saints, as you still do" (6:10). He cites the example of Abraham, to whom God made a promise that he kept, and notes how Abraham, by "patiently enduring," obtained that promise (v. 15). Melchizedek, too, obtained the promise, not, however, because he had any descent to which he could appeal, "but by the power of an indestructible life" (7:16). In other words, we are not to ask why it is necessary to suffer, as the people of Israel did during their wanderings in the desert, but we are to endure patiently, proving by our endurance that we are indestructible. Thus, we need to be able to show that we can take it, that we can endure his chastisements without whimpering, whining, or complaining. In the passage that links the punishment of sons by their fathers to God's chastisement, there is the same emphasis on endurance, on taking one's punishment like a man, and not "shrinking back," for those who shrink back will be destroyed. His authority here is Habbakuk (Hab. 2:3–4), who does not, however, speak of "shrinking back" but simply of waiting patiently for the one who is coming, that is, endurance is demonstrated in the capacity to wait. Shrinking back has the further and more ominous connotation of seeking to avoid one's punishment by moving backward as one's abuser advances and eventually corners his victim.

There are numerous references in the letter to the Hebrews to those who suffered abuse, and, as a result, received the promise of God. In 10:32–33, there is reference to the abuse that his own readers have suffered. In 11:26, Moses is cited as having "considered abuse suffered for the Christ greater wealth than the treasures of Egypt, for he looked to the reward." In the same chapter there is a list of judges and kings who "won strength out of weakness" and are judged by the author to be great men of faith. This list includes Jephthah, the harlot's son who was thrown out of the house by his brothers because his mother was not their father's wife. He subsequently sacrificed his virgin daughter to the Lord because he felt he could not renege on his intemperate, ill-considered vow (Judges 11). That he murdered his innocent daughter has little if any influence on the author's judgment that Jephthah was a great man of faith because he suffered at the hands of his military enemies and prevailed. In Hebrews 13:12–13, Jesus is described as having "suffered outside the gate in order to sanctify the people through his own blood," and "therefore let us go forth to him outside the camp, and bear the abuse he endured."

These references to abuse could be due to the possibility that those to whom the author is writing are under threat, subject to imprisonment and even martyrdom for their faith. The fact that he centers on the abuse suffered by Moses and others who died in their faith supports this conclusion: "They were stoned, they were sawn in two, they were killed with the sword; they went about in skins of sheep and goats, destitute, afflicted, ill-treated— of whom the world was not worthy—wandering over deserts and mountains, and in dens and caves of the earth" (11:37–38). But the author's basic theme throughout the letter is that his readers' sufferings are due to their sinfulness. Even if there is some evidence that they have struggled against sin, they "have not yet resisted to the point of shedding [their] blood" (12:4). It is not as though they are innocent victims of whatever suffering they are being made to endure, but that they are being chastized for their sinfulness, and, even then, they have not yet been chastised to the point where they have actually shed blood. (Is he recalling those times when, as a child, he was beaten so badly that blood *was* shed?)

Another possible allusion to the punishment scenario in childhood is an image that recurs throughout the letter to the Hebrews, that of the voice of God, a voice that one ignores at one's peril. Chapter 1 begins with the observation that God spoke to our fathers in many and various ways, and chapter 2 begins with the admonition to "pay the closer attention to what we have heard, lest we drift away from it" (2:1). To ignore the voice of God is the most foolish thing one can do, for his voice can shake the very foundations of one's existence:

> See that you do not refuse him who is speaking. For if they did not escape when they refused him who warned them on earth, much less shall we escape if we reject him who warns from heaven. His voice then shook the earth; but now he has promised, "Yet once more I will shake not only the earth but also the heaven." This phrase, "Yet once more," indicates the removal of what is shaken, as of what has been made, in order that what cannot be shaken may remain. Therefore let us be grateful for receiving a kingdom that cannot be shaken, and thus let us offer to God acceptable worship, with reference and awe; for our God is a consuming fire. (Heb. 12:25–29)

This image of the voice that strikes terror and fear is reminiscent of the childhood punishment scenario, in which the adult thunders at the child while the child shivers and quakes, and then dissociates from the scene by tuning out the voice of the parent and imagining being in some other place, far removed, a place of peace and quiet. Even the author's observation that Noah, Abraham, and Sarah could have returned to the land from which they had gone out but chose not to, for they desired a better home (11:13–16), may express the feelings of adults who have no desire to return to their childhood homes, where they were objects of parental abuse.

Thus far I have centered on the paranoid tone of the letter, as reflected in its anticipation of harm from outside, and its keen and persistent sense that the body, the will, and the self are at risk. I want also to comment on its dissociative features as reflected in its style, which is so disconnected and disjointed that the reader is often confused and unclear about the point that the author is trying to make. One example will need to suffice, as it will alert the interested reader to similar instances throughout the text:

> For you have not come to what may be touched, a blazing fire, and dark-ness, and gloom, and tempest, and the sound of a trumpet, and a voice whose words made the hearers entreat that no further messages be spoken to them. For they could not endure the order that was given, "If even a beast touches the mountain, it shall be stoned." Indeed, so terrifying was the sight that Moses said, "I tremble with fear." But you have come to Mount Zion and to the city of the living God, the heavenly Jerusalem, and to innumerable angels in festal gathering, and to the assembly of the first-born who are enrolled in heaven, and to a judge who is God of all, and to the spirits of just men made perfect, and to Jesus, the mediator of a new covenant, and to the sprinkled blood that speaks more graciously than the blood of Abel. (Heb. 12:18–24)

The basic idea here is clear enough. The God with whom we have to do is more terrifying than anything we have ever experienced, and this God re-quires a sacrifice that is equally powerful. The blood of Jesus is such a sacrifice, as it is far more perfect than the blood of Abel, and, because it is, it ushers in a new covenant. This is all logical enough. Yet the passage lurches along in run-on fashion, with the author making several connections at once: God's injunction to the people of Israel not to touch Mount Sinai on pain of death; the author's own theme of Jesus as mediator or high priest in our behalf; the story of Abel's death at the hands of Cain. The passage seems excessively compressed and, at the same time, oddly disjointed, as image is piled on image.

Because this passage begins by depicting a terrifying threat (God's order that no living thing touch the holy mountain or it will be instantly killed), and because it occurs shortly after reference to the author's own experience of being abused by his father, this simultaneous compression and disconnect-edness is reminiscent of the terror the author experienced as a child. In the threatened child's world, the experience of being severely beaten produces a dissociative effect wherein the discrete elements of the event are compressed (i.e., there is not much recall of the separate features of the episode), and are disconnected from one another (i.e., following no discernible temporal sequence). This compression and disjointedness reveals the extent to which the child feels threatened and defenseless. These stylistic features of this particular passage are also true of the letter as a whole, as it gives the appearance of following a logical progression of thought (e.g., frequent use of the word "therefore" contributes to the impression that the author is developing an argument that moves from premise to conclusion). Yet its content is so filled with threatening, even violent imagery, that the experience of reading the letter is not at all like reading a letter written by Paul, where a logical progression of thought may actually be far less apparent, yet communicates a far more settled and self-confident mind at work. From passage to passage, and page to page, the profound insecurity of the author of Hebrews is apparent to the reader, at least to the reader who is not under the thrall of the abusive structure itself. Even the author's claim that Christ's sacrifice puts an end to the need to propitiate God offers no real comfort or relief, because for those who persist in sinful behavior, not only is Christ's sacrifice of no avail, but the punishment will be even more severe than if Christ had made no sacrifice at all. That there is no final resolution is communicated both in the content and in the style of the letter. There is a pervasive sense of endangerment throughout, and the source and cause of such endangerment is God, the very one on whom one's hope for ultimate rest and peace depends. Get close to him and you may get burned.

Jesus: The Enlightened Witness

What purpose is served by interpreting the letter to the Hebrews as the work of an adult who was abused as a child and who has not, in adulthood, repudiated this abuse? For one thing, it challenges the use that is made of this letter to justify and legitimate the beating of children. It does so by asking what else would we expect of an author who was abused as a child and now, as an adult, uses the abuse he suffered as a child to support the idea of God as one who similarly chastizes us? For another, it establishes the intimate relationship between child abuse and intellectual heteronomy, for there is no other book in the New Testament that quotes other biblical sources to the extent that Hebrews does. The author does not believe that his ideas can stand on their own merits (which would be a sign of intellectual autonomy), but instead quotes from other biblical sources so extensively, so copiously, that his own voice can barely be heard apart from theirs. Furthermore, he conforms his ideas to the quotations he uses, often getting distracted by a phrase in the quotation that has little relevance to his main point, the reason for selecting this quotation in the first place. Third, the interpretation of the letter offered here points up the need for us to have the courage to confront biblical literalism where it is responsible for the suffering of innocent victims. This is the one way in which we can be enlightened witnesses. Rather than seeking to make sense of the letter to the Hebrews, and instead of deferring to it, on the supposition that if we do not "understand" it the problem must be with us, we need to have the courage to say that there is something fundamentally wrong with the way in which the author portrays God and understands the relationship of human selves to God.

While the letter to the Hebrews may have gained inclusion in the biblical canon because it represented itself as written by Paul (cf. all or parts of chapter 13), the best argument for its inclusion in the Bible today is that it witnesses to the fact that child abuse is a terrible thing, for consider what it did to the author of Hebrews. As Alice Miller writes in the concluding paragraph of her essay on Friedrich Nietzsche's struggle against the truth: "If Nietzsche had not been forced to learn as a child that one must master an 'unbearable fit of sobbing,' if he had simply been *allowed* to sob, then humanity would have been one philosopher poorer, but in return the life of a human being named Nietzsche would have been richer. And who knows what that *vital* Nietzsche would *then* have been able to give humanity?"[16] Similarly, if the author of Hebrews *had* been illegitimate, and not a "valued" son, then he would not have been beaten "for his own good," and he would not then have written words that justify the abuse of children, nor given us an image of God as an abuser too.

Opposing the author—and witness—of Hebrews we have the Gospels, and their witness to Jesus: Not only did he enjoin us never to despise a single child, but he also rejected the notion that the adult is superior to the child. There is perhaps no more touching story in all the scriptures than Matthew's account of the time when Jesus' disciples came to him and said, "Who is the greatest in the kingdom of heaven?" and Jesus called to him a child, and placing him in the midst of his disciples, said: "Truly, I say to you, unless you turn and become like children, you will never enter the kingdom of heaven. Whoever humbles himself like this child, he is the greatest in the kingdom of heaven" (Matt. 18:1–4). Perhaps this episode recalls that earlier one when Jesus, at age twelve, was accorded the same respect by the great teachers in Jerusalem. In any event, by singling out this child, Jesus honored him and gave him lasting grounds for self-pride. After all, this child had had his day in the sun. And had Jesus' eyes first fallen on the face of a girl in the crowd, surely he would have summoned her instead.

The author of Hebrews says that we become like God—holy like him—when we endure his chastisements. Jesus had a very different message: We become like God when we become like children, so an assault against a child is an assault against God. For this reason, we are to treat the children in our midst with kindness. As Micah asks, "What does the LORD require of you but to do justice and *to love kindness*, and to walk humbly with your God?" (Micah 6:8, emphasis added). Because he attested to a nonviolent God, and gave his life in order that this attestation would never be doubted or compromised, Jesus experienced identity with God. He is our true enlightened witness.

5

Abraham and Isaac:
The Sacrificial Impulse

Throughout human history, children have been used, against their will, in adults' attempts to satisfy or placate their gods. Children have been sacrificed to deities because adults believed this was what the deities required of them. In most instances, the adults have been motivated to comply with these demands out of fear, the same fear that children themselves exhibit when they are the object of parental abuse. Adults are afraid not to comply with the demand that they sacrifice their children to the gods because they are afraid of the consequences, not only to themselves personally but also, and more important, to the community in which they live. Children have been offered up to various deities in order to protect the community against war, disease, pestilence, and drought. They have been offered to the gods as an expression of the community's repentance for acting against the deities' will.

The people of Israel were critical of the Canaanites' sacrifice of children to Molech, as was Augustine of Carthaginians' child sacrifices to Saturn. Although Christianity has dissociated itself from actual rites of child sacrifice, it has not denounced the theory of sacrifice. In fact, because there are no periodic reminders of its consequences via rites of child sacrifice, there has been little social pressure to rethink the idea of a religion of sacrifice. As a result, Christianity has legitimated the physical and psychic deaths of hundreds of thousands of children throughout the centuries.

As Lloyd DeMause shows in *The History of Childhood: The Untold Story of Child Abuse*, Jesus' attitude toward children—"Do not despise one of these little ones"—did not inaugurate a new era in which children were endangered no longer. He writes: "The history of infanticide in the West has yet to be written, and I shall not attempt it here. But enough is already known to establish that, contrary to the usual assumption that it is an Eastern rather than a Western problem, infanticide of both legitimate and illegitimate children was a regular practice of antiquity, that the killing of legitimate children was only slowly reduced during the Middle Ages, and that illegitimate children continued regularly to be killed right up into the nineteenth century."[1]

During the first few centuries of the Christian era, infanticide was still an accepted, everyday occurrence. Children were thrown into rivers, flung into dung heaps and trenches, "potted" in jars to starve to death, and exposed on hills and roadsides, a prey for birds and wild beasts. Girls were valued far less than boys, and it was very rare for a family to raise more than one daughter. The others were exposed to die. Households consisted of one or two children, rarely three or more. Deformed children were almost always exposed to die. The theme of exposure loomed large in myth, tragedy, and even comedy, which was built around the subject of the misadventures involved in trying to chop up and roast a baby. The killing of legitimate children even by wealthy parents was so common that Polybius blamed it for the depopulation of Greece, and in the two centuries after Augustus, some attempts were made to pay parents to keep children alive in order to replenish the dwindling Roman population. Yet, it was not until 374 c.e. that killing an infant was declared to be murder (25–27).

DeMause acknowledges that the church fathers opposed infanticide, and yet, such opposition "often seemed to be based more on their concern for the parent's soul than with the child's life. This attitude can be seen in Saint Justin Martyr's statement that the reason a Christian should not expose his children is to avoid meeting them later in a brothel: 'Lest we molest anyone or commit sin ourselves, we have been taught that it is wicked to expose newly-born children, first because we see that almost all who are exposed (not only girls, but boys too) are raised in prostitution'" (28). After the Council of Vaison (442 c.e.), the finding of abandoned children was supposed to be announced in church, and by 787 c.e., Dateo of Milan founded the first asylum for abandoned infants. Yet, in DeMause's view, infanticide continued to be widespread, especially in the case of baby girls, as church records show typical ratios of boys to girls of 156 to 100 (in 800 c.e.) and 172 to 100 (in 1400 c.e.):

> Detailed studies are just beginning, but it is possible that infanticide may have been only sporadically punished prior to the sixteenth century. Certainly when Vincent of Beauvais wrote in the thirteenth century that a father was always worrying about his daughter "suffocating her offspring," when doctors complained of all the children "found in the frost or in the streets, cast away by a wicked mother," and when we find that in Anglo-Saxon England the legal presumption was that infants who died had been murdered if not proved otherwise, we should take these clues as a signal for the most vigorous sort of research into medieval infanticide. And just because formal records show few illegitimate births, we certainly shouldn't be satisfied with assuming that "in traditional society people remained continent until marriage," since many girls managed to hide their pregnancies from their own mothers who slept beside them, and they certainly can be suspected of hiding them from the church. (29)

DeMause claims that a high incidence of infanticide continued throughout the eighteenth and nineteenth centuries in Europe:

> Even though Thomas Coram opened his Foundling Hospital because he couldn't bear to see the dying babies lying in the gutters and rotting on the dung-heaps of London, by the 1890s dead babies were still a common sight in London streets. Late in the nineteenth century Louis Adamic described being brought up in an Eastern European village of "killing nurses," where mothers sent their infants to be done away with "by exposing them to cold air after a hot bath; feeding them something that caused convulsions in their stomachs and intestines; mixing gypsum in their milk, which literally plastered up their insides; suddenly stuffing them with food after not giving them anything to eat for two days. . . . " Adamic was to have been killed as well, but for some reason his nurse spared him. (29)

The history of childhood in Christian nations is a disturbing chronicle of systematic and deliberate abuse and neglect.

Why were Jesus' words of compassion for "the little ones" so casually disregarded? Why have Christians been so cavalier regarding the physical and emotional fate of their own offspring? A possible clue is in the frequent charge by nonChristians that Christians were engaged in the killing of babies in secret rites. As DeMause points out, when so accused, Christians were quick to point out that their accusers were guilty of putting their own offspring to death in public rituals. Yet, while these accusations against Christians were self-serving, what is striking about them is that they accused Christians of doing in secrecy what they themselves were doing publicly.

I am not here concerned with the literal truth of these accusations, but rather with the perception that Christianity was no less a sacrificial religion than the religions it sought to replace. That this perception was extant could only be due to the fact that, while it renounced the ritual of child sacrifice, its theology was deeply informed by the sacrificial idea itself. In his writings on infanticide, David Bakan has suggested that the Christian Eucharist takes the place of the ritual of child sacrifice in other religions, making Christ, rather than a child, the holy victim. By emphasizing that Christ is "truly present" in the sacrament, the sacrifice is repeated Sunday after Sunday, and participation in this real sacrifice is substituted for the law as a way of restraining infanticide.[2] Thus, in his view, one purpose of the Eucharist was to forestall actual acts of infanticide by reenacting the sacrificial death of Christ instead.

Yet, if this was the intention behind the Eucharist, the high incidence of infanticide in Christian nations indicates that the ritual has had little success in this regard. It replaces one ritual with another, but does not address the more fundamental problem that Christianity has not been able to shed the sacrificial idea itself. In fact, while we might have expected Christianity to have defined itself over against the religion of sacrifice, it has, instead, allowed itself to be defined as a religion of sacrifice. And this means that it has become a religion that requires an innocent victim who pays for the sins of the community. This self-definition of Christianity needs itself to be exposed, for its construal of the relationship of God to believers is reminiscent of the abusive relationship of parent to child.

The Aborted Sacrifice of Isaac

For Christians, the initial source of the sacrificial idea is the story of Abraham's aborted sacrifice of Isaac. This powerfully disturbing story has made a deep impression on the psyches of readers of the Bible. It is surely the best known of biblical "texts of terror."[3] We may well deplore the great notoriety of the Abraham and Isaac story, especially the fact that it so eclipses the story of the actual sacrifice of Jephthah's daughter, but the basic fact that this story is among the best-known stories in the Bible cannot be ignored. It is also a story that Christians, through the ages, have applied to their own lives. In *The Bible in Pastoral Care*, Wayne Oates tells about a woman who, on hearing a sermon on this story, returned home and assaulted her daughter with a knife, believing that this is what God had commanded her to do. The fact that Abraham was a father and Isaac was a son was unimportant to her. Nor did the fact that the story ends with Isaac being spared seem to affect her understanding of it. All that mattered is that the story was about a parent being commanded by God to kill the child whom he loved.[4]

We should not be surprised that Alice Miller has written about the Abraham and Isaac story since it is central to her theme of parental abuse of children. In a chapter in *The Untouched Key* titled "When Isaac Arises from the Sacrificial Altar,"[5] she tells about her search for an illustration for the jacket of the British edition of her earlier book, *Thou Shalt Not Be Aware*. Two Rembrandt depictions of the sacrifice of Isaac came to mind. In both, the father's hand completely covers the son's face, obstructing his sight, his speech, and even his breathing. As Abraham's use of his hands to control forcibly Isaac's powers of sight, speech, and even breath fit the themes of her book, Miller recommended this detail of Rembrandt's paintings to her publisher for the cover. But recollection of these paintings also prompted her to go to an archive to look at other portrayals of Abraham and Isaac. She found thirty in all, painted by very dissimilar artists, and with growing astonishment she discovered that all of them depicted Abraham with eyes turned upward, "as though he is asking God if he is carrying out His will correctly. . . . In all the portrayals of this scene that I found, Abraham's face or entire torso is turned away from his son and directed upward. Only his hands are occupied with the sacrifice" (138).

Also, as she looked at depictions of Isaac, she was struck by the fact that he was invariably portrayed as an adult at the peak of his manhood, and that he was simply lying there, quietly waiting to be murdered by his father. In some of the versions he was calm and obedient; in only one was he in tears, but in none was he rebellious or even questioning. He does not ask: "Father, why do you want to kill me, why is my life worth nothing to you? Why won't you look at me, why won't you explain what is happening? How can you do this to me? What crime have I committed? What have I done to deserve this?" (138).

Miller suggests that such questions cannot even be formulated in Isaac's mind because they can only be entertained by someone who feels himself to be on an equal footing with the person being questioned, and only if he can look the other in the eye: "How can a person lying on a sacrificial altar with hands bound, about to be slaughtered, ask questions when his father's hand keeps him from seeing or speaking and hinders his breathing? Such a person has been turned into an *object*. He has been dehumanized by being made a sacrifice; he no longer has a right to ask questions and will scarcely even be able to articulate them for himself, for there is no room in him for anything besides fear" (139).

Nor does the father ask any questions. He submits to the divine command as a matter of course, the same way his son submits to him: "He must—and wants to—prove that his obedience is stronger than what he calls his love for his child. . . . If the angel didn't intervene at the last moment, Abraham would become the murderer of his son simply because God's voice demanded it of him" (140).

As she continued to review these depictions of the scene, Miller was also struck by the fact that none of the artists gave this dramatic scene an individual, personal stamp. While the dress, colors, surroundings, and positions of the bodies varied, the "psychological content" was remarkably uniform. An obvious explanation for this is that the artists were attempting to be faithful to the biblical text, but this does not satisfy Miller, for one would expect that artists—of all persons—would allow their imaginations to range freely, and to question the validity of the biblical story: "Why did all of these artists accept the story as valid? The only answer I can think of is that the situation involves a fundamental fact of our existence, with which many of us became familiar during the first years of life and which is so painful that knowledge of it can survive only in the depths of the unconscious. Our awareness of the child's victimization is so deeply rooted in us that we scarcely seem to have reacted at all to the monstrousness of the story of Abraham and Isaac" (141).

In her own imaginative revisioning of the story, Miller considers two possible scenarios: One is that an enraged Isaac uses every ounce of his strength to free his hands to wrest the knife from his father's hands, so as to plunge it into his father's heart. The other is that he uses every ounce of his strength to free his hands so that he can remove Abraham's hand from his face. Then, "he would dare to use his eyes and see his father as he really is:

uncertain and hesitant yet intent on carrying out a command he does not comprehend. Now Isaac's nose and mouth would be free too, and he could finally draw a deep breath and make use of his voice. He would be able to speak and ask questions, and Abraham, whose left hand could no longer keep his son from seeing and speaking, would have to enter into a dialogue with his son, at the end of which he might possibly encounter the young man he had once been himself, who was never allowed to ask questions" (143–44).

In this second scenario, there would be a confrontation between the two, with the son challenging the assumptions behind the father's actions. If Abraham explains his action as a matter of his desire to obey the will of God, then Isaac will ask him how he can set aside his own feelings in deference to the deity, and he will ask him what kind of God this is who would demand such a thing as the murder of one's own child. In this scenario, the son does not want to be rescued by the angel who rewarded Abraham for his obedience. Instead, the son refuses "to let himself be killed, and thereby not only saves his own life but also saves his father the fate of being the unthinking murderer of his child" (145).

Thus, what Miller envisions is the child's refusal to be a sacrificial victim. He steps outside the sacrificial frame, challenging its validity, exposing it as spurious. If, for the parent, the sacrificial frame is so entrenched that he is unable to extricate himself from it, the child, at least, can refuse to participate in it by frustrating the parent's efforts to carry out what he believes to be his God-given duty.

But Miller's alternative scenario is likely to raise questions of its own: Why does Isaac allow himself to be his father's victim? Surely, one or both of the alternative scenarios that Miller envisions has been considered by Isaac himself. He must have considered using his physical strength either to resist his father's knife or even to turn the knife against him. Yet he does not act upon these revisionings. Is this because he believes that he will eventually be delivered, that his father will come to his senses or that some "angel" (the other parent or a sympathetic sibling) will intervene? Or is it because he identifies with his aggressor, sharing his father's belief that it is his father's God-given duty to attack the child because it is the child's God-given duty to be a sacrificial victim? Miller seems to imply that Isaac has no beliefs of his own, that he accepts his fate unquestioningly simply because "there is no room in him for anything besides fear." But the biblical Isaac believed in the same God that his father believed in. Otherwise, his father's answer to his question about the identity of the sacrificial victim—"God will provide, my son"—would merely have generated additional questions: "What do you mean, God will provide?" "And who is this God you serve anyway?"

Thus, believing in the same God that Abraham believes in, and believing that he has been ordained to be the sacrificial victim this God requires him to be, Isaac does not ask questions because he hasn't any. He so much identifies with his aggressor that we might even expect him to assist his father in the murderous act should his father's nerve begin to fail him and his hand begin to tremble. The dilemma here is that the child adopts the parent's perspective as his own, and the fact that he is filled by fear only reinforces this basic fact.

Another concern that Miller's alternative scenario raises is its assumption that Abraham can be reasoned with, that if Isaac questions what his father is doing, the older man may be persuaded to listen to reason. But can we assume this? If Abraham were acting only on his own initiative—if he were, in fact, only acting out of personal anger or vengeance—perhaps, then, he could be talked out of what he was intending to do. But we should not forget that he understands himself to be carrying out the will of God. He is a true believer, and true believers are not disposed to listen to reason. Isaac's questions are likely to strengthen this resolve, for they would only reinforce Abraham's view that what he is doing is in response to divine—not human—will.

A third consideration has to do with the very notion of sacrifice. The idea of sacrifice—that payment is demanded—is so deeply rooted in the human psyche, and in the structure of human society, that we rarely question its validity. Abraham does not challenge the notion that a sacrifice is required, nor does Isaac. Nor do most readers of the story question the storyteller's assurance that Abraham was commanded by God to do this thing, and that it was also by divine agency that Isaac was spared. Why do most readers of the text accept this claim and why do they not entertain the alternative theory that Abraham—like the woman in Wayne Oates's story—was out of his mind? Why we do not dispute the storyteller's assurance that God commanded Abraham to act as he did, thus questioning the whole premise of the story, tells us something about how deeply rooted is the sacrificial view of human life, both personal and societal, and how deeply rooted is the belief that this view has a religious legitimation.

Perhaps the fundamental reason that none of the artists was tempted to give this dramatic scene an individual, personal stamp is that the sacrificial idea is so deeply rooted in the human psyche, and in our understanding of how human society must work, that an alternative scenario is hardly imaginable. The biblical story itself accepts the sacrificial frame as a fact of human existence, so that it envisions only a variation within this frame—an alternative victim—and not the abrogating of the sacrificial frame itself. To put their individual, personal stamp on the scene, the artists would also have had to challenge the religious legitimation of the whole sacrificial event, to convey somehow that Abraham was not in fact hearing the voice of God but listening to voices in his own tortured mind. In this sense, the alternative scenario that Miller envisions—of Isaac speaking up to his father and questioning him—does not go nearly far enough, as it does not raise fundamental questions regarding the biblical story's effort to provide a religious legitimation for the sacrificial idea itself: That God requires a victim and if one is not offered there will be hell to pay.

It is true that Miller relates the story of Abraham and Isaac to the contemporary situation in which older men prepare wars that younger men are sent to fight and die in, and that she strongly advocates resistance to participation in war by the current generation of Isaacs who are in a position to know precisely what their fathers are doing, that is, sacrificing them on some altar because the older men are listening to the voice of their governments without questioning its validity.[6] But any vision of massive resistance to the victimization of the younger generation would be as utopian as the vision of life that Miller abhors is apocalyptic. Moreover, it does not seriously challenge the religious claims that are made in behalf of the sacrificial idea itself, the idea that the sacrifice is demanded by God himself. The most that Miller has to say in this regard is her suggestion that Isaac ask Abraham what kind of God is this who would demand such a thing as the murder of one's own child? This is a valid question for Isaac to ask, and the asking of it does take us a significant step beyond the perspective of the biblical storyteller who does not think to ask this question. But to ask this question is not yet to have asked the much more fundamental question, Why should we give the idea of sacrifice—in whatever form—a religious legitimation, invoking the will of God in its support?

The Religious Legitimation of Sacrifice

The issue of the religious legitimation of sacrifice is taken up by Søren Kierkegaard in his well-known interpretation of the Abraham and Isaac story in *Fear and Trembling*.[7] I will not attempt here a thoroughgoing study of this fascinating text, but will focus only on the first section where Kierkegaard does what Miller says the artists ought to have done, namely, imagines the different scenarios that might have substituted for the one presented in the biblical text itself. In envisioning these alternative scenarios, Kierkegaard seeks to penetrate the mind of Abraham, who might have been expected to consider the various ways he might deal with the situation at hand and to evaluate the short- and long-term consequences of these various alternatives.

Before presenting these alternative scenarios, however, Kierkegaard begins with his own interest in the biblical story, noting that a "man"—presumably himself—had heard the story of Abraham and Isaac as a child and had found it "beautiful": "Once upon a time there was a man who as a child had heard that beautiful story of how God tempted Abraham and of how Abraham withstood the temptation, kept the faith, and, contrary to expectation, got a son a second time" (9). Later, when the man read the story, it impressed him even more: "When he grew older, he read the same story with even greater admiration, for life had fractured what had been united in the pious simplicity of the child" (9). He kept returning to the story as he grew up: "The older he became, the more often his thoughts turned to that story; his enthusiasm for it became greater and greater, and yet he could understand the story less and less." Finally, "he forgot everything else because of it, his soul had but one wish, to see Abraham, but one longing, to have witnessed the event" (9). His craving was not to see the beautiful regions of the East, not the earthly glory of the Promised Land, not the God-fearing couple whose old age God had blessed, not the remarkable figure of the aged patriarch, not the vigorous adolescence God bestowed on Isaac. No, "his craving was to go along on the three-day journey when Abraham rode with sorrow before him and Isaac beside him. His wish was to be present in that hour when Abraham raised his eyes and saw Mount Moriah in the distance, the hour when he left the ass behind and went up the mountain alone with Isaac—for what occupied him was not the beautiful tapestry of imagination but the shudder of the idea" (9). The idea that Isaac must be sacrificed because God commanded it.

Kierkegaard then proposes four possible scenarios that the man who accompanied Abraham and Isaac up Mount Moriah may have witnessed. In the first, Abraham's party travels for three days until, on the morning of the fourth day, Abraham sees Mount Moriah looming in the distance. He leaves the young servants behind and takes Isaac's hand, and they walk up the mountain together. Suddenly, Abraham stands still and lays his hand on Isaac's head to bless him, and Isaac kneels to receive the blessing. Abraham's face epitomizes fatherliness, his gaze is gentle. But Isaac does not understand his father's action, and his soul is not uplifted. He begins to beg for his life, suspecting that something strange is going on, and for his beautiful hopes. But Abraham is reassuring as he lifts Isaac up and they continue walking, though Isaac still does not understand what is going on. Then Abraham turns away from his son for a moment, and when Isaac sees Abraham's face again, it has changed. His gaze is wild, his whole being is sheer terror. He seizes Isaac by the chest, throws him down on the ground, and says, "Stupid boy, do you think I am your father? I am an idolater. Do you think it is God's command? No, it is my desire." Then Isaac trembles and cries out in his anguish: "God in heaven, have mercy on me, God of Abraham, have mercy on me; if I have no father on earth, then you be my father!" Whereupon Abraham says quietly to himself, "Lord God in heaven, I thank you; it is better that he believes me a monster than that he should lose faith in you!" Kierkegaard concludes this scenario with an allusion to the mother who blackens her breast so that it is no longer inviting to the child who needs to be weaned: "So the child believes that the breast has changed, but the mother—she is still the same, her gaze is tender and loving as ever. How fortunate the one who did not need more terrible means to wean the child!" (11). Thus, in scenario one, Abraham falsely attributes the divine command to his own murderous desires so that Isaac would have faith in God instead.

In scenario two, Abraham and Isaac ride along the road in silence for three days, and Abraham stares continuously and fixedly at the ground. On the fourth day, he methodologically arranges the firewood, binds Isaac, and silently draws the knife. Then he sees the ram that God provides, sacrifices it, and goes home: "From that day henceforth, Abraham was old; he could not forget that God had ordered him to do this. Isaac flourished as before, but Abraham's eyes were darkened, and he saw joy no more" (12). Kierke-gaard concludes this second scenario with another reference to the weaning of a child, this time noting that a mother will conceal her breast and then the child has no mother: "How fortunate the child who has not lost his mother in some other way." Thus, here, Abraham performs as commanded, the outcome is precisely as the biblical story tells it, but Abraham has lost faith in God because of what God commanded him to do.

In the third scenario, Abraham rides thoughtfully down the road, and he thinks of Hagar and his son—Ishmael—whom he drove out into the desert. When he reaches Mount Moriah, he throws himself down on his face and prays God to forgive him his sin, that he has been willing to sacrifice Isaac, having forgotten his duty to his son. From that time forth, he often rides this lonesome road, finding no peace: Was it a sin that he had been willing to sacrifice to God the best that he had? And if it was a sin, how could it ever be forgiven, for what more terrible sin is there than a father's willingness to sacrifice his own son? Kierkegaard concludes this scenario with still another reference to the weaning of a child, and focuses on the mother's sorrow, because in the weaning process "she and the child are more and more to be separated," and they will never again be so close: "How fortunate the one who kept the child so close and did not need to grieve anymore!" (13). Here, Abraham discerns that it was wrong for him to have been willing to give up his son, and he is left to struggle with the moral and spiritual implications of his having forgotten his duty to his son. Hadn't he already abandoned Ish-mael to an uncertain fate in the desert? Isn't it a father's duty to value his son's life and protect it as even more precious than his own? And hasn't his willingness to give up his son—even if he subsequently thought better of it—cast a permanent shadow on their relationship together? In this scenario, it is the father who is left with all the questions, and who is unable to find any peace.

In the fourth scenario, Abraham and Isaac arrive at Mount Moriah, and Abraham, calmly and gently, makes everything ready for the sacrifice. But when he draws the knife, Isaac sees that Abraham's left hand is clenched in despair and that a shudder is running through his whole body. When they return home, Sarah comes out to meet them, but Isaac has lost his faith:

"Not a word is even said of this in the world, and Isaac never talked to anyone about what he had seen, and Abraham did not suspect that anyone had seen it" (14). Kierkegaard again alludes to the weaning of a child, and notes that, when the child needs to be weaned, the good mother has stronger sustenance at hand so that the child does not perish: "How fortunate is the one who has this stronger sustenance at hand" (14). Thus, in this scenario, Abraham believes that he has carried out his role as required of him, but Isaac has seen his father's own despair, his own fear and trembling, and this makes such an impression on Isaac that he can no longer believe in Abraham's God. Unlike the first scenario, where Abraham ensures that Isaac will believe in Abraham's God by representing the sacrifice as his own malevolent idea, here Abraham unwittingly undermines Isaac's belief because his left hand—the one that does not hold the knife—betrays him.

Kierkegaard notes that these four scenarios plus many others occurred to the "man" as he pondered the story, but all left him as uncomprehending of Abraham as was the Isaac of scenario one. Following these scenarios, he offers a brief eulogy on Abraham, in which he considers what it was that made Abraham the greatest of all men, for, unlike men whose greatness was in their power, wisdom, hope, or love, Abraham was "great by the power whose strength is powerlessness, great by that wisdom whose secret is foolishness, great by that hope whose form is madness, great by that love that is hatred to oneself" (16–17). As the very meaning of Abraham's life involved his son Isaac, the "test" to which God put him challenged his life's very meaning, "for what meaning would it have if Isaac should be sacrificed!" (19).

What impresses Kierkegaard about Abraham's decision to go through with the sacrifice of Isaac is that by doing so he was a man of absolute faith. Had he doubted, he would have placed himself on the altar—"for what is an old man compared with a child of promise"—and plunged the knife into his own heart. Instead, he arose early in the morning, hurrying "as if to a celebration," and prepared the sacrifice without a shred of hesitation or doubt:

> And there he stood, the old man with his solitary hope. But he did not doubt, he did not look in anguish to the left and to the right. . . . He did not challenge heaven with his prayers. He knew it was God the Almighty who was testing him; he knew it was the hardest sacrifice that could be demanded of him; but he knew also that no sacrifice is too severe when God demands it—and he drew the knife. (22)

As if he had studied the same paintings of the scene that Miller reviewed, Kierkegaard goes on to note that "anyone who looks upon this scene is paralyzed. Who strengthened Abraham's soul lest everything go black for him and he see neither Isaac nor the ram! Anyone who looks upon this scene is blinded" (22). But Abraham was neither paralyzed nor blinded. He never doubted, and this made the difference:

If Abraham had doubted as he stood there on Mount Moriah, if irresolute he had looked around, if he had happened to spot the ram before drawing the knife, if God had allowed him to sacrifice it instead of Isaac—then he would have gone home, everything would have been the same, he would have had Sarah, he would have kept Isaac, and yet how changed! For his return would have been a flight, his deliverance an accident, his reward disgrace, his future perhaps perdition. Then he would have witnessed neither to his faith nor to God's grace but would have witnessed to how appalling it is to go to Mount Moriah. (22)

Kierkegaard concludes his eulogy to Abraham with the observation that, of all remarkable fathers, Abraham does not need a eulogy, for eulogies are for fathers who need someone to snatch their memories from the power of oblivion. This is not the case with Abraham, "for every language calls you to mind." The man who heard the story of Abraham as a child, who struggled with it throughout his early youth and manhood, will never forget the Venerable Father Abraham who in his one hundred thirty years of life "got no further than faith" (23).

The reader of Kierkegaard's eulogy on Abraham cannot but be inspired by his stirring endorsement of Abraham's witness to his faith. What makes Abraham's faith so powerful is precisely that he does not even consider the alternative scenarios that entered the mind of the man who pondered this event. What is so truly startling and incomprehensible about Abraham is that he did *not* think of alternative scenarios, such as pretending to be the one who contrived the sacrifice so that Isaac would not lose his faith in God; or going through the motions of sacrificing Isaac and relinquishing his faith in the process; or asking God to forgive him for even considering the sacrifice of his beloved son; or going through with the sacrifice but with such despair that Isaac cannot but notice and lose his own faith in God because of his father's own fear and trembling. No, Abraham's faith is incomparable precisely because he does not ponder these alternative scenarios but instead hurries up the mountain, "as if to a celebration," and prepares to sacrifice his child without a shred of hesitation or doubt.

Kierkegaard's Idealization of Abraham

The question we have to ask is, Why does Kierkegaard himself, once having envisioned the alternative scenarios, which take account of the moral and religious ambiguities of the sacrificial idea, proceed to extol Abraham for his own utter disregard of these moral and religious ambiguities? If readers of the biblical story have difficulty comprehending Abraham, is this because Abraham is a man of such great faith that he allows nothing—even his beloved son—to come between himself and his God, or is it because he is so certain of himself, so sure that he is acting in response to the command of

God, that we necessarily wonder—precisely because he *is* so certain of him-self—whether he is not deluding himself? Why should he not consider the alternative scenarios that Kierkegaard has put forward? Why are they not even worth his consideration? And why is Kierkegaard so willing to reject these scenarios in favor of the one in which Abraham proceeds with the sacrifice as though it were a celebration? Why should Abraham not ask God to forgive him for even considering the sacrifice of his son? Why should Abraham not exhibit such despair that Isaac cannot but conclude that the God his father is trying to serve is unworthy of him?

I think that Kierkegaard is willing to reject these scenarios as the mere "ponderings" of a "man" who has been gripped by the story since childhood because he is unable or unwilling to face the initially disturbing but ulti-mately liberating truth that human sacrifice, whatever form it may take, has absolutely no religious legitimation.[8] Which is to say that, if Abraham thought he was acting in response to a command from God, he was deluding himself. Moreover, if the biblical storyteller thinks that Abraham was hear-ing a voice from God and not merely "hearing voices"—in the same way that paranoid and dissociative personalities hear voices—then he is also self-deluded, and his "alternative scenario" that God accepts alternative victims is based on the fallacious idea that God, and not humans, is the author of victimization.

I believe that Kierkegaard was unable to accept this conclusion because, like Isaac, he identified with the aggressor, adopting the perspective of the abusing father as his own, which included the abusing father's religious legitimation for the abuse. In this, he is not significantly different from contemporary Christian fundamentalists who provide a religious justifica-tion for the physical punishment of children. But why was he unable to accept this conclusion? I believe it was because of his intense desire to be a son to a man like Abraham. Note that he says that, as a child, he heard "that beautiful story of how God tempted Abraham and of how Abraham withstood the temptation." Since Kierkegaard's own father was a man who was known to have given in to various temptations (Kierkegaard's own mother had been his father's sexual partner before his first wife's death), the child Søren was introduced through the beautiful story of Abraham to a father who was above temptation, and who was therefore reliable, a father on whom a son could always depend. Conversely, consider what it would be like to be a son of such a father! Would he not be able to bask in his father's glory, to take great personal pride in the fact that he was the son of such a man as this?[9]

This desire to be the son of Abraham is reflected in the fact that Kierke-gaard chose to eulogize Abraham, as if to imply that he, Kierkegaard, is among those who grieve the death of Abraham, experiencing it as a deep, personal loss. Toward the end of the eulogy, he refers to himself as "a late lover" of whom Abraham had no need, as his memory will survive without Kierkegaard's celebratory words, but whom Abraham continues richly to reward: "You reward your lover more gloriously than anyone else. In the life to come you make him eternally happy in your bosom; here in this life you captivate his eyes and his heart with the wonder of your act."[10] He then goes on to ask Father Abraham to "forgive the one who aspired to speak your praise if he has not done it properly."[11]

All of this is spoken like a son for whom Father Abraham is a powerful ideal, a father figure who fully satisfies his son's desire for a father who is inwardly secure and, because he is secure, is able to secure his son's own self. As psychoanalyst Heinz Kohut points out, parents who are inwardly secure, who have a healthy narcissistic self, will not be put off by their child's idealization of them, but will accept it, recognizing that it serves a vital role in enabling the child to feel secure and protected. Conversely, parents who are bored, embarrassed, or rejecting of such idealizations will withdraw, leaving the child confused, despairing, and inwardly empty. Such parents fail to realize how much the children's own sense of self depends on their idealization of parents being mirrored back to them. In their paper on the disorders of the self, Kohut and his colleague Ernest Wolf offer the following illustration:

> A little boy is eager to idealize his father, he wants his father to tell him about his life, the battles he engaged in and won. But instead of joyfully acting in accordance with his son's need, the father is embarrassed by the request. He feels tired and bored and, leaving the house, finds a temporary source of vitality for his enfeebled self in the tavern, through drink and mutually supportive friends.[12]

Kierkegaard's own father made him feel self-conscious, aware of his insecurity and self-depletion. In his *Journals*, he recalls the impression it made on him some years earlier when, "filled with a youthful and romantic enthusiasm for a *master-thief*, I went so far as to say that it was only the misuse of powers, and thus such a man might still be converted," to which his father replied very solemnly, "There are offences which one can only fight against with God's continual help." Whereupon, the young Kierkegaard "hurried down to my room and looked at myself in the glass."[13] Instead of mirroring his son's idealization of a resourceful criminal, his father used the occasion to teach a lesson about how continual must be the struggle against sin, leading Kierkegaard to view himself in the mirror as a guilty, despicable culprit. In contrast, Kierkegaard saw in Abraham a father who represented the romantic, exciting, and risky attitude toward life with which the child Søren identified the master thief, but which his own father dismissed with a routine truism about the struggle against sin, a struggle that his father often lost. Given the contrast between Abraham and his own father, one can easily imagine that Kierkegaard envied Isaac, who had a father who could be idealized because he was a man of absolute faith.

If this is what Abraham means to Kierkegaard, it is not surprising that Kierkegaard does not question Abraham's treatment of Isaac, or suggest (with Miller) that Isaac engage in the questioning of Abraham. But Kierkegaard's own desire to be Abraham's beloved son need not deter others of us from challenging Abraham and from raising questions about the biblical story's effort to provide religious legitimation for the idea of sacrifice. In fact, if we take exception to Kierkegaard's own embracement of Abraham for the personal reasons we have just adduced, we are then free to consider alternative scenarios that he himself imagines, and others besides. What is striking about his alternative scenarios is that each concludes with a reference to a mother weaning her child. In the context, these maternal images seem out of place, as the story is clearly focused on what is occurring between father and son, not on the mother who has been left at home. And yet, the weaning theme offers an alternative way of understanding the disunity between parents and children, and the roles that both play in the working out of this disunity.

Isaac: Son of Sarah

If the father and son view the disunity in terms of sacrifice—and therefore assume that the son is destined to be a victim—the mother and son take a more measured view, seeing their disunity as the inevitable consequence of the separation of mother and child, as an experience over which both must grieve. If weaning and not sacrifice becomes the key metaphor for the deep fissures that exist at the core of human society, then this experience has its own legitimation, and there is no need to put forward a religious legitimation for what is an entirely natural, if profoundly sad and sorrowful event. Weaning has its costs too, but, as Kierkegaard puts it, "How fortunate the child who has not lost his mother in some other way." Which is also to say that fortunate is the child whose fate is not taken over by the fathers, who will demand sacrifice, but whose fate instead remains in the hands of the mothers (or the fathers with a mother's heart), who see to it that as the weaning occurs, strong sustenance is at hand so that their children do not perish without them.

If it seems strange to speak of weaning in the case of Isaac, who, as Miller shows, is on the verge of adulthood, these words by Bert Kaplan are apropos:

> While many children, sadly, do meet great severity, privation, and harshness early in life, I believe the full seriousness of weaning is ordinarily encountered . . . by the young adult who has recently left his or her family, that most womb-like of human institutions and has "come into the world." Students report that the sense of being weaned from family care develops

slowly over a period of years and that it is experienced partly as a function of their own desire for independence and freedom. Nevertheless, the full force of the fact of being alone in an indifferent world is a good deal more than they have bargained for.[14]

Thus, while the story of Abraham and Isaac directs our attention to the threatened killing of Isaac by his father, the "event" that goes unnoticed is the fact that father, son, and servants set off on their journey to Mount Moriah—where presumably important things happen—leaving the mother Sarah at home to grieve and to fear for her son's fate in the world that men have made for him. In each of Kierkegaard's alternative scenarios, Sarah is briefly mentioned: In one version she watches them from the window as they go down the valley until she can see them no longer. In another she kisses Isaac, the one who "took away her disgrace, Isaac her pride, her hope for all the generations to come." In still another she kisses Isaac, "her delight, her joy forever." In the fourth scenario, the one in which Abraham's despair is seen by Isaac, she is again mentioned, but this time as running out joyfully to meet them as they return, only to discover that her son "had lost the faith."

The critical event in this story is not, as the storyteller claims, what happens between Abraham and Isaac, but what is happening between Sarah and her son. The weaning of a son from his mother is a sad event, made the sadder because it happens almost without notice, as though it is a mere detail in an otherwise momentous tale about fathers and sons. It goes unremarked in the biblical setting because it *is* such a natural event, and the Bible intends to be a religious book, a book about our struggles with our thoughts and feelings toward God. Yet if weaning is a mere natural event, having none of the power and glory of the sacrificial event on Mount Moriah, it does have its religious consequences, as, in the weaning process, the son is sent into an indifferent world that is a good deal more than he bargained for, and, as one of Kierkegaard's scenarios suggests, it is possible that a son will lose his father and will return home to his mother's arms, disillusioned and demoralized. The question this scenario raises, a profoundly religious question, is whether she will have even stronger sustenance at hand so that his spirit does not perish, so that he is fortified to go out again, believing in himself when he can no longer believe in his father and his father's God.

If there is no religious legitimation for what Abraham proposed to do to his son Isaac, how do we explain his behavior? Why would a father do such a thing? While Kierkegaard eulogizes Abraham as a man of "'absolute faith,'" in David Bakan's view, the "paradigmatic sacrifice tale" reveals a profound ambivalence on the part of Abraham. For Bakan, Abraham has "the wish to kill Isaac," but projects this wish onto God, so that it appears as God's command to Abraham: "When a human being inflicts pain upon another human being, he characteristically believes that he does so out of necessity. In the case of Abraham, it is out of obedience to God."[15] But, Bakan points out, we can reasonably ask about the locus of the necessity: "A common psychodynamic mechanism is to convert desire so that it appears as external necessity. It is thus an open question in each instance whether what appears to be external necessity really is that, or is simply a facade concealing some internal pressure."[16]

Bakan suggests that the internal pressure may have to do with questions in Abraham's own mind, questions concerning who was in fact the father of Isaac. In Bakan's view, the biblical story of Sarah's conception of Isaac "allows for an interpretation of dubious paternity of Isaac." He hastens to add that he is not making an effort to find out what "really happened," as this would be rather odd when one has to do with a mythic figure, but that he is "seeking to understand the nature of the biblical text as a document which renders a state of mind for our understanding."[17] He notes that on two occasions Abraham conceals the fact that Sarah is his wife, allowing her to appear to be married to someone else, indicating that their marriage had its share of opportunism and deceit. The story of the visit of angels to Sarah's tent can be interpreted to mean that she conceived Isaac while Abraham was outside the tent, and that her expression of fear on hearing the prediction that she would give birth to a child, together with her explicit denial that the prediction had caused her to laugh, was because she anticipated Abraham's anger at her and possible revenge against the child.

Bakan notes that the allegation that Isaac was not Abraham's but Abimelech's son was known to the rabbis, and suggests that such doubt may even have been on Saint Paul's mind in Romans 9:6–8: "For not all who are descended from Israel belong to Israel, and not all are children of Abraham because they are his descendants; but 'Through Isaac shall your descendants be named.' This means that it is not the children of the flesh who are the children of God, but the children of the promise are reckoned as descendants." Thus, in Bakan's view, the point of the Abraham and Isaac story is that Abraham had "some internal pressure" to attack Isaac, but that he does not in the end act on this pressure but instead exercises restraint. Isaac is spared, and, as Kierkegaard puts it, Abraham "got a son a second time"— that is, Isaac now becomes Abraham's son because Abraham had the power to kill him but he did not. Rather, he adopted Isaac as his own.

In emphasizing Abraham's resentment owing to the particular circumstances of Isaac's birth, however, Bakan does not give sufficient attention to the jealousy of *any* father who is aware that his son is his wife's true delight, and who cannot bear the thought that he, the son of another woman, perhaps one whom his wife fears or despises, is not himself her true delight. It is the child in him that finds this situation frustrating and demeaning, and it is the child in him that seeks to do something about it. In this sense, Venerable Father Abraham is a child with murderous impulses against another child, as it is also only a child who would believe that killing a small animal instead will solve the problem of his murderous jealousy.

Whether Bakan's explanation for Abraham's inner provocation to harm Isaac is convincing is not the critical point. What *is* critical is his point that "a common psychodynamic mechanism is to convert desire so that it appears as external necessity." The sacrificial impulse is an instance of this psychodynamic mechanism. A very human desire is attributed to God and represented as a divine command. To persuade the reader that Abraham was acting on the command of God, the storyteller has the angel of the Lord call to Abraham at the critical moment when he is about to plunge the knife into Isaac's heart, telling him not to lay a hand on the child. This divine intervention seems to establish the validity of the storyteller's claim that it was God—external necessity—who commanded Abraham to do this thing, thereby dissuading the reader from exercising a healthy skepticism regarding the very idea that the sacrificial impulse has any other source than the heart and mind of Abraham himself.

If Abraham is finally worthy of being remembered, it is not, as Kierkegaard supposes, because he was a man of unquestioning faith, but because he finally came to his senses and repented of what he had intended to do to Isaac. This does not mean that Isaac was not traumatized and terrorized by the episode, and it does not mean that no harm was done to him. Yet, we can say that it was the staying of Abraham's hand that is the sole basis for viewing him as a man of faith, for it is an expression of faith when a man is able to see the error of his ways and to repent of the evil he has planned in his heart.

6

The Child Jesus as Endangered Self

If Kierkegaard perceived Abraham as an idealized father—one who could meet emotional needs his natural father could or would not meet—I suggest that Jesus, too, engaged in a similar idealization, but that, in his case, the idealized father was God himself.

When I was a seminary student, my student colleagues and I were warned by our New Testament professors not to view the four Gospels as historical documents. We were especially cautioned against our natural but naïve inclination to use these texts to gain access to the historical Jesus. The Jesus of history, we were told, is inaccessible because the sources that attest to what he said, did, and intended were not written as history, much less biography, but for purposes of proselytizing in behalf of the early Christian movement.

Since the time that I was in seminary, there has been a dramatic resurgence of interest among New Testament scholars in the historical Jesus. This renewed interest has been prompted by the discovery and accessibility to scholars of extracanonical writings (notably, the Dead Sea Scrolls), and also by the emergence of new hermeneutical theories that are applicable to the Gospel texts, especially theories derived from literary criticism. There has also been renewed interest in the use of sociological theories that shed new light on the social and political context in which Jesus lived. Lagging far behind, and considered the most suspect of these new "secular" (or nontheological) approaches, is the use of psychological theory in the interpretation of the Gospels. While the sociological study of the early Christian movement has gained some acceptance within biblical studies, psychology remains quite suspect, and what little has been done to date has to some extent validated such suspicion.

It is noteworthy, however, that some very penetrating psychological interpretations of various biblical texts have been made by feminist biblical scholars, none of whom view themselves as psychologists per se, but who in fact engage in psychological interpretation by virtue of the topics they choose to address. The topic of women's victimization is, for example, inherently psychological. It is impossible not to engage in psychological interpretation when one addresses the theme of the victimization of women as revealed, directly or indirectly, intentionally or unintentionally, in selected biblical texts. This theme is inherently psychological.

When I was a graduate student at The University of Chicago in the late 1960s, I became familiar with the work of David Bakan (referred to in the previous chapter), who taught in the psychology department. In his writings, but especially in his lectures in his course on the psychology of religion, Bakan spoke with considerable passion and urgency about the theme of child abuse, and sought to demonstrate that this was a central, perhaps *the* central psychological theme in the Bible. His interpretations of the stories of Abraham and Isaac, of Job and his sons, and of Jesus, all in terms of the "infanticidal impulse" of parents toward their offspring were met with considerable skepticism by divinity students who attended his lectures, but, for reasons that I did not then understand, and now only imperfectly understand, I found them compelling and persuasive. I will never forget the evening when he pointed out that Freud's oedipal theory is a half-truth. Yes, it is true that Oedipus wanted to kill his father, but this desire was not inherent in Oedipus. He was not born with murderous impulses, but was provoked by his parents' prior action of exposing him in the forest, in the dead of winter, fully expecting him to die. Instead, he was found by a shepherd and reared as the shepherd's own child. It is not, as Melanie Klein and her followers have suggested,[1] that children are innately hateful toward their parents. These attitudes have been provoked by their parents' aggression against them. The same theme, according to Bakan, runs throughout the Bible, the most dramatic instance being the story of Abraham and Isaac, which Bakan, as we saw in chapter 5, interprets as the murderous impulses of Abraham against a child who was fathered by another man. This interpretation left my divinity school cohorts incredulous, and yet, the issue of illegitimacy is a very important theme in the Bible, reappearing (as briefly noted in chapter 3) in the case of Jesus, and I, for one, did not then or now find Bakan's interpretation difficult to swallow. As feminist biblical scholars have now begun to open up the whole question of women's victimization as a pervasive (or, should we say, evasive) theme in the Bible, Bakan's interpretations of biblical texts as concerned with the victimization of children no longer seem so far-fetched. What I will explore in this chapter is the convergence of these two themes in the life of Jesus.

Looking back on my own work as a psychobiographer, I recognize a common theme in my studies of John Henry Newman, Orestes Brownson, Abraham Lincoln, and Saint Augustine, namely, the theme of the suffering of children due to parental mistreatment or to emotional neglect, sometimes but not always owing to tragedy and misfortune.[2] Newman was raised in his grandmother's home during the first years of his life, prior to boarding school, even though his parents were both living.[3] Brownson was raised by foster parents because his mother, after his father's death, could not support her family. Lincoln's mother died when he was a child, and his father, himself emotionally incapable of providing care and nurture, became the object of lifelong resentment. And, as we saw in chapter 2, Augustine was beaten by his teachers at school, and when he complained about his mistreatment, his parents mocked him, siding with the teachers. My studies of these particular historical figures—religious personalities—have supported Erik Erikson's much-debated interpretation of Luther as a child who experienced considerable emotional trauma, the victim of his father's abusive behavior and of his mother's acquiescence.[4]

My exploration here on Jesus as a victimized child continues the same line of inquiry. In centering on Jesus, I am aware that I am undertaking an unusually perilous task, as we lack the usual sources of information that are commonly used to develop a psychobiography. There are no personal letters and diaries, no reminiscences from the pens of siblings, parents, and friends, and no contemporary accounts of what it was like to be a child growing up in Galilee at the time that Jesus lived. The lack of such evidence would probably be enough to dissuade any responsible historian from embarking on this particular project. Even if there were no paucity of evidence, there is also the fact that such an investigation comes up against strong taboos that are present with any revered historical figure, but are dramatically magnified in the case of Jesus.

When I was describing the general argument that I planned to develop in this chapter to a group of our summer school students at lunch, one of the students, a pastor, said, "I have a church in a small town near Peoria, and I can tell you that what you are saying would never play there." He went on to say that the circumstances of Jesus' childhood are of no interest to his parishioners, or to him personally, as these things simply do not matter. What matters is that Jesus brought a new message of hope and deliverance, one that is as relevant today as it was in his own day. I responded by noting that even if we today may not be concerned about the circumstances of Jesus' childhood, we can assume that he himself was keenly interested in them, and it is his own concern with his childhood that I am trying to understand. How did *he* feel about his experience as a child? How did *his* feelings about these experiences influence his adult life, including his desire to bring a new message of hope and deliverance? Could it be that this very message had its origins in his childhood experience?

While I was basically satisfied with my response, I came away from this conversation with a much greater appreciation for the fact that the psychobiographical study of Jesus is a terribly risky enterprise, because it flies in the face of some deeply established taboos within the Christian community against opening up the whole issue of the victimization of children. By continuing to assert that we should not even be curious about Jesus' childhood, we place a veil of secrecy over the experiences of all children, including our own childhoods, using our religion to legitimate such secrecy, and to support the suppression of our curiosity, as adults, about our experiences as children.

As we saw in chapter 1, Alice Miller argues that we have very strong taboos against wanting and seeking to know what we experienced as children.[5] Such taboos serve mainly to spare the parents, to keep what they have done to their children a deep secret. Moreover, the theories we adults put forward to "explain" what occurs in childhood are typically designed to maintain the secrecy. She is especially critical of Freud's backpedaling on the issue of the sexual abuse of children, placing his own concerns for professional ostracism above his commitment to the truth as he knew it.

I am not primarily concerned here with Miller's criticism of Freud, as this whole issue has already been discussed. What concerns me instead, as I mentioned briefly in chapter 3, is the similar use of certain theological theories, particularly the theory that Jesus was born of a virgin. This theory serves a similar purpose, that of keeping what really happened in Jesus' case from coming to light, and thereby giving the practice of sparing the parents a religious legitimation. Once we as children learn how babies are actually conceived, we can then be introduced to the theory that Jesus was born of a virgin, the "father" being the Holy Spirit. Before the time that we know how children are conceived, this theory is not very relevant to us. After we know, it is incomprehensible to our natural thought processes ("Why should the conception of Jesus be any different from the conception of all the other children?"), but its very incomprehensibility enables the promoters of this theory to say that this is a matter of faith, and that we should not rely on our own powers of thought, but instead accept and believe what adults are telling us is so. How was he really conceived? What were the real circumstances of his conception? To ask such questions is to begin to lift the veil of secrecy which, in Miller's view, can only serve the purpose of sparing the parents. It does not serve the interests of the children, or of the adults who want to discover the origins of their present emotional distress in what happened to them as children.

Much contemporary biblical scholarship maintains this same prohibition against the desire to know about the circumstances of Jesus' conception, and their possible influence on his adult life. Today, however, the theories that are used to dissuade us from our natural curiosity about his childhood are less overtly theological and more related to historical method. While some biblical scholars today may actually believe that Jesus was born of a virgin, many probably do not believe this to be literally the case. Most believe that Joseph was his father. For them, the theory of the virgin birth is no longer a sufficient basis for maintaining the taboo against inquiring into the circumstances of Jesus' conception. Alternative grounds for suppressing our natural desire to know become necessary, and the most common argument is now that as Jesus' childhood was not of primary concern to the Gospel writers, it should not be of great concern to us. As the Gospel writers have other more important issues they want to address (they are not, after all, biographers), we should take their cue and not pursue an issue that is tangential and ultimately unimportant. In support of this position, biblical scholars also note that there is very little evidence in the Gospels about Jesus' childhood, thus confirming that it was not of primary concern to the Gospel writers. They have reinforced this position by pointing out how unsuccessful have been the attempts of psychologists and others to create a psychological profile of Jesus, frequently citing Albert Schweitzer's conclusion, in his thesis written for his medical degree in 1913, that such efforts have been exercises in futility.[6]

I must admit that, throughout the years that I was engaged in psychobiographical studies of the figures noted above, I shared the same skepticism regarding a psychobiography of Jesus, and largely for the same reasons. I felt that the best one could do with a figure like Jesus would be to develop an interpretation similar to those frequently found in psychoanalytic and analytic psychology (Jungian) journals, which focus on a literary character in a novel or play. One would, for example, offer a psychological interpretation of Matthew's Jesus in much the same way that others have developed psychological interpretations of William Shakespeare's Hamlet or Herman Melville's Ahab. It would be understood that one was merely applying one or another psychological theory to a literary text, one that, in this case, happens to be of the genre of gospel rather than play or novel. A literary, not historical, Jesus would be the object of psychological interpretation.

I am now convinced, however, that to settle for half a loaf in this fashion is to accept uncritically the assumption by which biblical scholars have been able to dissuade us from our natural curiosity about Jesus' childhood, the assumption that his childhood was not of urgent concern to the Gospel writers themselves. I am persuaded that his childhood was of very great concern to the Gospel writers precisely because they were aware that the circumstances of his conception and birth were of great interest to prospective converts to the Christian movement. Even if the Gospel writers had not been curious themselves, and even if they had been personally disposed to the view that all that really matters is the fact that Jesus brought a message of hope and deliverance, the issue could not be ignored, and they knew this. Questions were being raised concerning the legitimacy of Jesus' conception, and two of the four Gospel writers—Matthew and Luke—were sufficiently concerned with these questions that they began their Gospels with these very questions in mind. While their manner of addressing these questions was partly influenced by the taboo against lifting the veil of secrecy, mainly in order to spare the parents (especially Mary, who was probably alive at the time they wrote their Gospels), it was also influenced by their desire to show that Jesus' conception and birth were related to his message of hope and deliverance.

We might also ask: What is it that men and women, in their time and ours, seek deliverance from? And why is it that we are so much in need of the hope that Jesus' message offers? I believe that our desire for deliverance can be traced all the way back to childhood, when we experienced ourselves as captive and vulnerable selves, selves who were emotionally imprisoned and decidedly not the carefree individuals that adults imagined us to be. We were endangered selves. In fact, it is not too much to claim that childhood is the period in life when our selfhood is most endangered. This makes a certain kind of obvious sense, as it is in childhood (also in old age) that we are especially vulnerable, greatly dependent on others, mainly parents, for our very survival. But we need to go beyond the obvious, and beyond the issue of our physical survival, and to ask why it is that the *self*—the very core of our being and the locus of our self-reflective capacities—is most endangered in childhood.

Again, I find myself agreeing with Alice Miller that, for most of us, our endangerment as selves was not primarily because we felt physically threatened, but because we were learning to suppress our awareness of ourselves, of our own experiencing. We learned to deny our experiences, that which we most deeply felt within us, thus splitting off our conscious selves from much of what we felt. We did this, in Miller's view, largely from a need to spare our parents. Instead of expressing our deep grievances against them, we created excuses for them, rationalizing for them, and telling ourselves that our anger and hurt is immature, if not shameful, unbecoming of good children. After all, our parents deserve our gratitude, not our anger and accusations.

So we created a kind of fictive self, based on a romanticized or idealized view of our experience in the world, a self based on the assumption that we cannot bear to be aware. Once formed, this fictive self not only survives childhood, but its influence expands, as we find more and more reasons to be sparing: not only of other persons on whom we depend, but also of social institutions, on which we cannot but rely. We rationalize for them, finding plausible reasons for why they had no choice but to betray us and cause us to suffer.

On the other hand, childhood may also be a time when our sense of selfhood is *least* endangered, when we are still relatively free to be aware of what we are experiencing, and free to disclose such awareness to others. Miller's picture of childhood as a time when our true self is seriously endangered is undoubtedly one-sided, borne of her experience of being a therapist to adults who had miserable childhoods, and of the fact that her own awareness of her experience of being abused as a child emerged only after years of therapeutic practice and personal self-analysis. Childhood, then, may also be a time when we may still exhibit a refreshing freedom to see things as they are, and to be unsparing in what we say about what we see. As Ralph Waldo Emerson, in his essay "Self-Reliance," notes:

> The nonchalance of boys who are sure of a dinner, and would disdain as much as a lord to do or say aught to conciliate one, is the healthy attitude of human nature. A boy is in the parlor what the pit is in the playhouse; independent, irresponsible, looking out from his corner on such people and facts as pass by, he tries and sentences them on their merits, in the swift summary way of boys, as good, bad, interesting, silly, eloquent, troublesome. He cumbers himself never about consequences, about interests: he gives an independent, genuine verdict. You must court him: he does not court you.[7]

In contrast, says Emerson, "the man is, as it were, clapped into jail by his consciousness. As soon as he has once acted or spoken with *éclat*, he is a committed person, watched by the sympathy or the hatred of hundreds whose affections must now enter into his account. There is no Lethe for this. Ah, that he could pass again into his neutrality!"[8]

Here Emerson, himself deprived as a boy of love and affection by Calvinistic parents whose austere child-rearing practices included depriving the children of food while the parents ate their fill (an instance of what Miller calls poisonous pedagogy), reveals another side of childhood, the freedom to say whatever one pleases and not to measure the consequences. It is this freedom—the freedom to be unsparing in his attack on those social forces and conventions that deplete the true self, leaving it feeling empty and powerless—that Emerson now evidences in his celebrated paean to self-reliance, and that I want to believe is the impetus behind my own decision to explore the childhood of Jesus. As Miller shows, children learn very early to imprison themselves in their consciousness by learning not to be aware. But, as she also insists, such self-imprisonment is not irrevocable, as one can just as surely learn to violate social taboos and prohibitions against being aware, and to reject the theories about ourselves that not only keep us in the dark but also undermine our confidence in our natural, God-given capacity to know what we see and feel. It is in the spirit of such freedom that I now invade the parlor long dominated by professional biblical scholars, and offer my own "independent, genuine verdict" about Jesus. This is a verdict that I have presented previously in oral form as a respondent to a paper by John W. Miller on Jesus' "age-thirty transition,"[9] but am now emboldened to set down in writing because confirmation of my intuitions has recently been provided by a biblical scholar, Jane Schaberg, who, in spite of being a woman, has managed to gain entry to the parlor, as an adult!

Yet, from what I gather from the preface to her book on the illegitimacy of Jesus,[10] her efforts have been criticized for being "too imaginative." In what I take to be a kind of Emersonian protest, possibly borne of nonchalance regarding from whence *her* next meal is coming, Schaberg says, "Now that this book is finished, one of my own criticisms of it is that it is not imaginative *enough*."[11] It goes without saying that one of the ways adults squelch the awareness of children is to suggest that these little ones may be allowing their imaginations to run away with them. Yet, as Miller points out in her essay on the emperor's new clothes: "The cry of the child in Andersen's fairy tale—'But [the emperor] doesn't have anything on!'—awakens people from a mass hypnosis, restores their powers of perception, frees them from the confusion caused by the authorities, and mercilessly exposes the emptiness to which rulers as well as masses have fallen victim. All of this happens suddenly, sparked by the single exclamation of a child."[12] So, my views on the child Jesus are those of an adult who has nonetheless tried to take the perspective of a child for whom the real self lives in the free exercise of the gift of true imagination.

The Illegitimacy Argument

The infancy narratives in Matthew and Luke are concerned to tell the reader that Jesus' conception and birth were very special, that these events, as interpreted by Matthew and Luke, establish that he was God's chosen son, the one whose coming was foretold by the prophets. In making this affirmation, these narratives also reveal that Matthew and Luke were very much aware of the fact that many people had serious difficulty with such a claim because Jesus' conception and birth could easily be viewed as disconfirming evidence for this very claim. As Schaberg points out, one of the most persistent arguments mounted against the Christian movement's claim that Jesus was the promised one was the allegation that he was illegitimate, fathered not by Joseph, the man to whom Mary was engaged at the time and whom she subsequently married, but by some other man. While biblical scholars have traditionally dismissed this allegation on the grounds that it was concocted by the movement's adversaries in order to discredit it, Schaberg wonders whether these allegations may have had a basis in fact, as the two Gospel writers do not discount or even try to refute these allegations. Instead, through carefully chosen language that, especially in Luke's case, almost obscures the fact that such allegations were extant, the Gospel writers show that there is another way to consider the allegation of Jesus' illegitimacy, viewing the circumstances to which these allegations point not as merely scandalous but as positive evidence that God was acting in Jesus' life from the very moment of his conception. For both Matthew and Luke, Mary was the culmination of a long succession of biblical women whose victimization was transformed from being merely a scandalous event to ushering in a new era of hope for those who longed for liberation from oppression and abuse.

Schaberg's argument is based on textual analyses, the details of which cannot be thoroughly discussed here. Her central argument, however, is that both Matthew and Luke assumed that Mary's early pregnancy was by another man, not Joseph. Joseph's actions on learning of Mary's pregnancy, especially his decision to end their engagement quietly, are ones that would be expected if another man was involved. If Joseph had been the real father, his reaction to news of Mary's pregnancy would have been to proceed with the marriage on schedule, for it was not considered scandalous for a woman to become pregnant by her fiancé during the traditional year of betrothal prior to marriage. In one of the two traditional options available to Joseph and Mary, the man and woman would live together during the second half of their engagement year, and it was not unusual for conception to occur during this period. Matthew states, however, that Joseph and Mary had not yet "come together," which would suggest that they were either following the alternative traditional option of remaining apart for the entire betrothal period or that her pregnancy occurred during the first six months of their engagement. The scandal, then, was that another man was involved, and Schaberg suggests that apparent confusions in Matthew's genealogy of Jesus are actually indirect clues to this fact (e.g., only thirteen men are mentioned by name in a list which is supposed to include fourteen; the missing name is that of the natural father). So also is Luke's reference to Jesus as the "supposed" son of Joseph, which has traditionally been interpreted as Luke's way of saying Jesus had no "natural" father, an interpretation that Schaberg disputes on the grounds that neither Luke nor Matthew could have believed in the possibility of a conception without the involvement of a human father.

Assuming the involvement of another man, there were several options available to Joseph. One would be to take legal action on the grounds that the man took Mary by force. However, to bring charges of rape against the man, Joseph would have needed to be able to demonstrate that the episode occurred where Mary's screams for help could not have been heard (e.g., in an isolated location), or if it did occur where her screams for help could have been heard by others, that she in fact cried out and someone was prepared to testify to this fact. We have no way of knowing whether Joseph's initial decision to pursue another option, terminating their engagement quietly, was because he felt he could not prevail in court, or whether he wanted to avoid adverse publicity for himself and/or for Mary. We assume that he knew the circumstances of what had happened, that is, whether Mary was raped or whether she was a willing participant in an illicit sexual act (that she was twelve years old, the traditional age for a woman to marry, would be prima facie evidence for us today that she was not a consenting participant in the sexual act, but this may not have been the prevailing view in Joseph's day). We do not, in any case, know how Joseph felt about what he knew, and, therefore, we do not know why he had decided to end the engagement quietly. Was it because he knew that Mary had been the victim of rape, but that he had no stomach for a legal battle against the man who did this to Mary, even though this would exonerate Mary and bring the offender to justice? Or was it because he understood that Mary had willingly entered into a liaison with another man, and therefore he decided to end their engagement out of personal hurt, anger, and self-pride?

Admitting that we cannot use the Gospel texts to get at what was in Joseph's mind at the time, Schaberg is nonetheless of the view that the Gospel writers themselves believed that Mary was a victim of rape, and that Joseph, while knowing this to be the case, had chosen to end their engagement quietly instead of seeking to bring the offender to justice. Presumably, he believed that it would involve a legal battle that he could not win. While Schaberg only mentions the rabbinical tradition that Jesus' natural father was a Roman (named Panthera), using it to support her argument that allegations of Jesus' illegitimacy were widespread, it is worth noting that this could be a reason Joseph would not have dared to seek legal remedies, as it would have been dangerous for a Jewish man to make a charge of rape against any Roman in a court of law, especially when it is notoriously difficult to get a conviction for rape.

Still this does not explain why Joseph would change his mind and agree to honor his prior commitment to Mary after all, in spite of the fact that she was pregnant with the child of another man. Joseph's change of heart is viewed by the Gospel writers as evidence of God's intervention, comparable, we might say, to the divine intervention that occurred on the mountain in the land of Moriah, when Abraham was about to murder the child he believed to be the son of another man. A child had been conceived, and this child, in the absence of the natural father, needed a father. Like Abraham, Joseph set aside his feelings of anger and resentment and agreed to adopt the child as his own. The very fact that he did so testifies to the uniqueness of this child, to the fact that God had protected him because he had important plans for his life. While the Gospel writers here offer a theological rationale for Joseph's decision, this rationale incorporates within it an assumption concerning Joseph's moral obligation to set aside his own feelings in the matter and accept Jesus as his own child. Given the strong emphasis within Judaism on adults' obligation to care for the children (including the children that others have callously abandoned), we have here a plausible explanation for why Joseph, after his initial reaction of anger, would agree to raise Mary's son as his own.

As far as Mary herself is concerned, Schaberg believes that her pregnancy was a result of forced rape, though she acknowledges that this is what Matthew and Luke expect the reader to assume, as they are both concerned to present Mary as blameless. The fact that Joseph chose to stand by Mary, and that she was likely only twelve years old, supports the view that she was taken by force. Also, mistranslations have created the impression that Mary was inwardly thrilled with the realization that she was pregnant, when, in fact, the two writers want to convey the idea that it was in great fear, anxiety, and confusion that she went to her cousin Elizabeth for help and advice. This *could* imply that she was experiencing fear and remorse over the fact that the liaison would now be revealed, but in Schaberg's view, the emotional atmosphere created by the writers is more akin to that of the rape victim whose pain and suffering is compounded by the fact that she discovers, to her horror, that she is also pregnant. Schaberg also notes that, as Jesus' family, including Mary, were deeply involved in the Christian movement following his death, it is likely that family members, and probably Mary herself, were the source of the Gospel writers' information about these terribly personal events. It is certainly possible, therefore, that Mary disguised her willing involvement in the liaison and represented this as an act of rape, but Schaberg's point is that this is not the Gospel writers' own view of what happened, and that they would not be likely to present Mary as an innocent victim if they did not themselves believe this to be the case. After all, they had a personal stake in what they were claiming to be true, as they had committed their own lives to the Christian movement. It was important to them that they were communicating the truth, presenting it, of course, as delicately as possible, out of respect for the family's, and especially Mary's privacy.

Admittedly, an entirely different construction of the infancy narratives is possible, and, among biblical scholars with whom I have talked about these narratives, it is by far the most common: This is to argue that Matthew and Luke wanted to present Jesus as having been conceived without human insemination, and therefore attributed Mary's conception to the Spirit of God. Those New Testament scholars who take this position suggest or imply that it is likely that Joseph was Jesus' natural father, that in order for the Gospel writers to make the case that Jesus was "fathered" by the Spirit of God, Joseph had to be relegated to a secondary position, that of Jesus' adoptive father.[13]

Thus, in *Jesus: A Revolutionary Biography*, John Dominic Crossan states, "Both Matthew and Luke agree on the virginal conception of Jesus."[14] In his view, they both use Isaiah 7:14, "The young woman is with child and shall bear a son, and shall name him Immanuel," to support this idea, in spite of the fact that the "prophecy in Isaiah says nothing whatsoever about a virginal conception." Because it doesn't, Crossan believes that "somebody went seeking in the Old Testament for a text that could be interpreted as prophesying a virginal conception, even if such was never its original meaning. Somebody had already decided on the transcendental importance of the adult Jesus and sought to retroject that significance onto the conception and birth itself" (18). As for the widespread charge of illegitimacy, Crossan believes that these allegations did not precede the writing of the infancy narratives (Schaberg's argument) but were instead the consequence of Christians' claims for the virginal conception:

> Once opponents of Christianity heard claims of virginal conceptions and divine generation for Jesus, they would reply with instant and obvious rebuttal: his having no known human father means he was a bastard! The pagan philosopher Celsus, writing in the last quarter of the second century, declares, in the name of both Judaism and paganism, that a cover-up for bastardy must have been the real reason for such claims. The illegitimate father was, he claims, a Roman soldier named Panthera, in whose name we catch a mocking and reversed allusion to *parthenos*, the Greek word for the young woman from Isaiah 7:14. (18)

Crossan also notes that the infancy narratives are the only basis we have for assuming that Jesus was Mary's first child. What if one or more of his siblings were actually older? Would this not cast doubt on the illegitimacy claim?

But Schaberg argues that neither Matthew nor Luke would have entertained the idea that Jesus did not have a natural father, nor would this have been conceivable to their original readers. The idea of a nonnatural conception could only have come later, after asceticism with its renunciation of sexuality had gained significant inroads in Christian thought and practice (though she acknowledges that such an idea is already evident in the Gospel of John). Thus, if a natural conception was assumed, there would be no need for the Gospel writers to relegate Joseph to the status of adoptive father. Rather, for Schaberg, Joseph is represented as Jesus' adoptive father because this is what he actually was. When Luke refers to Jesus as the "supposed" son of Joseph (Luke 3:23), he is not making a theological point (i.e., that Jesus was conceived in an unnatural manner), but is noting that Joseph was not Jesus' natural father. As Schaberg points out, such alternative theories fail to "take seriously the claim of both evangelists that Joseph was not the biological father of Jesus."[15]

The identity of the man who fathered Jesus is not disclosed by either Gospel writer. As Schaberg notes, to have done so would have been to give him recognition that he assuredly did not deserve. As noted, an early rabbinical tradition held that he was a Roman, and some rabbinical writers further alleged that he was a member of the Roman army occupying Palestine at the time. While this view would support her thesis that Mary was the victim of rape, as it is consistent with the universal human experience of soldiers' sexual abuse of the women who live in the towns over which they have military control, Schaberg is understandably reluctant to speculate on the man's identity. Her concern is with Mary's victimization, and with the Gospel writers' view that God was able to reverse the effects of her victimization, and to use this horrible experience to usher in a new era in God's own struggle against oppression and innocent suffering. Yet, unlike the vast majority of biblical scholars, she does not dismiss these early rabbinical writings as mere polemics, but believes that they address, certainly from a partisan, even hostile perspective, a widespread assumption that Jesus was illegitimately conceived. In fact, there is the suggestion in another Gospel, that of John's, that the charge of illegitimacy figured prominently in Jesus' own controversies with those among the Jewish establishment who opposed his movement. When critics of Jesus say that they are descendants of Abraham and imply that Jesus cannot make the same claim, that he was born of fornication, he responds by saying that they are just as liable to the charge of illegitimacy as he is, because they behave as though the devil is their father (John 8:41–47). Says Schaberg, "The Jews meet Jesus' challenge to their religious or spiritual legitimacy by a challenge to his physical legitimacy. The suggestion of Jesus' illegitimacy here is subtle and is drawn from pre-gospel tradition."[16]

While this interchange between Jesus and his adversaries implies that wherever Jesus went he was vulnerable to attack as illegitimate, and, quite possibly, as the son of a non-Jewish father, what Schaberg does not address is the effect that awareness of his illegitimacy would have had on Jesus himself. While it is impossible to know at what age Jesus would have become aware of the circumstances surrounding his birth, we may assume that he would have learned of them as a young child, and that he would view his illegitimacy as a personal tragedy, and himself as the innocent victim of a situation he could do nothing to alter or change. The questions that beg to be asked, therefore, are: How, then, would knowledge of his illegitimacy affect him personally as a child? How would it influence his self-understanding? What measures would he take as a child to shield himself from the fact that he was perceived by those around him as deeply and irrevocably flawed?

Some scholars would argue that knowledge of the circumstances of Jesus' conception would have little impact on his self-understanding. The church historian, Roland Bainton, once observed that Martin Luther's adult life and theology would have been precisely the same had he been raised in an orphanage.[17] Against the tendency to minimize the impact of childhood experience, I want to offer the very opposite thesis, that virtually everything that Jesus said and did as an adult is traceable, in one way or another, to his awareness of being an illegitimate child. His illegitimacy would be profoundly self-defining, and his career as a prophet would not have taken the form that it did were it not for his illegitimacy. Especially noteworthy would be the relationship between his knowledge of his illegitimacy and what is commonly judged to be the core of his own religious experience and public message, his unusually close and personal relationship to God, whom he called "my father." His awareness of his illegitimacy and his deeply personal experience of God as father would be deeply related, for his experience of

God as father would enable him to transform the self-endangerment caused by his illegitimacy into a new sense of self-empowerment and inner freedom, one that challenged the negative self-image resulting from awareness of his illegitimacy.

Jesus' View of God as Father

Joachim Jeremias is widely credited with having noted the fact that Jesus not only spoke of God exclusively as father but also used a very informal, colloquial Aramaic word for father ("Abba"), one roughly equivalent to the English word "Daddy" or German word "Papa."[18] On the other hand, this English equivalent may be somewhat misleading as Jeremias emphasizes that the use of Abba was not limited to children, for adults in Jesus' time also addressed their fathers as Abba. (While adults in the Southern states of America often continue to call their fathers Daddy, this practice is not very common elsewhere.) Noting that there are no instances in the Hebrew Bible where God is directly addressed as father, Jeremias suggests that "the use of the everyday word 'abba' as a form of address to God is the most important linguistic innovation on the part of Jesus" (36). Not only is it most unusual that Jesus "should have addressed God as 'my father'; it is even more so that he should have used the Aramaic form 'Abba,' as 'Abba' was a most intimate form of address." Also, "the complete novelty and uniqueness of 'Abba' as an address to God in the prayers of Jesus shows that it expresses the heart of Jesus' relationship to God." Thus, his use of Abba for God was not merely a linguistic innovation, but also, and more profoundly, it was an expression of his own personal experience of God (64–67). (If it seems odd to speak of Jesus' "experience of God" when Christians affirm that Jesus *is* God, we need to remind ourselves that the Trinitarian formulation came about after his death, and that, as far as Jesus himself was concerned, God was Abba, or Father.)

Jeremias acknowledges that we "are not told when and where Jesus received the revelation in which God disclosed himself to him like a father to his son" (61). He guesses that this may have happened at the time of Jesus' baptism by John, a view, however, that I find quite unconvincing, as it discounts Jesus' childhood experiences, and flies in the face of overwhelming evidence that prayer—direct address to God—usually originates in childhood, particularly when such prayer takes the form, as it did in Jesus' case, of petition for help and protection. This view also dismisses the episode portrayed by Luke (2:41–51) where the twelve-year-old Jesus remained behind in the temple at Jerusalem to sit among the teachers, responding to his mother's complaint that he had treated her and Joseph badly with the question: "How is it that you sought me? Did you not know that I must be in my Father's house?" This earlier reference to "my Father" suggests that the baptism, with its affirmation of Jesus as the son with whom his Father is well pleased, was a culminating event in a long-standing relationship that went very far back into childhood. The idea that a relationship as deeply personal as this would suddenly be revealed, out of the blue, is simply not supported by what developmental psychology teaches us, that is, that a relationship this profound would have its roots in Jesus' childhood experiences, especially his awareness of being an illegitimate child and his struggle to come to terms with the implications of this fact for his personal self-understanding. Moreover, it is Luke's own view, portrayed through the temple episode, that the "disclosure" of God's identity as personal father to Jesus occurred during Jesus' early childhood. Perhaps there is a compelling reason to disagree with Luke on this point, but, if so, I cannot claim to know what it would be.

While some might contend that Jeremias overemphasizes the centrality of God's fatherliness to Jesus' teachings and self-understanding, it is notable that recent scholarship on the book of Q, the common source on which Matthew and Luke both rely, indicates that references to the "father above" attributed to Jesus are found in the earliest of the three strata that make up the book of Q. Also noteworthy is the fact that there is no other image of God than that of father in these early materials.[19]

Jeremias's recognition of the uniqueness of Jesus' view of God as his personal father, one of the few universally accepted "facts" relating to the historical Jesus, prompts us to ask this fundamental question: Would it be merely happenstance that an illegitimately conceived child, a child raised by an adoptive father, not only addressed God as father, but did so in an unusually intimate manner? As one who believes that religious innovations—especially profoundly imaginative ones—have deep psychological significance for those who are responsible for them, I find it implausible that this would all be a mere coincidence. Rather, the circumstances of Jesus' conception and his relationship to God as personal father would be profoundly related. The questions we must try to answer are: How would they be related? What would be the psychological connection between them? How would the experience of God as personal father be a reflection of Jesus' struggle with his endangerment as a child illegitimately conceived?

I can think of at least three ways to interpret this relationship, three readily imaginable scenarios. One is that his image of God as personal father would be a projection of his image of his natural father, the father he never really knew. In spite of the fact that this man would have been guilty of a terrible crime against Jesus' mother, Jesus, as a child, might not have given the actual circumstances of his conception—including Mary's terrorization—much thought, but instead, he might have idealized the man in his mind, viewing him as his secret protector whenever he found himself in difficulty or trouble. If his childhood as the adopted son of Joseph were less than happy, if his relations with Joseph were strained, or if he felt that Joseph favored his own children over Jesus, he might well have longed for his natural father, and thought of how his life would be different, for the better, if he were being raised by the man who fathered him. Or perhaps he had real grievances against his mother and therefore found himself aligned with his natural father against her. The physical inaccessibility of this man would prompt Jesus to direct this longing toward a heavenly father, one very much like the image he held of his natural father. Against those who viewed his illegitimacy as a stigma, Jesus, in this scenario, would be rather defiant, claiming that he was actually special by virtue of the qualities he shared with his natural father. His image of his father above would support his repudiation of that which he despised in his mother and adoptive father, whatever this might be.

A second scenario is that Jesus' image of God as father was largely a projection of Joseph, his adoptive father, and had roots in his awareness that Joseph had chosen to remain faithful to Mary, to be her and her unborn child's protector, in spite of the circumstances of the child's conception. Here, as in the first scenario, there is a direct projection, but of the father whom Jesus experienced on a daily basis, toward whom he felt profound gratitude for saving his mother and him from the usual fate that befell unmarried women with children. His image of God as father would then be based on his experience of his adoptive father, the one who assumed the responsibilities of fatherhood at the critical moment when Mary and her unborn child's future were in serious jeopardy. This is a father who sets aside his own personal feelings, placing himself and his own future at risk for the sake of an innocent woman and her unborn child.

A third scenario would be that Jesus' image of God, while that of a father, was diametrically opposite to his perception of his natural father, that the operative dynamic was not one of direct projection but of image-splitting. In this scenario, he would view the natural father as an immoral, reprehensible man, as the one who sexually violated his mother, a twelve-year-old virgin, and who was directly responsible for his own spoiled identity. If this man were also a Roman, and therefore talked about in Joseph's household with great hatred and disgust, Jesus would be intensely motivated to envision himself as the son of a very different father, one to whom he could always turn for help, and who, unlike his real father, would never act treacherously, or take advantage of the vulnerability of another, but would always consider the consequences of his actions for his son's own life and future. Such a father would be caring and protective, and, above all, he would be the source of a much-needed positive identity ("You are my beloved Son, with whom I am well pleased"). In this scenario, the heavenly Father counteracts the negative self-image that Jesus cannot otherwise overcome as the son of a man who is viewed by everyone in his family and community as despicable and subhuman. While this scenario does not require that we take Jesus' natural father to be a Roman—he could also be Jewish—this view has a certain internal logic. As Paul Hollenbach has pointed out in his interpretation of Jesus' healing of the Gerasene demoniac, mental illness among young Jewish men was a political act—the demons' cry "We are Legion" is an allusion to the Roman army—an act of defiance against the Roman occupation of Jewish communities and against the Jewish leaders who were cooperating with the Roman colonial government.[20] In this scenario, Jesus, aware of the fact that his mother was sexually assaulted by a Roman soldier, had a natural affinity for these young Jewish men who were defiant toward Rome. His "pathology" is that he has the genes of a Roman, and is therefore occupied by a foreign element that can only be exorcized by replacing this inner demon with a new internalized father, the one he affectionately calls "my father."

The Desire to Be Another Man's Son

Which of these interpretive schemas or scenarios is the most persuasive? Which one rings most true? I have not found this an easy question to answer, as there is much more involved here than simply assembling Jesus' recorded allusions to his heavenly Father and reading back to their probable antecedents in the perceptions and emotions of the child Jesus. Assuming, however, that Jesus' experience of God as father is rooted in his struggle against his own endangerment as a child, what is involved for one who seeks to get inside Jesus' own experience as a child is a kind of self-abandonment, that is, an imaginative entry into Jesus' own situation where I personally take the view of a child who is aware of his illegitimacy, and who has already begun to reflect on the fateful implications of this inexorable fact for his life. If this were my situation, how would I receive it? How would I experience it? How would I respond? This has proved to be a difficult, even painful exercise,[21] as it has necessarily involved recalling experiences in my own childhood which most nearly approximate his experience, realizing, of course, that Jesus' sense of being a child with a deep sense of personal tragedy was always with him, whereas my personal grievances against my own life fate were more episodic and less integral to my ontological sense of myself, my core identity.

Still, what I discovered in myself was something of the desire, reflected in the first interpretive schema, to have experienced my own father more forcefully than I did, and to have had a greater sense of his palpable presence and support, counteracting my mother's commanding, if not controlling presence. I also discovered in myself something of the profound gratitude reflected in the second scenario for my father's dependability and personal sacrifices for me. He was, indeed, a kind of Joseph to me, hovering in the background, rather self-preoccupied and not very talkative, but stable and steady, and, above all, a man who was moral without making a special point of it. Yet the more I pursued this exercise in introspection, a rather darker atmosphere emerged, as I became aware in myself of the feelings associated with the third scenario. Surely not the sense that my father was evil or despicable, or that he had violated or abused my mother. No, not that. But the sense, nevertheless, that it may have been better for this child to have had a different man for his father. Such feelings, long repressed, came to my awareness, and I reexperienced what must be one of the most painful experiences of childhood and possibly the strongest impetus for repressing our childhood experiences, that of feeling shame not for myself but for a parent whom I also deeply loved. As Helen Merrell Lynd points out, the shame we feel for others is often deeper and more painful for us than the shame we feel for ourselves.

Of course I immediately found myself reliving my guilt for entertaining thoughts like this, for my father had done nothing explicitly to warrant these feelings of mine, this sense of being inexplicably ashamed to be his son. I also found myself reliving the blame I had placed on my mother for her role in activating this desire to be another man's son, as she frequently belittled her husband in the presence of her children and revealed through her behavior toward the men her sisters had married that she deserved better. Yet I believe this desire in me to be another man's son was the beginning of my own religious consciousness, as this longing was not directed toward one of my uncles—for unlike my own father these men openly violated my mother's own prohibition against the use of alcohol, even in her presence—but toward the one whom Jesus called Father. He, the Father of Jesus, was the answer to my prayers to be a beloved son, the object of a father's affection and love. This father was not just anyone's father. He was Jesus' Father, accessible to me because Jesus shared him with me. My favorite Bible verse throughout childhood—one proudly but reverently borne—was John 14:6: "I am the way, and the truth, and the life; no one comes to the Father, but by me."

After engaging in this exercise in introspection, I was startled to find that Freud's introspections—his reliving of long-repressed childhood perceptions—led to a similar discovery. Puzzled by the fact that, in the writing of his great classic, *the Interpretation of Dreams*, he substituted the name of the general Hannibal's brother Hasdrubal for his father's name of Hamilcar, he relates his experience of visiting his half brother in England and discovering that he and his half brother's oldest son were exactly the same age. On recalling this incident in connection with his confusion of the names of Hannibal's father and brother, he became aware of a deeper recollection, the fact that he had wished at the time that he was not the son of his father (who was much older than his mother). As he writes in *Psychopathology of Everyday Life* of his correction of the original error in subsequent editions of *The*

Interpretation of Dreams, "I could have continued and recounted [there] how my attitude toward my father was changed by a visit to England. . . . How much pleasanter it would be had I been born the son of my brother instead of the son of my father!"[22]

The desire to be another man's son: I think this is a far more powerful and potent emotion for a child than the desire for a father whose presence is more palpable and protective, or the sense of gratitude one feels for his father's steady dependability. And I think this is precisely what the child Jesus would feel and experience with special keenness, as he had unusually powerful and urgent grounds for wishing he was not the son of the man who impregnated his mother. This strong wish to be another man's son is the deep inspiration for his view of God as a personal father, a father who effectively replaces human fathers in his understanding of himself as someone's son. He would know himself as the son of Abba, and thus, as no longer illegitimate or adopted. He was the true son of Abba and thus of no other.

As son of Abba, Jesus would thereby successfully challenge his fate, the stigma of his illegitimate birth, and insist on his right to an alternative identity, one that was more authentic, more true, because it was not based on social judgments and expectations, but on one's inherent, God-given freedom to be the self that one truly is. Here is an alternative identity whose essential core is one in which his self-affirmation is itself affirmed ("You are my beloved Son, with whom I am well pleased"). Perhaps it would take a man who was considered to be illegitimate to point out that it was not himself, but the social order on which others were depending and feeding that was illegitimate. Social institutions and conventions are powerful because we treat them as though they are real, as though they have the right and privilege to define us. We transfer our power to them, thus allowing them to drain us of our own power, leaving our spirits empty, weak, depleted, and degraded.

As a healer, Jesus would understand how this transfer of power works. A woman who had been rendered powerless by the loss of her own lifeblood for twelve years could take hold of his garment and regain power as the strength in his body was transferred into hers (Mark 5:25–34). Or a man who was rendered powerless because there was a "legion" of demons in his body, his life energy dispersed among them, would have his power restored when the demons left his body and took residence, instead, in a herd of swine (Mark 5:1–13). Such healings, such new infusions of power and strength, would occur because Jesus affirmed the self-affirmations of others, even as his heavenly Father did for him, while simultaneously disaffirming their negative self-judgments imposed by social convention and labeling. When a woman came and anointed his feet—an act of self-affirmation that Jesus named her "faith"—he ignored the obvious fact that she was a "bad woman," prompting the man in whose house this disruptive episode is said to have taken place to observe, "If this man were a prophet, he would have known who and what sort of woman this is who is touching him, for she is a sinner" (Luke 7:36–50). As Jesus would understand from his childhood struggles with his own inexorable fate, dramatic changes occur when we view ourselves and others as persons of inherent worth, celebrating one another's expressions of self-affirmation as a most "beautiful thing" (Matt. 26:10).

Of all selves, children are surely the most endangered, as they have few resources to defend their emerging selves against the institutions and forces that would cheat them of their unique individuality, and would label them instead. Moreover, children, as they become adults, are prone to rationalize in behalf of these institutions and forces, to spare them as they once spared their parents. This is their way of apologizing for the feelings of shame they felt for their fathers and mothers, feelings reflected in their desire to be the offspring of someone else. Against such conventional labeling and rationalization in behalf of the myriad social institutions that have no feelings for us, Jesus' own self-affirmation is itself a very beautiful thing to behold: "See that you do not despise one of these little ones; for I tell you that in heaven their angels always behold the face of my Father who is in heaven" (Matt. 18:10).

The Garden of Gethsemane

A further question that my own exercise in introspection prompts me to ask, however, is this: For those of us for whom Jesus' solution to his own identity problems was key to our own self-survival as children, what is the meaning of this solution as we live out our adult lives? Just as Kierkegaard struggled to understand his responses to the Mount Moriah story, I have struggled in my adult years to understand the Garden of Gethsemane story, where Jesus' alternative identity met its deepest test. What meaning has it for me?—one for whom Jesus' Father satisfied the desire to be another man's son?

This story, like the story of Abraham and Isaac, aptly fits Phyllis Trible's beautifully suggestive phrase, "text of terror," as it concerns the terror of a young man facing almost certain death. I doubt that this story is historical, for it is likely that a Galilean who caused public commotion in Jerusalem would immediately be arrested and crucified that very day. Yet in a sense it does not matter, for, whether historical or not, it addresses my dilemma as one for whom Jesus' solution to his identity problem was also my own. The story tells us that Jesus went to the garden to pray on his own behalf ("My Father, I pray that this cup be removed; nonetheless, not my, but thy will be done") and that his Father sent an angel to minister to him. The detail about the angel would suggest that the Abraham and Isaac story was somewhere in the consciousness of the author of this story. Against this background, the story has a truth for us, a dark but ultimately liberating truth.

Key to this story is the fact that, unlike the Mount Moriah tale, God, not Abraham, is the father in the story (the God-role and the father-role are conflated),[23] and, unlike Isaac, the son is able to speak freely to his father. Not only does he make his desire known to his father—his desire that his life be spared—but, even after accepting that his father's will should prevail, we are told that he "entreated some more," as if to indicate that, having accepted that his father's will would be enacted, it became all the more imperative that he try to change his father's mind. In effect, Jesus does what Alice Miller recommends that Isaac do: Speak freely to the father, and ask questions about why it is necessary for the son to die.

If this were only a story about parent-child relationships, we would conclude that it offers a better model for the settling of parent-child disputes than the Abraham and Isaac story, as Jesus is able to speak freely to his father, without restraint, in the hope that his father may reverse his earlier decision. It also suggests that, where a good parent-child relationship exists (as it does in the case of Jesus and his heavenly Father), the child can come to know the parent's mind, and to anticipate what the parent feels about an issue even before being asked or questioned about it; furthermore, even if the child is not in fundamental agreement with what the parent thinks or feels, the child can be sympathetically disposed to it, accepting that the parent has a valid point of view that is worthy of the child's respect. Conversely, it suggests that the parent need not become angry or feel threatened if the child asks the parent to reconsider the issue at hand, knowing from the child's tone of voice and demeanor that the parent's authority is not being challenged or contested. Thus, whereas this story has been used throughout the generations to support the superiority of the parent's will over that of the child, and of the need for parents to curb or break the child's will, often by means of harsh childrearing practices, it may be understood instead as a story that supports free and unrestrained, though respectful, communication between child and parent over their differences in viewpoint, perspective, and desires.

However, this is much more than a story about how parents and children may respectfully disagree. It is a story in which a son pleads with his father to be spared the death that almost certainly awaits him, and who believes that his father has the power to intervene in his behalf but chooses not to. Unlike the Abraham and Isaac story, it is not about how a human father's loyalty to God was tested by the threat of the loss of his son, but is, instead, the story of a son's unfailing loyalty to his father—even unto death—and of a father who, while deeply sympathizing with his son and moved by his ordeal, remains unyielding, and does not accede to his beloved son's request that he be spared the death that awaits him. It is not a story about how God spoke to a human father at the critical moment, charging him to stay his hand, but a story in which God the father chooses not to intervene in his son's behalf, and instead sends an angel of mercy to comfort his son as he endures his lonely ordeal, abandoned even by his friends.

What kind of story is this? What does it mean to tell us? Many have viewed it as a story about a father's painful yet courageous sacrifice of his son for a "higher cause," the son being a "ransom" for many (as the Gospel of Mark puts it). Others, like Paul Tillich, have said that Jesus had to be sacrificed so that there could be the Christ.[24] Still others have considered this a father's act of "self-sacrifice," since, in giving up his son, he gave up that which meant more to him than any other. These interpretations focus on a similarity between this and the Abraham and Isaac story, that of the sacrifice of the son for a higher purpose: the ransoming of sinners who are otherwise without hope, the sacrifice of the historical Jesus so that we may know the Christ who triumphs over sin and death, and the new self-disclosure of God as the one who does makes the ultimate sacrifice.

I confess that I find these interpretations unconvincing for, as René Girard points out, Jesus himself opposed the very logic of sacrifice, including self-sacrifice, on the grounds that sacrifice is a self-perpetuating social dynamic, each sacrifice demanding another, and another. This is what the author of the letter to the Hebrews has to acknowledge, for Jesus' "sacrifice" does not in fact end the process once and for all, it merely raises the stakes. Instead of sacrifice, Jesus' whole message, as Crossan points out, was based on egalitarian commensality, meaning that the rules of simple table fellowship were for him the model for human association and socialization.[25] Commensality, not sacrifice, was the central theme of his life and message.

These interpretations are also unconvincing because they provide justifications for the failure of God the Father to protect his Son, and thus, in Alice Miller's words, they *spare the parent*. The very fact that Christians have given so much attention to providing an explanation for the death of Jesus is itself an indication of how powerful is this need to spare the parent. We do not presume to ask God why he did not put his Son's life above all other considerations, nor do we even consider the enormous implications this would have had for humankind: If God the Father had intervened in behalf of his Son, as God the voice intervened in behalf of Abraham's son Isaac, this would have served as a powerful impetus for Jesus' followers to place the highest value on the protection of children against poverty, disease, war, and death. Instead, we have the sorry record of Christians, who, no less than their pagan neighbors, exposed their children to physical death and to a living hell as the victims of exploitation. What we have witnessed since the time of Jesus' death are theological attempts to provide an explanation for why God the Father was unyielding when his Son pleaded with him to be spared the fate of death. Thus, the history of Christian theology is replete with efforts to do precisely what Miller says the Freudian tradition has done, that is, to spare the parents by offering one explanation after another for why God the Father, fully conscious of the fact that his beloved Son was in mortal danger, did nothing about it.

To attempt to explain Jesus' death as a redemptive act of God is to shift responsibility for human treachery onto God. Girard instead attributes his death to the need of those in power to find scapegoats for their failure to govern effectively and wisely.[26] As Crossan points out, crucifixion had the purpose of depriving the accused of any identity he might otherwise claim: the body was left for animals and birds to devour as the ultimate shame, the culprit literally reduced to a nobody, leaving no trace behind.[27] The meaning of Jesus' death is that his murderers could not deprive him of his identity because it was based on his realized desire to be his Father's son, an identity they were powerless to take away.

The Meaning Is in the Setting

But, if so, where does this leave Jesus' understanding of God as father? And where does this leave us with respect to the story of the Garden of Gethsemane? In chapter 4, I suggested that Jesus, with his attestation to a nonviolent God, is an "enlightened witness" in the child's behalf against those who support the abuse of children.[28] While not an actual witness to the events that occurred in childhood, the enlightened witness is nonetheless able to affirm the likelihood of their occurrence, and thus to lend her strong support to the adult who is struggling to call these events to mind and to reinterpret them in the light of subsequent adult experiences. I would suggest that *each of us* needs to approach the Garden of Gethsemane story as an enlightened witness, and thus to provide a perspective on the story that is unequivocally on the side of the suffering one against those who acted violently against him, rejecting such violence as willed by God and proclaiming it unable to destroy his identity as son of the Father above.

For those who have been taught to view the death of our Lord as a ransom or even as a father's act of self-sacrifice, this may not be an easy position to take, and we are likely to be attacked as Alice Miller has been attacked, for her view that there can be no redemptive value in any violent act against any child. By challenging the idea that Jesus' death was willed by his Father above, and therefore has redemptive value for others, we challenge the idea that acts of violence against children, whatever form they may take, may also have redemptive value. One often hears adults proclaim, "Yes, I was beaten as a child, but it didn't do any lasting harm, for look at me now. I survived and, in fact, I'm a better person for it." Miller says, "No, this cannot be, for, as long as you believe this, you will inflict the suffering you endured on someone else. The problem is that you are not aware of this simple but tragic fact, for you have not been encouraged to make the connection between the sufferings you experienced as a child and the sufferings that you, as an adult, are inflicting on innocent others." Therefore, the real lesson of the suffering and death of Jesus is that as long as children are suffering abuse, we will continue to have innocent sufferers, both children and adults, who are paying for the abuse that was inflicted on them as children.

The fate of Jesus is a powerful, continual reminder to us of innocent suffering, wherever it may be occurring, for he did not deserve the death that was inflicted upon him. To say that God "willed" his death is to betray Jesus and his own attestation to the Father who abhors violence, and who therefore will have no complicity whatsoever in any sacrificial system, especially the sacrifice of the one who knew him as his Father. If Jesus died because he dared to attack the temple in Jerusalem—the broad consensus of biblical scholars—then it would be a betrayal of Jesus himself to suggest that he is God's sacrifice in our behalf. In this act of public defiance, Jesus proclaimed that God abhors sacrifice, for sacrifice begets sacrifice in a never-ending cycle of violence and bloodshed. Why then would the God to whom Jesus attests turn around and sacrifice his own beloved Son? In the form in which it occurs in the gospels, the Garden of Gethsemane story takes a fateful step toward the sacrificial theology of the letter to the Hebrews.

What, then, remains of the story of the Garden of Gethsemane when its sacrificial implications are removed? Following Kierkegaard's approach in *Fear and Trembling* of envisioning alternative scenarios to the Abraham and Isaac story, I suggest something like the following recounting of the event (a composite of Matthew, Luke and my own reflections on the story):

> Then Jesus went with them to a place called Gethsemane, and he said to his disciples, "Sit here, while I go yonder and pray. And taking with him Peter and the two sons of Zebedee, he began to be sorrowful and troubled. Then he said to them, "My soul is very sorrowful, even to death; remain here, and watch with me." And going a little farther he fell on his face and prayed, "Strengthen me, father, for the ordeal that I am about to undergo." And as he lay there, alone and exhausted, he heard his father speak as he had heard him before as he bathed in the River Jordan, "You are my beloved Son, with whom I am well pleased." And there appeared to him an angel from heaven, strengthening him.
>
> So fortunate is the one who knows whose son he is, and fortunate is the one who, in his darkest hour, has a place of safety, where his enemies cannot touch him, and an angel of mercy is there to strengthen him.

When the sacrificial dynamic is removed from the story, a figure-ground reversal occurs, and we become more cognizant of the protections and solaces provided by the setting in which the story is placed—the garden itself. When I was a very small child, my father and my paternal grandfather devoted many summer evenings to the cultivation of a victory garden, one of various ways in which they could serve their country during wartime while my uncles were overseas. My childhood experience of being allowed to make furrows with a garden trowel and to place the seeds in the furrows at prescribed intervals has engendered in me a natural sympathy for understandings of God—and of God's world—based on the image of the garden. Ralph Waldo Emerson's essays have been especially important for me in recent years because they employ garden images to speak about the human soul: the inner landscape of the self. Rollo May's autobiography, *My Quest for Beauty*, has also been of great influence, as he writes about the serenity that he has experienced in the world of nature, adding:

> I knew that the flowers and the spring verdure were not in themselves God. But are we not given a glimpse of the beauty of God by these gay trumpetings of brilliant pink of the flowering Judas tree, and by the lemon blossoms with their magical odor and by the heavily scented lavender of the wisteria hanging from every branch?[29]

May also recounts a counseling session with a woman who began by saying she was very weary, fatigued from entertaining visitors for the past week, and didn't have much to say. May suggested that she might then simply free-associate, briefly explaining to her how it works. She expressed doubts about the procedure but began: "The first thing that comes to me, I stopped my car on the way here to look at the twilight. It was just beautiful, the purple hues with the green hills behind them. . . . " She then proceeded through the hour to speak about beauty, about how her mother always wanted her to notice the beauty of the world; about God, because the beauty in the world could not be there by accident; and about the relationship of beauty to death. When the session came to a close, she apologized to Rollo May because it was all such "superficial talk." He responded that he felt it was the most profound hour the two of them had ever shared, and then writes: "This person is like the majority of people in our western culture; we suppress our feelings of beauty; we are shy about them, they are too personal. . . . It is too soul-baring."[30] He might well have added that we learn to suppress our feelings of beauty in childhood, and that we often do so, as children, because our religion tells us that our sense perceptions are unreliable guides to ultimate truth, a view that is forcefully challenged by Joan Erikson in her book *Wisdom and the Senses*.[31]

Of all the authors who have employed the garden metaphor to speak of beauty and death, and of the presence of God, the poet Louise Glück is my personal favorite. Her book *The Wild Iris*[32] follows an earlier collection of poems titled *Ararat*, in which she explores her childhood against the backdrop of the biblical story of Abraham and Isaac.[33] In *The Wild Iris*, her husband's garden becomes the setting for her reflections on the meaning of life in the face of death, and on our perception of the presence of God in the world. As the book jacket puts it, she has created "an impassioned poly-phonic exchange among the god who 'discloses virtually nothing,' human beings who 'leave signs of feeling everywhere,' and a garden where 'whatever returns from oblivion returns to find a voice.' " The poem in which occurs her statement about the God who discloses virtually nothing is titled "Matins":[34]

What is my heart to you
that you must break it over and over
like a plantsman testing
his new species? Practice
on something else: how can I live
in colonies, as you prefer, if you impose
a quarantine of affliction, dividing me
from healthy members of
my own tribe: you do not do this
in the garden, segregate
the sick rose; you let it wave its sociable
infested leaves in
the faces of the other roses, and the tiny aphids
leap from plant to plant, proving yet again
I am the lowest of your creatures, following
the thriving aphid and the trailing rose—Father,
as agent of my solitude, alleviate
at least my guilt; lift
the stigma of isolation, unless
it is your plan to make me
sound forever again, as I was
sound and whole in my mistaken childhood,
or if not then, under the light weight
of my mother's heart, or if not then,
in dream, first
being that would never die.

Later, in "Vespers,"[35] she notes that God appeared to Moses in the burn-ing bush, and may, in a similar way, be appearing to her now, if not in her husband's garden, then in the surrounding pasture blazing with color:

Even as you appeared to Moses, because
I need you, you appear to me, not
often, however. I live essentially
in darkness. You are perhaps training me to be
responsive to the slightest brightening. Or, like the poets,
are you stimulated by despair, does grief
move you to reveal your nature? This afternoon,
in the physical world to which you commonly
contribute your silence, I climbed

the small hill above the wild blueberries, metaphysically
descending, as on all my walks: did I go deep enough
for you to pity me, as you have sometimes pitied
others who suffer, favoring those
with theological gifts? As you anticipated,
I did not look up. So you came down to me:
at my feet, not the wax
leaves of the wild blueberry but your fiery self, a whole
pasture of fire, and beyond, the red sun neither falling
      nor rising—
I was not a child; I could take advantage of illusions.

Finally, in another poem also titled "Vespers,"[36] she concludes that God is
in the garden, yet notes that the presence of God is more like her husband's
way with the garden than her own:

I don't wonder where you are anymore.
You're in the garden; you're where John is,
in the dirt, abstracted, holding his green trowel.
This is how he gardens: fifteen minutes of intense effort,
fifteen minutes of ecstatic contemplation. Sometimes
I work beside him, doing the shade chores,
weeding, thinning the lettuces; sometimes I watch
from the porch near the upper garden until twilight makes
lamps of the first lilies: all this time,
peace never leaves him. But it rushes through me,
not as sustenance the flower holds
but like bright light through the bare tree.

My purpose in citing these poems by Louise Glück is to make the simple
point that a powerful key to the meaning of the Gethsemane story is the
setting in which it occurred. Unlike Mount Moriah, with its exaggerated
sense of sacrifice and duty, its confident spirit ("God will provide . . . , my
son"), its histrionics ("and he took the knife to slay his son"), the garden is a
place for soul-searching and soul-baring, and soul-mending, a place where
God is agent of our solitude. It is a place where sorrow and grief, longing
and desire, serenity and pleasure mingle, like plants of many species, together. It is not a place of high stakes, of challenging tests of courage and
will, but a setting in which we find our own kind of peace: whether the peace
that holds and sustains, or the peace that rushes in and through, like a bright
and searching light.

I have often found myself praying in garden settings like the one in which
the Gospel writers envisioned Jesus in his last hours on earth. I feel his
presence about me in such moments. What makes this possible is the freedom that I have as an adult to take advantage of illusions. When I think of
him in his profound loneliness, having no witnesses to watch and to wait

with him in his agony and terror, I sense that he was not alone. Angels from heaven may appear in many places, including mountains where spirits are tested to the limit, but they are most palpably present in those garden places where souls are searched and bared and mended.

"Supposing Him to Be the Gardener"

The Gospel of John has another garden scene: Mary Magdalene was standing weeping outside the tomb where Jesus' body had been laid to rest, and as she wept she stooped to look into the tomb. She saw two angels in white, sitting where the body of Jesus had lain, one at the head and the other at the foot. They asked her why she was weeping, and she replied, "Because they have taken away my Lord, and I do not know where they have laid him." Saying this, she turned around and saw Jesus standing, though she did not know that it was he. He asked, "Why are you weeping? Whom do you seek?" Supposing him to be the gardener, she replied, "Sir, if you have carried him away, tell me where you have laid him, and I will take him away." He spoke her name, "Mary," and she answered, "Teacher." Then he said to her, "Do not hold me, for I have not yet ascended to the Father; but go to my brethren and say to them, I am ascending to my Father and your Father, to my God and your God" (John 20:11–18).

It was a brief conversation, the kind that not infrequently takes place between the one who has been bereaved and the one who has been taken away in death. Did this postdeath encounter really happen? Or was it a dream? For the bereaved, there is no distinction, for the encounter itself, however and whenever it occurs, is as real as real can be. What matters more is the fact that it occurred in a garden, and that Mary initially mistook Jesus for the gardener, supposing that he was the one responsible for removing the body from the grave. A case of mistaken identity. Or was it?

Could it be that Jesus is the one who continues to maintain and nurture the gardens of our lives, tending the fragile shoots until they are able to flower of their own accord? Perhaps Mary Magdalene was more right than she knew. The resurrected Jesus ascended into heaven where his Father received him, but his spirit took the form of a simple gardener who does the work of a thousand angels.

Alternative Scenarios

In this chapter, I have taken up Jane Schaberg's effort to bring a fresh perspective to bear on the infancy narratives. I am not a trained biblical scholar, and I have no professional stake in the controversy that her book has generated among these scholars. But I am a Christian, as are Schaberg and her critics, and I have a personal stake in the issue of whether the Christian faith we pass on to our children and children's children is a religion of abuse or a religion of love.

It troubles me, therefore, that some of the reactions of Schaberg's colleagues to her book are themselves illustrative of the problem that I have been addressing in this book: the abuse that is committed in the name of religion. I have not read all of the scholarly reviews of her book, but I have read several of them, and have been surprised at their dismissive, even sarcastic tone. Leander E. Keck, professor of Biblical Theology at Yale Divinity School, writes in his book *The Church Confident*: "Almost any idea gains credence today if its advocates claim to be motivated by identification with the poor, the powerless, and the oppressed. Even the long-discredited legend that Jesus was the illegitimate offspring of a vulnerable Jewish girl who, during her betrothal, was seduced or raped, perhaps by a Roman officer (whom the Nazis identified as an Aryan), has been rehabilitated because it is said to show God's concern for the marginalized and the subversion of patriarchy."[37] He cites the Schaberg book. Likewise, Luke Timothy Johnson, professor of New Testament at Candler School of Theology, in a review in *Christian Century* on John Shelby Spong's *Born of a Woman: A Bishop Rethinks the Birth of Jesus*, says that books like this one "belong on the 'Religion' shelf of the ever-proliferating self-help literature produced by those recovering from every imaginable form of dysfunction and addiction," and then summarizes Spong's "therapeutic rereading" of the infancy narratives: "Mary [according to Spong] was in reality a teenaged girl who was raped and became pregnant with an illegitimate child and was taken under the protection of Joseph. Spong offers no evidence for this speculation beyond Schaberg's already highly tendentious appropriation of anti-Christian slanders (apparently deriving from Jewish sources) peddled in the second century by Celsus."[38]

Keck's comments are puzzling to me. I was taught in a seminary course in New Testament that the Gospel of Luke, in which we find one of the infancy narratives explored by Schaberg, was written by an author who identified "with the poor, the powerless, and the oppressed." In Schaberg's view, the infancy narrative in Luke sets this very tone for the gospel as a whole, for it is one more in a sordid series of biblical "texts of terror" in which women (including young girls) were sexually abused. Keck's comment about what the Nazis believed is heavy-handed, as it implies that one should not even discuss the issues and questions raised by the infancy narratives because of the way the Nazis exploited such discussions. In his summary dismissal of Schaberg's work as nothing but a revival of a "long-discredited legend," Keck comes across like a parent declaring to an irksome child: "As far as I'm concerned, the matter is closed. You and I have nothing further to talk about."

If Keck raises the specter of Naziism, Johnson raises the specter of therapeutism. He worries that the gospels are being read from a "therapeutic" point of view, and are therefore in danger of falling into the hands of those who are recovering "from every imaginable form of dysfunction and addiction." This, too, is puzzling to me. One of the reasons I chose the field of pastoral care was that it seemed to have direct connections to the healing ministry of Jesus. If Crossan is right that "egalitarian commensality" was the central theme of Jesus' own ministry, then this instruction from the earliest strata of the book of Q is especially apropos: "And if you enter a town and they receive you, eat what is set before you. Pay attention to the sick and say to them, 'God's kingdom has come near to you.' "[39] Paying attention to the sick is a critical link between commensality and kingdom. Yet here, Spong is dismissed because he reads the infancy narratives with "therapeutic" eyes, and Schaberg, on whom Spong relies, is also dismissed for her "tendentious" argumentation (which is to say that she exhibits a definite point of view).

What I believe is occurring here is a not-so-subtle form of verbal shaming. Schaberg is being told by her colleagues in the field of New Testament that she crossed a line that she ought not to have crossed, that, in effect, she has committed a shameful act. Her critics undoubtedly miss the irony here, for this is precisely what her book is about: the shaming of a woman and the power of a patriarchal system to protect its own interests. I worry that such public shamings may have their desired effect. They may cause the woman to have doubts, to wonder if she should have kept her views to herself, or even to doubt her own perceptions and judgments. This is not an unfamiliar scene, for it is one in which you and I have found ourselves before, on many occasions: In a seminar, a committee meeting, a public forum, we may have expressed what we considered an important insight, a different angle on an issue that others assumed to be clear-cut and unambiguous, only to have our insight dismissed or ridiculed by someone who could not see the ambiguity, or who simply had a more persuasive way of speaking. We fell silent, left to ruminate about whether what we said was even worth saying, and why it is our lot in life to have insights that are so readily discountable.

So let me request this of those biblical scholars who find Schaberg's argument unpersuasive: Give those of us who are not biblical scholars an alternative scenario, one based on your view that Jesus was reared by his natural parents, Mary and Joseph. Imagine for us what his childhood was like. Explain to us the relationship between his experience of his father Joseph and his message about his Father above. To my knowledge, John W. Miller is the only biblical scholar who has offered such a scenario in anything near the depth and complexity with which Schaberg has formulated hers, focusing on the decisive role that Joseph's death may have played in Jesus' life and in the shaping of his message.[40]

In the meantime, what is certain is that the ridicule that Schaberg's work has received is uncomfortably close to the ways that abusive parents treat their children, and to the ways that ruling elites create scapegoats for their own failures to govern effectively and wisely.

II
Reclaiming The Garden

7

A Garden of Childhood Verses

Martin E. Marty's *A Cry of Absence*, written within months of his wife's death from cancer, is a deeply moving meditation on the Psalms. In explaining his decision to focus on the Psalms in this time of grief and despair, he confesses that he has always been a person for whom texts hold special meaning—more so than objects of art—so it was natural for him to turn to the book of Psalms for sustenance.[1]

It is significant that Psalms, the biblical texts to which individuals who are in physical and emotional pain turn for sustenance, is a book of poetry. While large sections of the book of Job and some of the prophetic books are mostly poetry, the book of Psalms is unique in being a collection of poems written by various authors and reflecting their own personal experiences. These authors' personal meditations have struck a deep, resonant chord with others because, as Carl Rogers once noted, "what is most personal and unique in each one of us is probably the very element which would, if it were shared or expressed, speak most deeply to others. This has helped me to understand artists and poets as people who have dared to express the unique in themselves."[2]

This study has been concerned with the pain and poignance of childhood, especially as experienced in and through the child-parent relationship. Many have written about this experience, including psychologists, autobiographers, and poets, yet, in my experience, none have written as sensitively about it as have the poets. For years, I have been an avid reader of psychological texts that provide much insight into what it is like to be a child. Psychologists, however, necessarily focus on the generic child, and when they write about a specific child and this child's experiences, they do so in order to make a point about childhood in general.[3] I would never denigrate these psychological studies, for they sensitize us to many of the central issues, themes, and problems of childhood. But they do not succeed very well in portraying how it was for you and for me, on any given day, to be a child. They paint in broad strokes, describing several years of our lives with a suggestive phrase that rings true, and yet leaves so much unsaid and unremarked. Psychologists, after all, are interested in the growth process, in how we develop, and in what aids and inhibits the maturing process. They cannot register the experiences—good, bad, or indifferent—that at the time may have seemed unremarkable, yet from that day forth, acquired a permanent place in the storehouse of our memories, affording pleasure or inflicting pain whenever called to mind.

I have also been an avid reader of autobiographical texts, as these texts invite the reader to witness the author's childhood, and to gain a feel for what it must have been like to be this child in this context or setting. Here the experiences that the psychological texts fail to register are not only called to mind but also written down and reflected on from the vantage point of adulthood, and thus of what came after. The reader is invited to witness the author's childhood experiences, and, if not always to express approval, at least to empathize, and thus—so the author hopes—to acquire a predisposition early in the reading to view with understanding what the author has to say about his or her life, and so to appreciate the life as it was lived. To be invited to witness the experiences of a child can have a powerful effect on the reader. I recall: Maxim Gorky's account of how he was struck repeatedly by his grandfather, and the efforts of his uncle to console him;[4] or Thomas Merton's account of his mother's death and of his relief that his father did not require him to go to the mausoleum to witness the final disposition of her ashes;[5] or Dorothy Day's account of living through the San Francisco earthquake, and being left in the bed she shared with her sister as her mother came to rescue her sister instead of her;[6] or Annie Dillard's experience of being terrified at night by blinding lights that played on her bedroom wall until she discerned that there was a simple explanation—the headlights of passing automobiles.[7]

Episodes such as these speak volumes about the pain, the worries, the fears, the confusions, the despair, and yes, the triumphs of childhood. But, however effective they are in inviting us to witness the childhood of another, childhood is the first chapter in a narrative that intends to press on and to give the lion's share of attention to the author's adulthood. This means that childhood experiences become a part of a larger project, and, more often than not, the author is so concerned to get on with the story that the childhood is related in rather cursory fashion. Annie Dillard's *An American Childhood* was written, in part, to counteract this characteristic of autobiography. Moreover, many autobiographers make little effort to penetrate deeply into their childhoods, to gain understanding of its hidden meanings. The task they have set for themselves is to take stock of where they have arrived—many autobiographies being written in midlife—so as to set the stage or agenda for what is yet to come. Writing about their childhood is, for many, a necessary evil or means to warm up to their task, for it seems more to be a requirement of the genre of autobiography than motivated by some deep, inner need to know and to understand the childhood years. This explains why so many initial chapters of autobiographies consist of clichés and superficial theories about how their authors came to be the persons they now are. Thus, however valuable autobiographies may be in disclosing the experiences of childhood, there is a price that autobiography pays for its intention to narrate a life, and to view childhood as a significant chapter—but often no more than this—in a story that has many chapters and is mostly concerned with recent experiences and their future implications.

I have found myself turning more often to the poets for insight into the experience of childhood—insight that discloses what it was like to be a child, and, even more significantly, insight that lays the foundation for reconciling ourselves to the fact that we were children of these, and not some other, parents. This is to say that poets invite us not only to witness but also to participate in the total experience of soul-searching, soul-baring, and soul-mending. Of all the texts that hold promise of enabling us to recover the child's song that has since been muffled by the sanctionings of adults and adulthood, poems are best able to make good on that promise. This is because, unlike psychological texts, they are concerned with the particular experiences, not the general flow, of childhood and because, unlike autobiography, they are content to explore a single childhood experience for its own sake and in its own right, without forcing it to fit an interpretive schema whose significant meanings emerge decades later.

In keeping with the biblical precedent of the Psalms, I have chosen for our meditation together poems written by a variety of authors. Unlike the psalms, the authors of these poems are not anonymous, but, while their names are known, I will make no effort to place or contextualize them, for who they are, or were, in their adult lives, is for us here, quite irrelevant. What matters is that they have written of their childhood experiences in an effort to give a voice to the child that continues to live within them. Unlike the parents who, in Alice Miller's recounting, made a secret pact with Saint Nicholas that had the effect of stifling the children's songs, these poets have made a pact with the child who is in them, to sing—as best they can and to the extent that they can recall—the songs they might have sung as children were they not so afraid, confused, and uncertain.

I have organized these poems according to four broad themes: poems that reveal the range of painful, poignant, and pleasurable experiences of childhood; poems that focus specifically on the child-parent relationship as experienced in childhood; poems that reach out to the parents now, usually after their deaths, in an effort to effect a reconciliation, an embracement after years of holding the parents, and being held by them, at arm's length; and poems that address the awkward but sustaining fact that our brothers and sisters are often our sole living witnesses to our experience as children, and are therefore, if for no other reason, forever bonded to us. These poems are merely a sampling of what is there, a sampling that has particular resonance for me. Some readers may feel that they do not speak to, or of, their own experiences. If so, this does not in itself discredit the exercise that I am recommending here, that of going into whatever constitutes a garden for each of us, and bringing along some verses that hold promise of evoking the child's song that lies buried beneath a heap of resentments and hurts. When that song is sung—at first, perhaps, in a low moaning, then in quivering voice amid tears and sobs and ragings, and finally in full-throated affirmation—may we then know the inner peace that surpasses all understanding, a deep satisfaction with the self that we are, a profound gratitude for our one and only life and those who made it possible, and a bracing embrace of the whole created order of things. The song of the soul. Amen and hallelujah.

How It Was to Be a Child

In writing about their childhood, poets are fully aware that they are viewing the past from their perspective as adults. Much of what they say about childhood is an adult's projection, and is therefore not advanced as incontrovertible truth, but more in the spirit of wondering and questioning: Could this be how it was? Is this how it felt? Poets are concerned about gaining insights from their reflections on the earlier years of their lives, insights that may serve them in their lives today. Thus, they view childhood as a period in life that possesses and discloses significant meanings for us if we, as adults, are open to reflecting on this distant past, much of it pleasurable, but much of it painful, and painful now to recall to mind.

In "True Confessional," Lawrence Ferlinghetti suggests that his life began with great anticipation because, after all, everything was new to him:[8]

> The world had been going on
> a long time already
> but it made no difference
> It was new it was like new
> i made it new
> i saw it shining
> and it shone in the sun
> and it spun in the sun
> and the skein it spun
> was pure light
> My life was made of it
> made of the skeins of light
> The cobwebs of Night
> were not on it
> were not of it
> It was too bright

to see
too luminous
to cast a shadow
and there was another world
behind the bright screens
I had only to close my eyes
for another world to appear
too near and too dear
to be anything but myself
my inside self
where everything real
was to happen

Some poets recall experiences in which they, as children, knew joy as they have never known it since. In "Adults Only," William Stafford tells about the time he and other unidentified children experienced a rather amazing epiphany at the state fair:[9]

Animals own a fur world;
people own worlds that are variously, pleasingly, bare.
And the way these worlds *are* once arrived for us kids
    with a jolt,
that night when the wild woman danced
in the giant cage we found we were all in
at the state fair.

Better women exist, no doubt, than that one,
and occasions more edifying, too, I suppose.
But we have to witness for ourselves what comes for us,
nor be distracted by barkers of irrelevant ware;
and a pretty good world, I say, arrived that night
when that woman came farming right out of her clothes,
by God,

At the state fair.

An unorthodox epiphany, no doubt, but these are the very experiences that disclose to us as children that life is good.

Mostly what poets recall from their childhood, however, is that they were engaged in the struggle for survival, and so often experienced a deep sense of inner desolation and despair. Another poem by Stafford, titled "Learning to Like the New School," conveys a child's despair that has somehow to be gotten over:[10]

They brought me where it was bright and said,
"Be bright." I couldn't even see. They tried
again: "Look up." I tried but it

was all sad to me. They turned and went
away. And then it all came on
to be a world like this—you learn only
the one clear lesson, "How It Is":
the rain falls, the wind blows,
and you are just there, alone, as yourself.
The world is no test—"So you got here, fine,"
any new place says. And you say, "Yes, I'm here."

While some poets point to specific experiences in which they felt life's
desolation, it is more typical of them to recall a mood or a pervasive sense of
desolation not attributable to any specific experience or event but, for that
very reason, all the more difficult to understand. In "Remorse for Time,"
Howard Nemerov writes of his awareness as a child of the fact that he would
not live forever:[11]

When I was a boy, I used to go to bed
By daylight, in the summer, and lie awake
Between the cool, white, reconciling sheets,
Hearing the talk of birds, watching the light
Diminish through the shimmering planes of leaf
Outside the window, until sleep came down
When darkness did, eyes closing as the light
Faded out of them, silencing the birds.
Sometimes still, in the sleepless dark hours
Tormented most by the remorse for time,
Only for time, the mind speaks of that boy
(he did no wrong, then why had he to die?)
Falling asleep on the current of the stars
Which even then washed him away past pardon.

When do we first become aware that we will die someday? When that
awareness comes, the anticipation of which Ferlinghetti writes is surely compromised, and the child is now tormented by remorse—not for wrongful
deeds but for time itself, which is already running out.

In "The Still Time," Galway Kinnell recalls the summer nights when
he was filled with a great inner craving that he knew would never be
assuaged:[12]

I remember those summer nights
when I was young and empty,
when I lay through the darkness
wanting, wanting,
knowing
I would have nothing of anything I wanted—
that total craving
that hollows the heart out irreversibly.

So it surprises me now to hear
the steps of my life following me—
so much of it gone
it returns, everything that drove me crazy
comes back, blessing the misery
of each step it took me into the world;
as though a prayer had ended
and the changed
air between the palms goes free
to become the glitter
on common things that inexplicably shine.

And all the old voices,
which once made broken-off, choked, parrot-incoherences,
speak again,
this time on the palatum cordis, all of them
saying there is time, still time,
for those who can groan
to sing,
for those who can sing to heal themselves.

"Young and empty"—a pervasive experience of childhood. And again the matter of time that seems to be running out. Yet here Kinnell also uses his childhood to make an affirmation, for there is still time "for those who can groan to sing, for those who can sing to heal themselves."

If despair and desolation were common to childhood, so, too, were experiences of fear for what others might do to us. In "Now I Lay Me," Sharon Olds recalls her great fear of her father and mother, both abusive of her, and the terror she would experience as night began:[13]

It is a fine prayer, it is an excellent prayer, really,
Now I lay me down to sleep—
the immediacy, and the power of the child
taking herself up in her arms
and laying herself down on her bed
as if she were her own mother,
Now I lay me down to sleep,
I pray the Lord my soul to keep,
her hands knotted together knuckle by knuckle,
feeling her heart beating in the knuckles,
that heart that did not belong to her yet
that heart that was just the red soft string in her
chest that they plucked at will.
Knees on the fine dark hair-like hardwood
beams of the floor—the hairs of a huge animal—
she commended herself to the care of some reliable keeper
above her parents, someone who had a

cupboard to put her soul in for the night,
one they had no key to, out of their reach
so they could not crack it with an axe, so that
all night there was a part of her
they could not touch. Unless when God had it
she did not have it, but lay there a raw
soulless animal for them to do their dirt on—
coming toward her room with those noises at night and their
fur and their thick varnished hairs.
If I should die before I wake seemed so
possible, so likely really,
the father with the blood on his face,
the mother down to 82 pounds, it was a
mark of doom and a benison
to be able to say *I pray the Lord
my soul to take*—the chance that, dead,
she'd be safe for eternity, which was so much
longer than those bad nights—
she herself could see each morning the
blessing of the white dawn, like some true god coming,
she could get up and wade in the false
goodness of another day.
It was all fine except for the word *take*,
that word with the claw near the end of it.
What if the Lord were just another one of those takers
like her mother, what if the Lord were no bigger than her father,
what if each night those noises she heard
were not her mother and father struggling to
do it or not do it, what if those
noises were the sound of the Lord wrestling with her father
on the round white bedroom rug,
fighting over her soul, and what if the
Lord, who did not eat real food,
got weaker, and her father with all he ate and
drank got stronger, what if the Lord
lost? *God bless Mommy and Daddy and
Trisha and Dougie and Gramma Hester and
Grampa Harry in Heaven*, and then the
light went out, the last of the terrible kisses,
and then she was alone in the dark
and the darkness started to grow there in her room
as it liked to do, and then the night began.

We are accustomed to thinking of adults experiencing "the dark night of the soul," but here Sharon Olds recalls that this was precisely what she experienced, night after night, as a child. For her, the only hope was that the Lord would be able to defeat her tormentors, but what if the Lord were not strong enough to prevail? Maybe the best the Lord could do was to "take" her away, to save her from all this.

Many poets experienced the threat of evil from without, but almost as painful was the realization that there was evil, inexplicable evil, within. In "Turning in Bed," Thomas Carper recalls his anguish over having treated another boy with a cruelty he could not understand or fathom:[14]

> The stench of early cruelty returns
> As I, a child, crouch underneath low boughs
> Playing with candles. In small pans the worms
> Writhe. Now I grow, and from a neighbor's house
> He runs at me, screaming that I have hid
> His toy gun, which I get and, with a blow
> That terrifies me, smash it to his head,
> Causing blood and my blinding tears to flow.
> The picture breaks. I ache. The sheets are taut.
> I turn for comfort, then return to hell,
> Fleeing across a fiery space and caught
> By images assaulting me until
> I fear I will not wake again, but keep
> Revolving painfully on the spit of sleep.

While not recalling that he was so overtly cruel, William Stafford has a painful recollection in "Remembering Brother Bob" of resenting his younger brother's vulnerability and reliance on him:[15]

> Tell me, you years I had for my life,
> tell me a day, that day it snowed
> and I played hockey in the cold.
> Bob was seven, then, and I was twelve,
> and strong. The sun went down. I turned
> and Bob was crying on the shore.
> Do I remember kindness? Did I
> shield my brother, comfort him?
> Tell me, you years I had for my life.
>
> Yes, I carried him. I took
> him home. But I complained. I see
> the darkness; it comes near: and Bob,
> who is gone now, and the other kids.
> I am the zero in the scene:
> "You said you would be brave," I chided
> him. "I'll not take you again."
> Years, I look at the white across
> this page, and think: I never did.

For Louise Glück, the struggle with her amoral self centered on her conflicts with her sister, conflicts owing to their shared perception that they were competing for their very survival. Her title "Animals" tells us what she now thinks of herself and her sister as children:[16]

> My sister and I reached
> the same conclusion:
> the best way
> to love us was to not
> spend time with us.
> It seemed that
> we appealed
> chiefly to strangers.
> We had good clothes, good
> manners in public.
>
> In private, we were
> always fighting. Usually
> the big one finished
> sitting on the little one
> and pinching her.
> The little one
> bit: in forty years
> she never learned
> the advantage in not
> leaving a mark.
>
> The parents
> had a credo: they didn't
> believe in anger.
> The truth was, for different reasons,
> they couldn't bring themselves
> to inflict pain. You should only hurt
> something you can give
> your whole heart to. They preferred
> tribunals: the child
> most in the wrong could choose
> her own punishment.
>
> My sister and I
> never became allies,
> never turned on our parents.
> We had
> other obsessions: for example,
> we both felt there were
> too many of us
> to survive.
>
> We were like animals
> trying to share a dry pasture.
> Between us, one tree, barely

strong enough to sustain
a single life.

We never moved
our eyes from each other
nor did either touch
one thing that could
feed her sister.

Yet, if poets recall having been cruel, indifferent, or suspiciously wary of other children, they also remember when they did feel deeply for another child. In "A Gesture toward an Unfound Renaissance," Stafford recalls going to bed at night thinking of another child's plight:[17]

There was the slow girl in art class,
less able to say where our lessons led: we
learned so fast she could not follow us.
But at the door each day I looked back
at her rich distress, knowing almost enough
to find a better art inside the lesson.

And then, late at night, when the whole town
was alone, the current below the rumbly bridge
at Main Street would go an extra swirl
and gurgle, once, by the pilings;
and at my desk at home, or when our house
opened above my bed toward the stars,
I would hear that one intended lonely sound,
the signature of the day, the ratchet of time
taking me a step toward here, now, and this
look back through the door that always closes.

Also, in "One Time," he remembers a time when he did act kindly, without hesitation, in a simple gesture of solidarity with another child:[18]

When evening had flowed between houses
and paused on the schoolground, I met
Hilary's blind little sister following
the gray smooth railing still warm from the sun
with her hand; and she stood by the edge
holding her face upward waiting
while the last light found her cheek
and her hair, and then on over the trees.

You could hear the great sprinkler arm
of water find and then leave the pavement,
and pigeons telling each other their dreams
or the dreams they would have. We were
deep in the well of shadow by then, and I

held out my hand, saying, "Tina, it's me—
Hilary says I should tell you it's dark,
and, oh, Tina, it is. Together now—"

And I reached, our hands touched,
and we found our way home.

If childhood had such moments of moral satisfaction, when we felt good about what we did for one another, still, poets mainly recall for us that childhood was a time of sadness, of longing, of yearning. They also recall that, very often, we felt a great heaviness of soul, of melancholy, and inner desolation. A recurrent theme in Galway Kinnell's poems is that, in his boyhood, he experienced inexplicable and unnameable yearnings and longings that he continues, even now, to feel. The boy of unaccountable yearnings is still a part of him. It makes him sad to think about this boy, yet he values him, and wants very much to remain in touch with him and to keep faith with him. In "The Old Moon," he speaks of returning to where he sat as a boy for there, in that place, he will find his very soul:[19]

I sat here as a boy
On these winter rocks, watching
The moon-shapes toil through the nights—
I thought then the moon
Only wears her mortality.

Then why to these rocks
Do I keep coming back, why,
The last quarter being nearly
Wasted, does the breath
come back dragoning the night?

Unless, perhaps,
The soul, too, is such a country,
Made of flesh and light,
And wishes to be whole
And therefore dark.

In "Young," William Stafford provides a kind of summation of what it is like to be a child—the dreams, the confusions, the failures, the good intentions that led nowhere, and, as time went on, the accumulated weight of it all:[20]

Before time had a name, when win
or lose were the same, in a forsaken
town I lived unnoticed, blessed.
Remember when shadows played
because there were leaves in the wind?
And people came to our door from a land
where stories were real?

Barefoot, we traveled the roads
all summer. At night we drew pictures
of home with smoke from the chimney.
And we frowned when we read,
so we could understand.

After the years came true, but before
their cost, I played in that big world, too,
and often won: this face was known;
gold came into these hands.
But unwieldy hours overwhelmed
my time. All I intended blew away.
The best of my roads went wrong,
no matter my age, no matter
how long I tried.
It was far, it was dim,
toward the last. And nobody knew how
heavy it was by the end,
for that same being who lived back then.

Don't you see how it was, for a child?
Don't you understand?

How We Struggled over Parents

If childhood was a time in which we came to know an unnameable
sadness and unaccountable and unassuageable yearning, it was also a time
when we struggled with our fears—real and fantasized—of our parents,
and with the fact that we had feelings toward them of which we were
ashamed and guilty. So often we wanted to please them, and so often we
failed, or thought we failed. Sometimes we experienced a sister or brother
as an ally in our struggle to come to terms with parents. Other times, a
sister or brother seemed allied with parents against us, and since we were
unable to view this alliance for what it was—each child endangered and
trying to find a way to survive—we often felt outnumbered and victim of
a sibling's treachery and betrayal.

It should not surprise us that poets, in writing about their childhoods,
have focused on their experiences with parents. Among the poets represented here, only one—Sharon Olds—has written about being sexually
abused by a parent. But many have written about their parents as the witting
or unwitting cause of emotional pain and torment. In "Vacation Trip," William Stafford relates how his mother, with her glum silence, could put a
damper on what was supposed to have been a pleasurable experience:[21]

The loudest sound in our car
was Mother being glum:

Little chiding valves
a surge of detergent oil
all that deep chaos
the relentless accurate fire
the drive shaft wild to arrive

And tugging along behind in its great big
balloon,
that looming piece of her mind:

"I wish I hadn't come."

In another poem, "Mother's Day," he recalls his and his sister Peg's effort
to placate their mother:[22]

Peg said, "This one," and we bought it
for Mother, our allowance for weeks
paid out to a clerk who snickered—
a hideous jar, oil-slick in color,
glass that light got lost in.

We saw it for candy, a sign for
our love. And it lasted:
the old house on Eleventh,
a dim room on Crescent where
the railroad shook the curtains,
that brief glory at Aunt Mabel's place.

Peg thought it got more beautiful,
Egyptian, sort of, a fire-sheened
relic. And with a doomed grasp
we carried our level of aesthetics
with us across Kansas, proclaiming
our sentimental badge.

Now Peg says, "Remember that candy jar?"
She smoothes the silver. "Mother
hated it." I am left standing
alone by the counter, ready to buy what
will hold Mother by its magic, so
she will never be mad at us again.

Parents given to their own unhappy moods could make life miserable for the
children who tried—but invariably failed—to make such parents happy for
any significant length of time. But, as children, we did not understand that
we were not the cause of their unhappiness and that it was not our responsibility to make and keep them happy.

As the daughter of a mother who did not have enough love to go around,
Louise Glück, in "A Fable," based on the biblical story of Solomon and the

two harlots, perceives that she sacrificed herself for the sake of her mother's survival:[23]

> Two women with
> the same claim
> came to the feet of
> the wise king. Two women,
> but only one baby.
> The king knew
> someone was lying.
> What he said was
> Let the child be
> cut in half; that way
> no one will go
> empty-handed. He
> drew his sword.
> Then, of the two
> women, one
> renounced her share:
> this was
> the sign, the lesson.
> Suppose
> you saw your mother
> torn between two daughters:
> what could you do
> to save her but be
> willing to destroy
> yourself—she would know
> who was the rightful child,
> the one who couldn't bear
> to divide the mother.

For Glück, her problem was made worse by her knowledge of the fact that her mother had been bereaved of her first child, also a daughter. If this other daughter, as the title "Lost Love" suggests, was the one her mother truly loved, why could her mother not express some of that same love toward the daughter who lived? Or is there only so much to go around?[24]

> My sister spent a whole life in the earth.
> She was born, she died.
> In between,
> not one alert look, not one sentence.
>
> She did what babies do,
> she cried. But she didn't want to be fed.
> Still, my mother held her, trying to change
> first fate, then history.

> Something did change: when my sister died,
> my mother's heart became
> very cold, very rigid,
> like a tiny pendant of iron.
>
> Then it seemed to me my sister's body
> was a magnet. I could feel it draw
> my mother's heart into the earth,
> so it would grow.

In "The Blue Dress," Sharon Olds reveals that she was so hungry for any expression of love from her parents that she would embrace it even if it came in a cruel package:[25]

> The first November after the divorce
> there was a box from my father on my birthday—no card, but a
> big box from Hink's, the dark
> department store with a balcony and
> mahogany rail around the balcony, you could
> stand and press your forehead against it
> until you could almost feel the dense
> grain of the wood, and stare down
> into the rows and rows of camisoles,
> petticoats, bras, as if looking down
> into the lives of women. The box
> was from there, he had braved that place for me
> the way he had entered my mother once
> to get me out. I opened the box—I had
> never had a present from him—
> and there was a blue shirtwaist dress
> blue as the side of a blue teal
> disguised to go in safety on the steel-blue water.
> I put it on, a perfect fit,
> I liked that it was not too sexy, just a
> blue dress for a 14-year-old daughter the way
> Clark Kent's suit was just a plain suit for a reporter, but I
> felt the weave of that mercerized Indian Head cotton
> against the skin of my upper arms and my
> wide thin back and especially the skin of my
> ribs under those new breasts I had
> raised in the night like earthworks in commemoration of his name.
> A year later, during a fight about
> just how awful my father had been,
> my mother said he had not picked out the dress,
> just told her to get something not too expensive, and then
> had not even sent a check for it,
> that's the kind of man he was. So I
> never wore it again in her sight

but when I went away to boarding school I
wore it all the time there,
loving the feel of it, just
casually mentioning sometimes it was a gift from my father,
wanting in those days to appear to have something
whether it was true or a lie, I didn't care, just to
have something.

If there is a dominant theme in poets' review of their relationship, as
children, to parents, it is that their parents seemed so unable to love their
children, and the children, in turn, could not understand why. Is it something I *did*? Is it something about *me*? Only later was it possible to recognize
that the fault was not with oneself, but had to do with the parent's own
emotional impoverishment that even a child could not assuage or counter.

On the other hand, the same poets who felt their parents' lack of love for
them have deeply cherished recollections of one or two events when the
child could truly admire the parent, and, in a most wonderful way, bask in
the thought of belonging to this man or woman. In "Regardless," Stephen
Dunn tells of being invited by his father to join him in one of his delightful
adventures that would lead without fail to unanticipated trouble:[26]

> Once, my father took me to the Rockaways
>   during a hurricane
> to see how the ocean was behaving,
>
> which made my mother furious, whose love
>   was correct, protective.
> We saw a wooden jetty crumble. We saw water
>
> rise to the boardwalk, felt the wildness
>   of its spray.
> That night: silence at dinner, a storm
>
> born of cooler, more familiar air.
>   My father
> always rode his delightful errors
>
> into trouble. Mother waited for them, alertly,
>   the way the oppressed
> wait for their historical moment.
>
> Weekdays, after six, I'd point my bicycle
>   toward the Fleet Street Inn
> to fetch him for dinner. All his friends
>
> were there, high-spirited lonelies, Irish,
>   full of laughter.
> It was a shame that he was there, a shame

                    to urge him home. Who was I then but a boy
                        who had learned to love
                    the wind, the wind that would go its own way,

                    regardless. I must have thought damage
                        is just what happens.

As Dunn's poem also reveals, to be a child was to be caught between the
two, mother and father, in their quiet but stubborn ways, struggling for
control over a child's very soul. In "Vocation," Stafford reflects on his sense
of helplessness in being the child of two parents so different from one another, yet both of them a part of him:[27]

> This dream the world is having about itself
> includes a trace on the plains of the Oregon trail,
> a groove in the grass my father showed us all
> one day while meadowlarks were trying to tell
> something better about to happen.
>
> I dreamed the trace to the mountains, over the hills,
> and there a girl who belonged wherever she was.
> But then my mother called us back to the car:
> she was afraid; she always blamed the place,
> the time, anything my father planned.
>
> Now both of my parents, the long line through the plain,
> the meadowlarks, the sky, the world's whole dream
> remain, and I hear him say while I stand between the two,
> helpless, both of them part of me:
> "Your job is to find what the world is trying to be."

Thus, if the child cannot avoid split loyalties, of being torn between love for
mother and for father, the even deeper and disturbing realization is that this
split has become internalized, so that the child's own self is hopelessly divided. "Vocation" suggests that when the child is thus split at the roots—a
self divided against itself—it helps if one of the parents can give some clear
direction, or, at least, be heard to speak words of wisdom even if the child,
years later, must supply them. The truth they teach is that the self's division
will be overcome, if ever it can be, by means of a third: the world that is itself
trying to be more than it is, possessed of a deep, unassuageable yearning.

Embracing the Parent Child

Poets envision several ways in which the children, now adults, may reach
out to their parents, whether living or deceased, and embracing them, find
that they can be at peace about the fact that they were the children of these
particular parents, no longer harboring the desire to be someone else's child.

They understand that such reconciliation does not come easily or cheaply. They also understand that it does not necessarily, or even usually, occur before the parents' death. More typically, it comes later, when one has had time to reflect on what happened and why. Often the parents' death itself is the initial catalyst for such reflection.

In "After 37 Years My Mother Apologizes for My Childhood," Sharon Olds captures the confusion that is created when an attempt is made, by one or the other, to reconcile this side of the grave:[28]

> When you tilted toward me, arms out
> like someone trying to walk through a fire,
> when you swayed toward me, crying out you were
> sorry for what you had done to me, your
> eyes filling with terrible liquid like
> balls of mercury from a broken thermometer
> skidding on the floor, when you quietly screamed
> *Where else could I turn? Who else did I have?*, the
> chopped crockery of your hands swinging toward me, the
> water cracking from your eyes like moisture from
> stones under heavy pressure, I could not
> see what I would do with the rest of my life.
> The sky seemed to be splintering like a window
> someone is bursting into or out of, your
> tiny face glittered as if with
> shattered crystal, with true regret, the
> regret of the body. I could not see what my
> days would be with you sorry, with
> you wishing you had not done it, the
> sky falling around me, its shards
> glistening in my eyes, your old soft
> body fallen against me in horror I
> took you in my arms, I said *It's all right,
> don't cry, it's all right*, the air filled with
> flying glass, I hardly knew what I
> said or who I would be now that I had forgiven you.

This is not to say that attempts to reconcile this side of the grave are not worthwhile, but they raise troubling questions about what child and parent will do in their remaining years together.

Thomas Carper, in "Even the Weariest River," writes about his mother, who, while still alive, is unable to "connect" with him, but, precisely for that reason, is strangely accessible to him, perhaps because she has become so like a child in an adult's body:[29]

> Her voice is childlike. "No man lives forever,
> Dead men rise up never. . . . " Looking at me,

Her eyes are bright. "But even the weariest river,"
My mother sighs, "winds somewhere safe to sea."
Sitting across the table, gaunt and small,
She murmurs, "I remember," as though I
Should praise her, as in school. She can recall
Only fragments from a history
That stopped, it seems, some fifty years ago—
Before my birth. The ruin of her mind
Is infinite. She says, "I do not know
Just who you are, but you are very kind."
Then, after a pause, "I'm very glad you came."
She smiles and calls me by my father's name.

The deepest indications we have that the child has reached out and embraced the parent—perhaps more strongly and fervently than ever the parent reached out and embraced the child—are those times, after the parent's death, when the child experiences love for the parent as a *child*. Denise Levertov describes such an experience in "The Opportunity":[30]

My father once, after his death,
appeared to me as a rose,
passed beyond intellect.
This time, he resumes
human form to become
a boy of six.
I kneel to hug him,
kiss the child's bare shoulder;
near us the ocean
sighs and murmurs,
firm sand reflects
the turn of the wave.

This is my chance to tell him,
"Much has happened, over the years,
many travels.
In the world,
in myself.
Along the way,
I have come to believe
the truth of what you believe."

The child, with good grace,
permits
my brief embrace; he smiles:
the words
are lazy waves above and around him,
he absorbs their tone,

knows he is loved.
Knows only that.

This was my chance
to speak, I've taken it,
we are both content.

Sharon Olds, in "Late Poem to My Father," writes of a similar experience, and, like Levertov, uses the word "love," knowingly and unselfconsciously, to express how it felt:[31]

Suddenly I thought of you
as a child in that house, the unlit rooms
and the hot fireplace with the man in front of it,
silent. You moved through the heavy air
in your physical beauty, a boy of seven,
helpless, smart, there were things the man
did near you, and he was your father,
the mold by which you were made. Down in the
cellar, the barrels of sweet apples,
picked at their peak from the tree, rotted and
rotted, and past the cellar door
the creek ran and ran, and something was
not given to you, or something was
taken from you that you were born with, so that
even at 30 and 40 you set the
oily medicine to your lips
every night, the poison to help you
drop down unconscious. I always thought the
point was what you did to us
as a grown man, but then I remembered that
child being formed in front of the fire, the
tiny bones inside his soul
twisted in greenstick fractures, the small
tendons that hold the heart in place
snapped. And what they did to you
you did not do to me. When I love you now,
I like to think I am giving my love
directly to that boy in the fiery room,
as if it could reach him in time.

By loving her father *as a child*, Olds avoids any temptation to spare her father for his adult cruelty toward her. What she does instead is to find a way to love him for what he was before he became a threat to her well-being, going so far as to imagine that her love—had he experienced it then—might have saved him from the future that his life became. This same opportunity is available to us all: to embrace our parents for the children that they were, giving them the love they need to enable them to return the love of which we have need. And so they love because we first loved them.

If it is possible for us to love our parents as children, it should not then be difficult to join e.e. cummings in his grand view of his parents who have found their way to the garden of heaven itself:[32]

> if there are any heavens my mother will(all by herself)have
> one. It will not be a pansy heaven nor
> a fragile heaven of lilies-of-the-valley but
> it will be a heaven of blackred roses
>
> my father will be(deep like a rose
> tall like a rose)
>
> standing near my
>
> (swaying over her
> silent)
> with eyes which are really petals and see
>
> nothing with the face of a poet really which
> is a flower and not a face with
> hands
> which whisper
> This is my beloved my
>
> (suddenly in sunlight
> he will bow,
>
> & the whole garden will bow)

The garden is the image of wholeness: father and mother together and their child experiencing how good it feels that they are at peace with one another. This is not the Garden of Gethsemane as described by the Gospel writers: a scene of struggle and conflict, a scene in which the flowers receive no mention at all. Rather, it is a garden where the setting is all, where flowers are not mere accessories to an important event, but *are* that event, bowing to one another. With this scene before him, the child experiences wholeness in himself, and he has regained the song suppressed in him for as long as he remembers. Among poets, e.e. cummings stands out for his capacity to write poems as though they were songs, songs that we can easily visualize a child singing when deep in play, mind-free and wandering. "My mother will be . . . " "My father will be . . . " and "the whole garden will bow." A child's fantasy, but so true, and so reassuring.

Faithful Witnesses

The significance of brothers and sisters is that, when we were young, they were there to witness. It is not that they experienced things as we did, or that their perceptions of a childhood lived among the same family members are similar to, or even compatible with, our own. We may, in fact, have radically different perceptions of father and mother, and of what it was like to be a child of theirs. But the fact is that we went through at least portions of it together, and, much like soldiers who return from fighting together in war, we feel there is something between us just because we went through it together, something that others, including our mates, will never fully be able to appreciate or understand.

In "Collecting Future Lives," Stephen Dunn tells of two brothers who sit up late one night, after the others have gone to bed, and talk about what their years together as children had really been about:[33]

> Now that everybody was dead
> only he and his brother knew
> the blood secrets, the unequal
> history each nervous system
> keeps and rehearses
> into a story, a life.
> Over the years they'd agreed
> to invent and remember
> a long hum of good times,
> love breaking through
> during card games,
> their father teaching them
> to skip stones
> under the Whitestone Bridge.
> The smart liar in them
> knew these stories
> were for their children
> who, that very moment
> over dinner, were collecting
> their future lives.
> But sometimes
> in their twice-a-year visits
> late at night
> when their wives had tired
> of the old repetitions,
> they'd bring up the silences
> in the living room
> after a voice had been raised,
> father's drinking, mother's
> long martyrdom before the gods
> of propriety and common sense.
> In their mannerisms
> each could see the same ghosts.
> And if they allowed themselves

to keep talking,
if they'd had enough to drink,
love would be all
that mattered, the love
they were cheated of
and the love they got,
the parental love
that if remembered at all
had been given, they decided,
and therefore could be given again.

If, for siblings, to recall childhood is like telling war stories, is it any wonder that poems about our brothers and sisters tend to have a sad, almost melancholy way about them? In "Two Set Out on Their Journey," Galway Kinnell describes the journey that he and his sister were setting out upon as being lighthearted at first, then taking on sorrow as they and time progressed:[34]

We sit side by side,
brother and sister, and read
the book of what will be, while the wind
blows the pages over—
desolate odd, desolate even,
and otherwise. When it falls open
to our own story, the happy beginning,
the ending happy or not we don't know,
the ten thousand acts which encumber
and engross all the days between,
we will read every page of it,
for if the ancestors have pressed
a love-flower for us, it will lie
between pages of the slow going,
where only those who adore the story
can find it. When the time comes
to close the book and set out,
whether possessing that flower
or just the dream of it, we will walk
hand in hand a little while,
taking the laughter of childhood
as far as we can into the days to come,
until we can hear, in the distance,
another laughter sounding back
from the earth where our next bodies
will have risen already
and where they will be laughing,
gently, at all that seemed deadly serious once,
offering to us new wayfarers

the light heart
we started with, but made of time and sorrow.

The same note of sadness is evident in William Stafford's "At the Grave of My Brother":[35]

The mirror cared less and less at the last, but
the tone of his voice roamed, had more to find,
back to the year he was born; and the world
that saw him awhile again went blind.

Drawn backward along the street, he disappeared
by the cedars that faded a long time ago
near the grave where Mother's hair was a screen
but she was crying. I see a sparrow

Chubby like him, full of promise, barely
holding a branch and ready to fly.
In his house today his children begin
to recede from this year and go their own way.

Brother: Good-bye.

Stafford here is aware that he may feel the loss of his brother even more deeply than his brother's children do, because he remembers his brother as a child—"full of promise"—and sees what the years have done to him.

So, however we felt about our brothers and sisters then, and however we have felt toward them since, they are witnesses to our past, and we to theirs, and this makes for a bond between us, one that grows stronger, it seems, as time goes on. They may not be "enlightened witnesses"—they were too close to the action to play that role—but they are faithful witnesses, and sometimes this is the sustenance for which we, in our postenlightenment state, have greater need. Stafford captures the uniqueness of this bond in "How It Is with Family":[36]

Let's assume you have neglected to write
a brother or a sister. The closeness you had for years
is gone. But now there's a need—let's assume
it's about money or something. You still know
them so well you feel right about it. You begin,
and even if they don't respond, your words and the whole
idea go along as part of the world: you don't have to
be correct. You say, "It's Bob," "It's Peg," "I'm just
writing them." Let's assume someone blames
you—the reaching out as if no time had passed.
You're surprised: there's a part of the way things are
that calculating people can't know. You don't
waste much time following out that strangeness, you
just write, "Bob," or "Peg," "It's me—send the money."

A Child Is Singing

Besides the Garden of Gethsemane, the most celebrated garden in Christian literature is the garden where Augustine experienced his conversion. As he relates the experience in his *Confessions*, the climactic moment comes when he sees a woman, whom he names Continence, beckoning to him from across the garden. She was, quite literally, his angel of mercy, for she saved him from a fate that he dreaded nearly as much as Jesus, in the Garden of Gethsemane, dreaded the fate that was crushing down on him.

But Augustine had another odd experience that day, an experience that set in motion the process of his conversion, his yielding to God. This was his hearing of a child singing. He writes:

> I was asking myself these questions, weeping all the while with the most bitter sorrow in my heart, when all at once I heard the singing voice of a child in a nearby house. Whether it was the voice of a boy or a girl I cannot say, but again and again it repeated the refrain "Take it and read, take it and read." At this I looked up, thinking hard whether there was any kind of game in which children used to chant words like these, but I could not remember ever hearing them before.[37]

Some have suggested that this was merely an auditory hallucination, comparable to his visual hallucination of the woman he named Continence. But Augustine means for us to assume that he heard the voice of a real child, leading others to wonder whether it may have been the voice of Adeodatus.

Setting aside such speculations, what matters is that he heard the singsong voice of a child from his place in the garden, and that the voice was life-changing. Perhaps it called to mind the song of the child within him, long suppressed, the song he idly sang when he was himself at play. Surely its invitation to "take it and read" was nothing like the threatening voices of his teachers who demanded that he apply himself to the books they set before him lest he be unmercifully whipped. For the voice came when he was already weeping, with the most bitter sorrow in his heart, and it was therefore the beginning of the mending of his soul. The child's song arises out of sorrow. It is not, originally, a song of joy, but of suffering and despair. Yet once it begins and grows in strength and resonance, it surprises even ourselves, as we find pleasure in the very sound of our own voice. And like the grievers who gather around the gravesite and sing their heartfelt hymn of praise to the One who gave this life that death has now taken away, we, too, find in our hearts a gratitude for this one and only life of ours. And we then discover that, in raising our voices, we have also raised our heads, eyes no longer downcast, no longer shamed, but firmly fixed on the horizon and the way that lies before us.

In " . . . That Passeth All Understanding," Denise Levertov captures this moment of the beginning of the mending of our souls:[38]

An awe so quiet
I don't know when it began.

A gratitude
had begun
to sing in me.

Was there
some moment
dividing
song from no song?

When does dewfall begin?

When does night
fold its arms over our hearts
to cherish them?

When is daybreak?

8

The Soul Made Happy

Childrearing is a difficult task. To us parents, it often seems like a very treacherous minefield. One false step, it seems, and everything blows up in our faces. No wonder, then, that we have latched onto whatever help we can get, and why Christian parents have made books like James Dobson's *Dare to Discipline* into bestsellers.

Throughout this book, I have taken a very critical view of theological legitimations for the physical and emotional abuse of children. Of course, those who offer such legitimations do not consider the resulting behavior as "abuse." They call it punishment, tough love, or teaching the child a lesson. This does not mean, however, that abuse is not taking place. In fact, the abuse is even greater when the interpretive framework used by parents to legitimate their actions disguises the fact that abuse is occurring. The abuse is compounded by its being misinterpreted.

Parents who read this book may legitimately complain, however, that I have only written about what not to do, that I have had very little to say about what they should do, especially when confronted with the inevitable conflicts that occur between parent and child in the normal course of things, and when their own best efforts as parents meet with little or no success. If I now find myself reluctant, in this final chapter, to offer a compendium of advice for struggling parents, this is only partly because I cannot claim any special expertise in the art of childrearing. More pertinent is the fact that this is a book about religion and about the ways in which religious practice and theological ideas have sanctioned the abuse and torment of children. So, I will skirt the issue of how we might all become better parents and will instead offer a concluding theological argument, one that sets the stage for what would be, in my judgment, a more appropriate approach to childrearing than is offered by authors like Dobson, Fugate, and others.

The Garden of Eden Story

I take here as my central text the very familiar story of the Garden of Eden as found in Genesis 2—3. This story provides an explanation for human unhappiness, and, specifically, it explains why men are condemned to onerous labor and why women experience pain in childbirth. Thus, the story is about the fate of two adults, named Adam and Eve, and yet it has had a powerful effect on childrearing, as the sin committed by them has been projected onto children, and the consequences of their sin have been used to justify the punishment of children. Study should be made of how this story has been applied to children down through the centuries, how it has been the basis for ascribing to children a natural disposition toward sinfulness—especially the sin of disobedience—and how it has been used to support the specific punishment method of forced separation and isolation from parents and other members of the family. But I am not an expert in church history or historical theology, so I will simply focus on the story itself and suggest that the story, as we have it in the Bible, invites us to draw a different conclusion from that of the storyteller, a conclusion that later I will refer to as the assumption of the second chance.

The story consists of three acts. The first is the act of God in creating humankind and placing them in the garden. As the curtain rises, the Lord God has just completed creating the heavens and the earth. There are no plants or herbs in sight because "the LORD God had not caused it to rain upon the earth, and there was no man to till the ground." But then God caused a mist to rise from the earth and it watered the whole face of the ground. Then God formed a man of dust from the ground, and breathed into his nostrils the breath of life, and the man became a living being. Next, God planted a garden in Eden and put the man there. God then made "every tree that is pleasant to the sight and good for food" to grow, and placed two trees in the very center of the garden: the tree of life and the tree of the knowledge of good and evil. A river flowed from Eden into the garden and there it divided and became four rivers.

It was the man's task to till and keep the garden. He was free to eat of every tree of the garden save one. Of the tree of the knowledge of good and evil he was not to eat, "for in the day that you eat of it you shall die." Then God caused a deep sleep to fall upon the man, and while the man slept God took one of his ribs and out of it he created a woman. They were both naked, but were not ashamed.

The second act of the story begins with the appearance of the serpent who, according to the storyteller, is "more subtle than any other wild creature that the LORD God had made." The serpent first spoke to the woman, asking: "Did God say, 'You shall not eat of any tree of the garden'?" She replied to the serpent, "We may eat of the fruit of the trees of the garden;

but God said, 'You shall not eat of the fruit of the tree which is in the midst
of the garden, neither shall you touch it, lest you die.' " But the serpent said
to her, "You will not die. For God knows that when you eat of it your eyes
will be opened, and you will be like God, knowing good and evil." So the
woman ate of the fruit of the tree and gave some to her husband, and he also
ate. And their eyes *were* opened, and "they knew that they were naked; and
they sewed fig leaves together and made themselves aprons."

The third act begins with the man and woman hearing the sound of the
Lord God walking in the garden in the cool of the day, and they hid from
God's presence among the trees of the garden. But God called to the man,
and said to him, "Where are you?" The man replied, "I heard the sound of
thee in the garden, and I was afraid, because I was naked; and I hid myself."
God replied to him, "Who told you that you were naked? Have you eaten of
the tree I commanded you not to eat?" The man answered that the woman
whom God had given him gave him the fruit of the tree and he ate it. God
turned to the woman and said, "What is this that you have done?" She
answered, "The serpent beguiled me, and I ate." Then God turned to the
serpent and placed a curse on it (the curse of having to crawl on his belly and
eat dust). Then God turned to the woman and placed a curse on her (the
curse of increased pain in childbearing and subservience to her husband).
Then God turned to the man and cursed him too (hard labor leading eventually to physical death). Then, after clothing the man and woman, God
drove them out of the garden. The reason? Because now that they had
gained knowledge of good and evil, they might try to reach up and eat of the
tree of life, and live forever. To ensure that they would not attempt to return,
God placed an angel with a flaming sword at the east end of the garden to
guard the way to the tree of life.

This story in three acts is commonly referred to as the Fall. The page
heading on the Bible I have used for recounting the story reads, "The Fall of
Man." The very use of the word "fall" to describe what occurs in this story
introduces, however subtly, an association with childhood, for as discussed in
chapter 3, a major fear in childhood is that of falling. (It is also one of the
greatest fears that parents have regarding an infant child because falling from
a dressing table, a crib, or down a flight of stairs may result in the child's
death.) In any event, the two humans had been placed in the garden as its
caretakers and there was only one restriction imposed on their freedom to
do whatever they pleased. Yet, aided and abetted by the subtle reasoning of
the serpent, they violated this restriction, and when God discovered what
they had done, God expelled them from the garden and made certain that
they would never return.

As noted, this story has been widely used to instruct Christian parents in
the rearing of their children. It has informed their understanding of the basic
nature of children and has provided guidelines for the punishment of chil-

dren when they have misbehaved. If the Garden of Eden story is viewed as an attempt to envision how life began for the human race, it has seemed a small step to use it as an account of the beginning of the life of each individual. If the Garden of Eden story is about the "childhood" of the human race, it has also seemed appropriate to view the story as being about the childhood of each and every one of us. Once this connection, this analogy, has been made, the conclusion seems inescapable: Children are disposed by nature to disobey the rules that adults have established for their own good (remember that God prohibited the eating of the fruit lest death result), and such disobedience, when it occurs, needs to be severely punished, for otherwise the children will gain the impression that they can disobey at will. If God swiftly and summarily punished the humans' first transgression, then surely parents cannot do otherwise than to punish children for their very first act of disobedience. It should not surprise us, therefore, that there has been much discussion and debate among advocates of severe punishment of children as to when these punishments should first be inflicted, with some arguing that it should begin when the child is still in the crib. Children, the story seems to say, are inherently rebellious. Tell them the one thing they are not to do and their natural disposition is to do it.

This interpretation of the Garden of Eden story supports the theological perspective that Philip Greven describes in great detail in *Spare the Child*: Sin is understood as rebellion, and parents do not do their children any favor by letting them get away with it. The only question is whether the willfulness of the child needs to be bent or broken, and the answer one gives to this question depends on whether one believes that the child's natural will is thoroughly perverse or only misguided.

Shame and Self-Alienation

But what if we were to view the Garden of Eden story from a different theological perspective, one in which we consider the act of disobedience to be symptomatic of a deeper problem. In this perspective, the idea that the problem resides in the "will" would be shown to be rather superficial. This alternative perspective would begin to ask questions that the first perspective does not ask, such as: Why was the serpent successful in creating doubts about the motives of the Lord God? And what about the fact that the act of disobedience made the two humans ashamed of themselves, self-conscious in their nakedness? By asking these questions, we question the first theological perspective on the grounds that it lacks depth, failing to take seriously enough the deeper psychological issues that lie beneath or behind the act of disobedience itself.

Thus, on closer inspection, a story that seemed to be primarily about guilt—the committing of a wrongful act—has a strong element of shame as well, and, furthermore, shame seems somehow to be the deeper, or the more problematic, element in the story. The couple is aware of having done precisely what they had been commanded by God not to do, yet, it was not the act of disobedience itself, but the effect that this act had on their whole bearing, their whole sense of self, that the storyteller wants us especially to notice. They were utterly ashamed, self-conscious in the presence of each other, and were also very, very afraid. Shame and fear, emotions that they had not experienced before this, were more prominent even than the guilt they felt for having disobeyed God. The theological word that best captures this deeper dimension of the story is alienation. In their shame, they are alienated from each other and from God, and their shame is intimately linked with fear—not, I would say, the fear of punishment (though this may be present to a degree) but rather the fear of exposure, of having their shame being mirrored back to them through God's appearance to them.

In the psychological literature on shame and guilt, there is now an emerging consensus that shame is a global emotion, involving the total self, whereas guilt is more specific to an action that one has taken. In *Shame: The Exposed Self*, Michael Lewis describes the phenomenological experience of shame: "In shame situations . . . the focus is upon the self, both as object and subject. The self becomes embroiled in the self because the evaluation of the self by the self is total. There is no way out. The focus is not upon the individual's behavior, but upon the total self. The individual who makes global attributions focuses upon herself, not upon her action. Focusing inward, such a person is unable to act, and is driven from the field of action into hiding or disappearing."[1] Thus, when we experience shame, we are terribly self-conscious, and we make global evaluations: "I am no good," "I am worthless," "I am an awful person." With guilt, "individuals evaluate their behavior as failure but focus on the specific features of the self or on the self's action that led to the failure. Unlike shame, in which the focus is on the global self, with guilt the individual focuses on the self's actions and behaviors that are likely to repair the failure" (76). Thus, the feeling that is produced in guilt is not as intensely negative as shame and does not lead to confusion and immobilization: "In fact, the emotion of guilt always has an associated corrective action, something that the individual can do—but does not necessarily actually do—to repair the failure. Rectification of the failure and preventing it from occurring again are the two possible corrective paths" (76). In fact, to speak of "corrective paths" has application only to guilt: "Whereas in shame we see the body hunched over itself in an attempt to hide and disappear, in guilt we see individuals moving in space as if trying to repair the action" (76).

Because Lewis views shame as a response to our failure to meet our own standards, rules, and goals, we may assume that the humans in the Garden of Eden story did not view their action in eating the fruit as a violation against

God only. It was also, and more profoundly, a violation against themselves. Yes, God had commanded them to avoid eating of the tree of the knowledge of good and evil. But they had believed that they were fully capable of honoring this command. It was not the fact that they had broken God's rule, but the fact that they had violated their own standard that caused them to feel shame. Had they been concerned only about violating God's command, their reaction would have been one of guilt: "We did something we ought not to have done, and now we have to find a way to repair the failure." But this is not how they reacted. Instead, they felt totally exposed as both object and subject of their action: "How could *I* have done such a thing?"

Lewis claims that his recent studies and those by Hans Heckhausen and Deborah Stipek indicate that by the beginning of the third year of life children already have their own set of standards, rules, and goals and seem to show distress when they violate them. He cites the example of one of his own experiments:

> Children are placed in a room and told not to look at an attractive toy that has been placed behind them. After a few moments the experimenter leaves the room, first informing the children that they should not look at the toy while the experimenter is gone. For most of the 2½-year-old children, temptation is too great, and they turn toward the toy almost immediately. When the experimenter reenters the room, the children are asked if they looked at the toy. At least 65% of these children report that they did not look at the toy. The children are videotaped before the experimenter leaves, while she is absent, and after her return. Examination of the children's expressions after the children look but before the experimenter returns reveal indications of guilt: a lowering of the eyes, no smile, and a certain tension in the body. By the time the experimenter reenters the room, the children no longer are exhibiting this facial expression. In fact, their facial expression might be described as neutral, innocent, or even "What? Me peek?" (67–68)

Note that Lewis here suggests that the children experience guilt, presumably on the grounds that the children do not experience this violation as one in which their whole self is involved. Yet, even here, there are the beginning signs of what will soon develop into experiences of shame, especially in the lowering of the eyes, a response that occurs even in the absence of the person who issued the command not to look. Thus, shame will occur when the child is unable to externalize the prohibition as nothing more than the command of another, but senses instead that her own standards have been violated. Then, the same scenario will be experienced as a shame event. It will be totally self-involving and it will be impossible for the child to compose the neutral facial expression that Lewis describes. Furthermore, the more central these standards are to the child's sense of self, the more likely the experience will be to elicit shame as opposed to embarrassment. Shame is the emotion felt when one has failed to meet one's own standards or goals and when these standards or goals are central to one's sense of self.

The conclusion is inescapable: Because they reacted with such intense emotions of shame, Adam and Eve were conscious of having violated their own standards, and these standards were central to their own sense of self. It is true that they had violated a command from God—much as the children in Lewis's experiment had succumbed to the temptation to look at the attractive toy—but, unlike these children, they were unable to compose themselves, but instead went into hiding and were ashamed to look at each other and to be seen by God. Adam's attempt to transfer blame to Eve is also symptomatic of a shame experience for, unlike guilt, where one can usually recognize how one might go about repairing the damage, there is no such corrective path to take in shame, so one is especially prone to do what Adam did: "I cannot deny that I did it, and there is nothing I can do to rectify what has happened, but *she* got me into this."[2] In short, what would appear to be a story about humans' violation of a prohibition placed upon them by God—and thus an instance of disobedience—becomes, in this deeper reading, a story about how humans violate their own standards, and find themselves utterly helpless to do anything about it. They are unable to think of a corrective path that might be taken, for there is none. Their reaction is not "I have committed a sin" but "I am utterly worthless. How could I have been so stupid as to have allowed the serpent to beguile me?" Their global self stands condemned.

In this alternative reading of the Garden of Eden story, how is the serpent's success to be explained? We must, of course, set aside the notion that women are especially naïve and gullible, nor is much to be gained by interpreting the serpent in sexual terms. Rather the serpent appealed to their hubris by making an invidious comparison between their own self-evident rectitude and God's alleged impurity of motives. Lewis suggests that hubris is to shame as pride is to guilt. Hubris and shame involve the global self, our self as a whole, while pride and guilt involve specific actions of the self. Thus, if shame is the feeling that our very self is a failure, then hubris is the feeling that our very self is a great success. In contrast, guilt is the feeling that there is something we have done that is not up to our standards or goals, and pride is the feeling that we have done something that meets our standards. Thus, pride is a good thing, while hubris is far more problematic:

> Hubris is a consequence of an evaluation of success according to one's standards, rules, and goals where the focus is on the global self. In this emotion, the individual focuses on the total self as successful. In extreme cases, hubris is associated with grandiosity or with narcissism. . . . Hubris is difficult to sustain because no specific action precipitates the feeling. Because hubris feelings are addictive, people prone to hubris derive little satisfaction from the emotion. Consequently, they seek out and invent

situations likely to repeat this emotional state. This can be accomplished either by altering their standards, rules, and goals or by reevaluating what constitutes success according to their actions, thoughts, or feelings.[3]

Lewis also notes that hubristic persons have difficulty in their interpersonal relations since their own hubris is likely to interfere with the wishes, needs, and desires of others, thereby promoting interpersonal conflict: "Moreover, given the contemptuousness associated with hubris, the other is likely to be shamed by the nature of the actions of the person having this emotion."[4]

Given that Adam and Eve respond so globally when they violate their standards, it seems quite plausible that they viewed their success in meeting their standards before the Fall in similarly global terms, and were therefore highly susceptible to hubris. The serpent appealed to their hubris when he raised questions about God's true motives: Was God's prohibition for their own good, as God had claimed, or was it because God did not want the humans to become as gods, equal in power to God? By raising the question, the serpent appealed to their hubris—not to their pride—for their pride was based on their success in meeting their own standards through concrete actions, while their hubris had a life of its own, over and above these specific achievements. Lewis is right to associate hubris with the narcissistic personality because it has a sense of self-importance and of entitlement that far exceeds actual achievements and accomplishments.[5] Thus, if the humans in the story were so susceptible to hubris, it makes perfect sense to view their shame experience as the Fall. Given the heights to which their global sense of self had taken them, the experience of shame was that much more devastating.

While some theorists believe that shame, guilt, hubris, and pride exist in infancy, Lewis believes that these four emotions emerge after the first two years of life. Unfortunately, his evidence focuses exclusively on shame, guilt, and pride, and hubris is basically ignored. Does this mean that young children lack hubris? More likely, hubris originates in experiences of pride, and is that feature of pride that manifests itself in contempt for those who are unable to perform the task in question. Thus, Lewis cites a study in which children were set the task of tower stacking. The children who finished first and succeeded raised their eyes, smiled, and looked triumphantly at the losers. They also sat up straight, and some of them threw their arms up in the air, as if to inflate themselves. In contrast, the children who failed exhibited body collapse, lowered heads, lack of eye contact with the winners, and hands that did not stray from their work.[6] Perhaps, then, there are emerging tendencies toward hubris in the successful children's look of triumph at the losers and in their self-inflation. These responses seem to go beyond pride in a job well done. Furthermore, they suggest that hubris is most likely to be evoked when there is opportunity for invidious comparison between children, and when they are conscious of being involved in a competition where there will be winners and losers. Somehow, the serpent appealed to the humans' predisposition to self-inflation. Perhaps this predisposition to hubris (though not to pride) is what original sin is all about, but if so, we should recognize that it does not originate in a social vacuum and is not innate, but occurs when adults place children in situations where they are expected to compete with one another, where there are winners and losers.

If hubris explains the susceptibility of Adam and Eve to temptation, one that led them to violate their own standards, we are still left with the question why God considered it necessary to punish them and why it was so severe (i.e., permanent expulsion from the garden)? We need to set aside ex post facto reasoning of the sort that says that since we humans are condemned to work by the sweat of our brow and to experience pain in childbirth, we must have done something wrong to deserve this fate. While the storyteller may have intended to provide an explanation for why humans are so unhappy, we need to find the rationale for their punishment in the dynamics of the story itself. And it is precisely here that I find the story to be highly problematic. Isn't the shame that the humans experienced as a consequence of violating their own standards punishment enough? Why does God need to compound the punishment they have already experienced by expelling them from the garden? What possible good can come from shaming them further, adding shame to shame?

This ending to the story implies that God's own sense of self is so insecure that God cannot respond in a calm and even manner to an expression of human hubris, one that in this case has already led to a devastatingly painful experience of personal shame. If they must be "taught a lesson," the lesson is already there to see in the shame that their actions have caused. No further purpose is served by subjecting them to further humiliation. Only a God who is threatened by the hubris of individuals less powerful will have a need to be punitive in the way that the God in the story is punitive. A God who is inwardly secure would instead conclude that if anything is to be done, it is not to punish further, and certainly not by increasing their already acute sense of alienation and isolation, but to initiate the work of restoration—the restoration of the "interpersonal bridges" that have been impaired if not destroyed by this overwhelming experience of shame.[7]

If I take exception to the ending of the Garden of Eden story, to the third act, it is not simply because I favor happy endings. Nor is it because I have a soft, romanticized view of God, a God who is lacking in backbone, timid, and wishy-washy. No, my objections to the ending of the story are that it fails to understand two important things: One is that Adam and Eve were acutely aware of having violated their own standards, rules, or goals. They were devastated by the knowledge that they had failed in terms of their own standards. Thus, the issue was not disobedience toward God but personal failure. The other is that shame is its own punishment. Anyone who is experiencing shame finds it impossible to imagine a worse punishment than shame itself. In fact, death would come as a welcome relief. In this regard, the *storyteller's* conclusion is the romantic happy ending: "If I can turn my story into one about guilt, and focus on the need for guilt to be appropriately punished, then perhaps I will succeed in distracting attention—my own included—from the painfulness of the second act in which shame is so palpably present that one can virtually reach out and touch it." Thus, the author is himself guilty of resorting to the happy, or, at least, happier ending, for, as Lewis points out, guilt is far more manageable than shame.[8] And so the final act of the story shifts the focus from the total global self to the specifics of why humans work by the sweat of their brow and experience pain in childbirth. As Erik Erikson points out: "'Shame is an emotion insufficiently studied, because in our civilization it is so early and easily absorbed by guilt.'"[9] Quite unintentionally, the story of the Garden of Eden explains why this is so. As a paradigmatic story about the very beginnings of our particular civilization, this story itself invites the absorption of the emotion of shame into the mechanisms and strategies of guilt.

Self-Alienation and the Return to Wholeness

Lewis does not offer any magic solutions to the problem of shame, for he assumes that we will continue to hold standards, rules, and goals for ourselves throughout our lives (even though these may change over time). However, he believes that there are better coping strategies than denial and forgetting. (As I once wrote, amnesia is to shame as rationalization is to guilt.)[10] These better strategies are laughter, especially the ability not to take oneself too seriously, and confession of one's shame, especially to a person whom one respects, who is perceived to have the respect of the community, and who is likely to respond with empathy and understanding.[11] Also, as Gershen Kaufman emphasizes, we should give particular attention to the importance of restoring interpersonal bridges. This would mean focusing on the harm that has been done to the relationship between Adam and Eve, especially by Adam's effort to transfer the blame to Eve.

But the consequence of shame that fails to receive much attention in the literature is its self-alienating effects and the problem of what can be done to restore our sense of inner wholeness. Given Lewis's view that shame arises from the failure to meet our own standards, rules, or goals, it is not at all difficult to see why the shame experience would also create a sense of self-alienation. This alienation occurs because the shame experience creates two conflicting perspectives within the self: One is the perspective that I have failed and ought therefore to be ashamed. From this perspective, one stands condemned, and appropriately so. The other is the perspective that the standard, rule, or goal to which I aspired was inappropriate or unworthy of my commitment. This perspective argues that shame, while it occurred, gives new insight, the insight that the standard, rule, or goal is itself suspect. After all, as Lewis points out, our standards, rules, and goals are very likely to change in the course of a lifetime. Thus, a standard that caused us to experience the shame of failure at one point in our life may subsequently be relinquished, and "failure" to adhere to this standard later in life may not result in shame at all. Indeed, one may take appropriate pride in the fact that one is no longer a slave to this particular standard.

Every shame experience elicits this internal controversy, this inner argument between "I have failed and am therefore no good" and "The standard according to which I failed is what is no good." The first perspective is overwhelmingly condemnatory, while the second perspective is somewhat more hopeful. On the other hand, the second perspective is typically mistrusted because it blames the standard, rule, or goal, and seems to countenance an attitude of defeat if not of fatalism: "If I cannot succeed at my standard, rule, or goal, I will lower my standard, I will abandon my rule, I will give up on my goal." Even to consider such lowering, abandoning, or giving up may create even more shame, shame compounded.

Yet, there is a solution to this problem: When we are still in the throes of a shaming experience, we are prone to view these two perspectives as absolutes: *Either* I am no good *or* the standards are no good. As the strength of the shame emotion dissipates, however, we can begin to see that they need not be viewed in such absolutist terms. I cannot deny that I have failed but the standard to which I held myself was also inappropriate, unrealistic, or both. Several decades ago, Carl Rogers employed a method for enabling his counselees and himself to discern whether therapeutic progress was being made. It consisted of having a client sort a large number of index cards with self-descriptive statements according to these two self-representations: Who I am now (the real self) and who I would like to be in the future (the ideal self). What Rogers found is that as the cards were sorted and resorted several times in the course of therapy, both the representation of the real self and the representation of the ideal self changed, and, if the therapy was going well, there was increasing congruence between the new real self and the new ideal self.[12] This move toward greater congruence between the real and the ideal self may reflect both modifications in standards, rules, and goals and a greater sense that one is realizing those standards, rules, or goals to which one has chosen to remain committed and faithful. This need not be viewed as a "lowering" of one's standards so that one can feel better about oneself, but may be viewed instead as a much more fluid process in which standards are being reevaluated and redefined, and the self is becoming more clearly— less globally—defined as well.

I do not mean to suggest that shame can ever be eliminated, but I am setting forth an image of wholeness, where the two sides of the self are not caught up in a hopeless quarrel but are discovering that they can live in peace. The righteous self—the one that insists on meeting standards—and the shameful self—the one that invariably fails—are no longer polarized, no longer engaged in recriminations and accusations, or threatening to divorce each other.

But there is another way to talk about this, a way that is not so clinical, not so psychotherapeutic, a way that is more inspirational: This is the language of return, of coming back to the Garden of Eden. The biblical story-teller views this desire to return as futile, for, according to him, God placed an angel at the east gate of the garden so that the banished ones could not gain entry to the garden. Yet, we need to reject this sense of futility, for the Garden of Eden is not a place on the face of the earth, but a place in the self, in the innermost core of the self—the soul. It is here in the soul where the enmity between our righteous and our shameful self is set aside, where we are at peace with ourselves, no longer engaged in self-condemnation.

To reject the idea that the Garden of Eden remains inaccessible to us is, of course, to engage in the very intellectual autonomy that the biblical story appears to condemn. Isn't this simply more of what occurred between the serpent and Eve, when questions about God's motives for the prohibition were raised and acted upon? Wasn't it the exercise of intellectual autonomy that got them into difficulty, and, if so, why would we not simply accept the story as told? Why? Because to accept the story as told is to accept the idea that we are condemned to a lifetime of unhappiness, a lifetime of being at enmity with self, others, and God. It is essential that we question the ending of the story of the Garden of Eden, that we envision another ending, one based on our longing to be whole again.

In support of our desire to have a different ending to the story than the one the biblical storyteller provides we have none other than our enlight-ened witness, Jesus himself, who told stories that seldom ended as their listeners expected. His power as enlightened witness derived from his ability to envision a different ending, and thereby to support those who also envi-sioned different endings. The role of the enlightened witness is precisely that of discerning the flaw in the story as originally rendered and exposing this flaw so that the whole story is brought into question. As any child could point out, the flaw in the story about how God made certain that we would never return to the garden is that only one of four possible points of access to the garden—its eastern end—is adequately guarded. The scenarios that this flaw in the story enables us to imagine are almost limitless. What of the west, the north, the south?

I find myself envisioning the return to the Garden of Eden as something akin to the experience of William Stafford and other unidentified children in his poem "Adults Only" (cited in chapter 7). The title strongly implies that the children were not allowed to be there, yet somehow or other they found themselves in the giant cage where a woman was about to come "farming right out of her clothes." As Stafford observes, "a pretty good world, I say, arrived that night." So, in my envisioning of the return to the garden, it occurs by cover of night, it is accomplished surreptitiously, and no one gets hurt, for nothing is to be gained by taking it by force.

But you, the reader, may have a different scenario, one that works better for you. How we accomplish the return is not the important thing. What matters is that we find our way back, reclaiming the sense of wholeness that we lost here so many years ago. William James expresses this sense of wholeness quite beautifully at the beginning of his chapter on conversion in *The Varieties of Religious Experience*:

> To be converted, to be regenerated, to receive grace, to experience religion, to gain an assurance, are so many phrases which denote the process, gradual or sudden, by which a self hitherto divided, and consciously wrong, inferior and unhappy, becomes unified and consciously right, superior and happy, in consequence of its firmer hold upon religious realities.[13]

This passage from James is often quoted in the context of discussion of the adolescent conversion experience, but the recovery of wholeness and the happiness that accompanies it may occur at any point in life, and is perhaps even more likely to occur in middle to late adulthood,[14] when we find ourselves reaching out over the seemingly impassable years to the child we used to be, taking this child in our arms and loving this child, perhaps for the very first time. To know such wholeness, to be at enmity with ourselves no longer, is the very essence of religion, for it is the purpose of religion to bind together that which was once broken asunder, and this must surely include the self which has been hopelessly divided.

The Garden of Eden has variety and is multiform. As the biblical storyteller notes, found within its borders are every tree that God has made to grow. It is also a place of fertility, for we are told that a river flows out of Eden to water the garden, and this river is divided and becomes four rivers in all. But, most of all, the Garden of Eden is a place where the self is reunited, and is consciously right, superior and happy. This is not hubris, but self-appreciation.

I am under no illusions about this experience of wholeness and its capacity to survive the ravages of daily living. Of course we will continue to hurt ourselves. Of course we will engage in self-condemnation. The luster of the Garden of Eden will diminish and the wholeness we have found will desert us. I know this and you know it too. Yet we also know that at the center of the garden, alongside the tree of the knowledge of good and evil—of our inherent division—stands the tree of life itself, and beneath this tree there constantly flows the river of regeneration.

We are, in any case, talking about the soul, and about its own inherent capacity to provide for itself. In a little-known essay on the treatment of the soul, Freud suggests that we make a serious mistake if we assume that *we* are the doctors or the curers of the soul, for, in his view, the soul is its own doctor, and its treatment originates within itself. The soul, in other words, has its own powers of regeneration.[15] The image of the garden and of the tree of life that stands in the midst of the garden enables us to visualize the soul's own regenerative powers. This is not hubris. We are not here talking about a self that does not know its own limits, but about the soul and its capacity to regenerate itself, over and over again. This is the garden that Jesus has been tending for us while we have been away.

In the introduction to this book, I cited Alice Miller's experience of stumbling onto a Saint Nicholas celebration on the edge of a forest. As we saw, this experience—this so-called "celebration"—filled the children with shame and dread. Against this image of the dark and threatening forest, I have put forward the image of the garden, and have suggested that the Garden of Eden need no longer be viewed as the place where humanity fell from grace, but as the place where we are safe, secure, and happy. It is a place where children are not put to shame, where they are not given reason to fear, where they are not made to feel inferior and wrong. It is a place where the sounds that children make are not in the form of sighings and sobbings, but are the familiar peals of laughter by which children let us know that they are at home in the world and at peace with themselves.

Jesus placed a child in the midst of his disciples, and said, "Truly, I say to you, unless you turn and become like children, you will never enter the kingdom of heaven" (Matt. 18:2–3). Like many other adults, I go to bed at night worrying for the children: Are they safe? Are they secure? Or are they, like little Sharon Olds, praying the Lord her soul to take on the chance that, dead, she'd be safe for eternity? But I also worry for us adults who may never experience again the happiness we glimpsed as children, before this happiness was clouded over by feelings of shame, inferiority, and self-doubt. It is in company with other adults who have found happiness to be so elusive, so inaccessible, so far beyond reach, that I join in Louise Glück's prayer that it would be God's plan "to make me sound forever again, as I was sound and whole in my mistaken childhood."

The Assumption of the Second Chance

I was nine years old. My younger brother, then four, had been unusually difficult that day. When my father came home from work, my mother told him about my little brother, how he was becoming more than she could handle. At dinner that evening we—my brothers and I—could feel the tension. No one was speaking. A sense of doom was in the air. After dinner my parents told all of us to stay close. We were not to go running off. Then my father pulled the car out of the garage and my mother came out of the house. They directed us to get into the car, my younger brother between my parents in the front seat and my two older brothers and I in the back. My father pulled out of the driveway and started up the street. "Where are we going?" one of us had the courage to ask. No answer. My father drove on. Dusk was approaching. Then, on our right, we recognized the building and began to realize what was going on. We felt dread in the pits of our stomachs. It was the orphanage, and our parents were about to send my little brother away. My father stopped the car and turned to my brother and said, "This is the end of the line." My mother opened the door and began to get out so that my brother could follow. The three of us in the back seat were stunned. I somehow found my voice and, amid sobs, pleaded: "Don't send him away. He'll be good. Just give him a second chance."

What I did not know, of course, is that they had no intention of leaving him at the orphanage that night. Years later he told me that he suspected it was a ruse because he noticed that no lights were burning on the first floor of the orphanage, suggesting to him that the offices were closed for the evening. But *I* took them at their word, first believing that they were going to abandon him; next assuming that my pleading in his behalf had made them change their minds. For a very long time—months, maybe even years—I assumed that my parents were capable of abandoning a child of theirs, and I did all in my power to make certain that it would never be me. But something surely died in me—in all of us—that night. Life before that night had not been perfect. There had been the usual conflicts between parents and children, the usual fightings and reconciliations. But this was different. This was the threat of abandonment. The sense of dread that this threat produced in me was nearly overwhelming.

If I have taken the child's side in this book, it is not because I have some romanticized view of children. Of course children are devious, manipulative, even vicious. Of course children treat their parents shamelessly, telling them lies, calling them names, challenging their rightful authority. I also know that some children are worse than others: more devious, more dishonest, more destructive, more demonic. There is no doubt in my mind—nor, for that matter, is there doubt in his—that my brother had provoked my parents beyond their patience and endurance. And perhaps my parents had good reason to believe that if they did not take decisive action then, they would come to regret it in future years.

And yet, even though I know now that it was not my pleadings that saved him, I believe, nonetheless, that there was wisdom in my contention that he should be given a "second chance." The original Garden of Eden story undermines this belief and, in so doing, leaves us feeling demoralized, as though we have been condemned to live in a world in which all of us must get perfect marks and any mistake or failure means that we are condemned for life. The author of Revelation also challenges the story, as he envisions all the children of the world gathering beside the river where stands the tree of life, with its twelve kinds of fruit and its healing leaves (Rev. 22:2).

Which is to say that the Bible itself, this book of our lives, this book that Augustine took up and read when he came to that moment in his life when he desperately needed a second chance, envisions our return to the garden, there to reexperience the inner peace that surpasses all understanding, a deep satisfaction with the self that we are, a profound gratitude for our one and only life and those who made it possible, and a wide embrace of the whole created order of things. The song of the soul.

As we gather beneath the tree of life, we remember—with heads bowed—the misbegotten ones who, like the child William Stafford recalls in "Thinking for Berky," could not make it back:[16]

> In the late night listening from bed
> I have joined the ambulance or the patrol
> screaming toward some drama, the kind of end
> that Berky must have some day, if she isn't dead.
>
> The wildest of all, her father and mother cruel,
> farming out there beyond the old stone quarry
> where highschool lovers parked their lurching cars,
> Berky learned to love in that dark school.
>
> Early her face was turned away from home
> toward any hardworking place; but still her soul,
> with terrible things to do, was alive, looking out
> for the rescue that—surely, some day—would have to come.
>
> Windiest nights, Berky, I have thought for you,
> and no matter how lucky I've been I've touched wood.
> There are things not solved in our town though tomorrow came:
> there are things time passing can never make come true.
>
> We live in an occupied country, misunderstood;
> justice will take us millions of intricate moves.
> Sirens will hunt down Berky, you survivors in your beds
> listening through the night, so far and good.

Even in the garden, the sirens that hunted down the others can still be heard in the distance, and no one of us here feels perfectly safe. Yet we have touched the tree of life—however warily, fearful that lightning might strike a second time—and we have found that it is good.

As children, many of us sang the simple gospel song, "Come into My

Heart, Lord Jesus." We asked him to come in today and to come to stay. I conclude by affirming the empowering truth of this simple gospel song we sang as children. In an article on Warner Sallman's "Head of Christ," a familiar painting found in millions of Christian homes, David Morgan reports that while many view it as sentimentalized, others "recalled incidents from their childhood which ranged from the mundane to the traumatic when Sallman's picture provided needed comfort."[17] One woman who had suffered repeated sexual abuse as a child recalled: "It helped me to keep sane in a world that felt very unsafe to me. After I spent hours praying for all the people who I was told would be hurt or killed if I told my secret, this picture would be the very last thing that I would look at before I closed my eyes. . . . Then I would dissociate out of my body and into the ceiling, but somehow I felt that I could at least internalize the image of Jesus and that He, as I saw Him in the picture, was on the ceiling with me" (14).

There are images, like that of the God of the author of Hebrews, that reflect and exacerbate fears for one's very survival, and there are images, like the internalized image of Jesus, that enable us to keep our sanity in a world that feels very unsafe to us. They save the child's self from fragmentation, but they also maintain their mending ways, enabling us, even as adults, to lay ourselves down to sleep at night, secure in the knowledge that no one, however vicious, can destroy the soul that grows within us.[18] As we sing the song about the Lord Jesus that we sang as children, let us not forget that even as our own souls are beginning to flower, there are children who are singing this song for the very first time, who though their lives are just beginning, have already felt the slashing cruelties of life. As Stafford observes in "Scars":[19]

> They tell how it was, and how time
> came along, and how it happened
> again and again. . . .
>
> Rows of children lift their faces of promise,
> places where the scars will be.

Notes

Introduction

1. Alice Miller, *Banished Knowledge: Facing Childhood Injuries*, trans. Leila Vannewitz (New York: Doubleday, 1990), ch. 1.

Chapter 1. Alice Miller on "the Mutilated Soul"

1. Søren Kierkegaard, *Purity of Heart Is to Will One Thing*, trans. Douglas V. Steere (New York: Harper & Brothers, 1956).

2. Alice Miller, *The Drama of the Gifted Child: The Search for the True Self*, trans. Ruth Ward (New York: Basic Books, 1981).

3. Alice Miller, *For Your Own Good: Hidden Cruelty in Child-Rearing and the Roots of Violence*, 2d ed., trans. Hildegard and Hunter Hannum (New York: Farrar, Straus Giroux, 1984).

4. Alice Miller, *Thou Shalt Not Be Aware: Society's Betrayal of the Child*, trans. Hildegard and Hunter Hannum (New York: Meridian Books, 1984).

5. Alice Miller, *The Untouched Key: Tracing Childhood Trauma in Creativity and Destructiveness*, trans. Hildegard and Hunter Hannum (New York: Doubleday, 1990).

6. Alice Miller, *For Your Own Good*, 43.

7. Ibid.

8. Ibid., 75.

9. Alice Miller, *Untouched Key*, 133.

10. Ibid., 29.

11. Ibid., 31.

12. Alice Miller, *Banished Knowledge*, trans. Leila Vennewitz (New York: Doubleday, 1990), 1.

13. Alice Miller, *Breaking Down the Wall of Silence: The Liberating Experience of Facing Painful Truth*, trans. Simon Worrall (New York: E. P. Dutton, 1991), 19–20.

Chapter 2. Augustine: The Vicious Cycle of Child Abuse

1. *The Confessions of Saint Augustine*, trans. John K. Ryan (Garden City, N.Y.: Image Books, 1960), 51–53.

2. See Alice Miller, *For Your Own Good*, 2d ed., trans. Hildegard and Hunter Hannum (New York: Farrar, Straus Giroux, 1984).

3. E. R. Dodds, "Augustine's *Confessions*: A Study of Spiritual Maladjustment," *Hibbert Journal* 26 (1927–28): 459–473.

4. Leo Ferrari, "The Boyhood Beatings of Augustine," *Augustinian Studies* 5 (1974): 1–14.

5. Alice Miller, "Friedrich Nietzsche: The Struggle against the Truth," in *The Untouched Key*, trans. Hildegard and Hunter Hannum (New York: Doubleday, 1990), 71–133.

6. See David Bakan, "Some Thoughts on Reading Augustine's *Confessions*," *Journal for the Scientific Study of Religion* 5 (1965): 149–52.

7. Here and below I use R. S. Pine-Coffin's translation of *The Confessions of Saint Augustine* (Baltimore: Penguin Books, 1961).

8. Carthage was well known in the ancient world as a city that engaged in the ritual sacrifice of children. Augustine himself comments on this practice in *The City of God*, noting that the God to whom children (usually small boys) were sacrificed was Saturn, who mutilated his father and devoured his children. That northern Africans sacrificed their children to the god Saturn was widely commented upon in classical and patristic writings. Especially noteworthy in this regard is Minucius Felix's comment that "in some part of Africa infants were sacrificed to [Saturn] by their parents, and their cries smothered by endearments and kisses for fear of a victim being sacrificed in tears." This prohibition against crying over a loss has relevance to our later discussion of Adeodatus's reaction to his grandmother's death. For classical and patristic references to child sacrifice, see John Day, *Molech: A God of Human Sacrifice in the Old Testament* (New York: Cambridge University Press, 1989), 86–91.

9. Here and below I use John K. Ryan's translation of *The Confessions*, 94.

10. Peter Brown, *Augustine of Hippo* (Berkeley, Calif.: University of California Press, 1969), 39.

11. Ibid., 135.

12. In discussing the fact that he believed many things without proof, Augustine offers the following examples: historical events, places he has never seen, facts about personal friends, and "so many things about physicians", *The Confessions of Saint Augustine*, trans. John K. Ryan, 139. The specificity of this last example indicates that there is, for him, something quite special about medical doctors.

13. John H. S. Burleigh, ed., *Augustine: Earlier Writings* (Philadelphia: Westminster Press, 1953), 69–101.

14. R. S. Pine-Coffin, *The Confessions of Saint Augustine*, 200.

15. On this point, see Paul Ricoeur, *Interpretation Theology: Discourse and the Surplus of Meaning* (Fort Worth, Tex.: Texas Christian University Press, 1976), 92–95.

16. Helen Merrell Lynd, *On Shame and the Search for Identity* (New York: Harcourt, Brace & Co., 1958), 57.

Chapter 3. Religious Sources
of Childhood Trauma

1. Alice Miller, *Banished Knowledge*, trans. Leila Vennewitz (New York: Doubleday, 1990), ch. 3.

2. Philip Greven, *Spare the Child: The Religious Roots of Punishment and the Psychological Impact of Physical Abuse* (New York: Alfred A. Knopf, 1991).

3. Alice Miller, 2d ed., *For Your Own Good*, trans. Hildegard and Hunter Hannum (New York: Farrar, Strauss Giroux, 1984), chs. 1–2.

4. Marshall Frady, *Billy Graham: A Parable of American Righteousness* (Boston: Little, Brown & Co., 1979), 49.

5. Ibid.

6. J. Richard Fugate, *What the Bible Says About . . . Child Training* (Garland, Tex.: Aletheiz Publishers, 1980), 145.

7. James Dobson, *Dare to Discipline* (Wheaton, Ill.: Living Books, 1970), 23.

8. Aimee Semple McPherson, *Aimee: The Life Story of Aimee Semple McPherson* (Los Angeles: Foursquare Publications, 1979), 13.

9. David Wilkerson (with John and Elizabeth Sherrill), *The Cross and the Switchblade* (Lincoln, Va.: Chosen Books, 1963), 83.

10. Ruth Wilkerson Harris, *It Was Good Enough for Father: The Story of the Wilkerson Family* (Old Tappan, N.J.: Fleming H. Revell Co., 1969), 96–97.

11. Greven, *Spare the Child*, 30.

12. Hart M. Nelsen and Alice Kroliczak, "Parental Use of the Threat 'God Will Punish': Replication and Extension," *Journal for the Scientific Study of Religion* 23 (1984): 267–77.

13. Clyde Z. Nunn, "Child-Control Through a 'Coalition with God,' " *Child Development* 35 (1964): 417–32.

14. Leonard Shengold, *Soul Murder: The Effects of Childhood Abuse and Deprivation* (New Haven, Conn.: Yale University Press, 1989), 4 and 28.

15. Dobson, *Dare to Discipline*, 19.

16. Greven, *Spare the Child*, 204–5.

17. Ibid., 206.

18. Ibid.

19. David Wilkerson, *The Vision* (New York: Jove Books, 1974), 114.

20. Ibid., 121.

21. David Wilkerson, *Racing Toward Judgment* (Old Tappan, N.J.: Fleming H. Revell Co., 1976), 134.

22. Greven, *Spare the Child*, 210–11.

23. Ibid., 211.

24. Ibid.

25. Paul Creelan, "Watson as Mythmaker: The Millenarian Sources of Watsonian Behaviorism," *Journal for the Scientific Study of Religion* 24 (1985): 194–236. Quotation on 194.

26. Ibid., 202–3.

27. Greven, *Spare the Child*, 168.

28. Alice Miller, *Banished Knowledge*, 38–41.

29. Sandor Ferenczi, "Confusion of Tongues between Adults and the Child," in *The Assault on Truth: Freud's Suppression of the Seduction Theory*, ed. Jeffrey Moussaieff Masson (New York: Penguin Books, 1985), 291–303. Quotation on 298.

30. Ibid., 298.

31. See Greven, *Spare the Child*, 159.

32. Ferenczi, "'Confusion of Tongues," 300–1.

33. Ibid., 300.

34. Alice Miller, "Buster Keaton: Laughter at a Child's Mistreatment and the Art of Self-Control," in *The Untouched Key*, trans. Hildegard and Hunter Hannum (New York: Doubleday, 1990), ch. 3.

35. Ibid., 37.

36. Buster Keaton (with Charles Samuels), *My Wonderful World of Slapstick* (Garden City, N.Y.: Doubleday, 1960), 151.

37. Ibid., 13.

38. Alice Miller, *Untouched Key*, 40–41.

39. Webster's *New World Dictionary of the American Language* (Cleveland: World Publishing Co., 1957), 1537.

40. Carl Goldberg, *Understanding Shame* (Northvale, N.J.: Jason Aronson, 1991), p. 3.

41. Russell C. Allen and Bernard Spilka, "Committed and Consensual Religion: A Specification of Religion-Prejudice Relationships," *Journal for the Scientific Study of Religion* 6 (1967): 191–206. Quotation on 200.

42. Jane Schaberg, *The Illegitimacy of Jesus: A Feminist Theological Interpretation of the Infancy Narratives* (San Francisco: Harper & Row, 1987).

43. Erving Goffman, *Stigma: Notes on the Management of a Spoiled Identity* (Englewood Cliffs, N.J.: Prentice-Hall, 1963).

44. Alice Miller, *Banished Knowledge*, ch. 4.

45. See James A. Mohler, *A Speechless Child Is the Word of God: An Interpretation of Saint Augustine* (New Rochelle, N.Y.: New City Press, 1992), 46–54.

46. Gordon W. Allport, "Religion and Prejudice," in *Personality and Social Encounter: Selected Essays* (Boston: Beacon Press, 1964), 257–67.

47. John Day, *Molech: A God of Human Sacrifice in the Old Testament* (New York: Cambridge University Press, 1989), 24–25.

48. See also David Bakan, *The Duality of Human Existence* (Chicago: Rand McNally & Co., 1966) and *Disease, Pain and Sacrifice* (Chicago: University of Chicago Press, 1968), on Jewish rejection of infanticide.

49. Kurt Vonnegut, *God Bless You, Mr. Rosewater* (New York: Laurel Books, 1965), 92–93. I am grateful to Steven Kraftchick for bringing this story to my attention.

Chapter 4. Letter to the Hebrews:
The Lasting Effects of Childhood Trauma

1. Christopher G. Ellison and Darren E. Sherkat, "Obedience and Authority: Religion and Parental Values Reconsidered," *Journal for the Scientific Study of Religion* 32 (1993): 313–29.

2. Ibid., 326.

3. Ibid., 315.

4. Martin Luther, *Table Talk*, vol. 54 of *Luther's Works*, ed. and trans. Theodore G. Tappert (Philadelphia: Fortress Press, 1967), 235, 300.

5. Ibid., 443.

6. Alice Miller, *Banished Knowledge*, trans. Leila Vennewitz (New York: Doubleday, 1990), 171. I am indebted to John Kuentzel for drawing my attention via a seminar paper to the importance of the "enlightened witness" theme in Miller's work.

7. Luther, *Table Talk*, 424–25.

8. Philip Greven, *Spare the Child* (New York: Alfred A. Knopf, 1991), p. 52.

9. Ibid., 53.

10. Ibid.

11. René Girard, *Things Hidden since the Foundation of the World*, trans. Stephen Bann and Michael Metteer (Stanford, Calif.: Stanford University Press, 1987), 182.

12. Thomas Jefferson, "The Life and Morals of Jesus of Nazareth," repr. in *An American Christian Bible*, ed. Eric Holden (Rochester, Wash.: Sovereign Press, 1982). Erik H. Erikson discusses Jefferson's selection in *Dimensions of a New Identity* (New York: W. W. Norton & Co., 1974) and "The Galilean Sayings and the Sense of 'I,' " *Yale Review* 70 (April 1981): 321–62. He critiques Jefferson's deletion of the accounts of Jesus' healings, as these accounts concern how Jesus empowered others.

13. Alice Miller, *Breaking Down the Wall of Silence*, trans. Simon Worrall (New York: E. P. Dutton, 1991), ch. 8.

14. Greven, *Spare the Child*, 168–69.

15. Ibid., 157–59.

16. Alice Miller, *The Untouched Key*, trans. Hildegard and Hunter Hannum (New York: Doubleday, 1990), 133.

Chapter 5. Abraham and Isaac: The Sacrificial Impulse

1. Lloyd DeMause, ed., *The History of Childhood: The Untold Story of Child Abuse* (New York: Peter Bedrick Books, 1988), 25.

2. David Bakan, *The Duality of Human Existence* (Chicago: Rand McNally & Co., 1966), p. 229.

3. Phyllis Trible, *Texts of Terror: Literary-Feminist Readings of Biblical Narratives* (Philadelphia: Fortress Press, 1984). Adopting Trible's theme of biblical texts of terror, Philip Culbertson in *New Adam* explores several texts of terror involving male relationships, including David and Absalom, Abraham and Ishmael, and Jonathan and David.

4. Wayne Oates, *The Bible in Pastoral Care* (Philadelphia: Westminster Press, 1953).

5. Alice Miller, *The Untouched Key*, trans. Hildegard and Hunter Hannum (New York: Doubleday, 1990), 137–45.

6. Ibid., 139–40. As Miller puts it, "In the face of mobilization for war—even a conventional one, a nonnuclear war—the questions of the younger generation are silenced. To doubt the wisdom of the state is regarded as treason. Any discussion or consideration of alternative possibilities is eliminated at a single stroke. Only practical questions remain: How do we win the war? How do we survive it? Once the point of asking these questions has been reached, the young forget that prosperous and prominent old men have been preparing for war for a long time. The younger generation will march, sing songs, kill and be killed, and they will be under the impression that they are carrying out an extremely important mission. The state will indeed regard highly what they are doing and will reward them with medals of honor, but their souls—the childlike, living, feeling part of their personality—will be condemned to the utmost passivity."

7. Søren Kierkegaard, *Fear and Trembling* (pseud. Johannes de Silentio), trans. Howard V. and Edna H. Hong (Princeton, N.J.: Princeton University Press, 1983).

8. See René Girard, *Violence and the Sacred*, trans. Patrick Gregory (Baltimore: John Hopkins University Press, 1977), and *Things Hidden since the Foundation of the World*, trans. Stephen Bann and Michael Metteer (Stanford, Calif.: Stanford University Press, 1987). In the latter, Girard points out: "When considered as a whole, modern research (of which our own project constitutes only a new, more advanced stage), can be seen as part of a much larger dynamic, that of the first society to become capable of deciphering a causal sequence and revealing it to be one of arbitrary violence—whereas in the history of all humanity this casual sequence has never appeared in any form other than that of mythology. . . . A society that replaces myth by an awareness of persecution is a society in the process of desacralization. We are not the first to note that the one and the other are related, but we are the first to understand the necessity of their relatedness" (126).

9. See, on this point, Heinz Kohut, *The Restoration of the Self* (New York: International Universities Press, 1977), 171ff.; and *The Analysis of the Self* (New York: International Universities Press, 1971), ch. 5.

10. Kierkegaard, *Fear and Trembling*, 23.

11. Ibid.

12. Heinz Kohut and Ernest S. Wolf, "The Disorders of the Self and Their Treatment: An Outline," in *Essential Papers on Narcissism*, ed. Andrew P. Morrison (New York: New York University Press, 1986), 175–96. Quotation on 184. Kohut cites a similar case of a failed attempt to set up one's father as "an admired idealized image" in *Analysis of the Self*, 139–40.

13. Søren Kierkegaard, *The Journals of Kierkegaard*, trans. Alexander Dru (New York: Harper & Brothers, 1958), 54.

14. Bert Kaplan, "The Decline of Desire as the Ultimate Life Crisis," in *Encounter with Erikson: Historical Interpretation and Religious Biography*, ed. Donald Capps, Walter H. Capps, and M. Gerald Bradford (Missoula, Mont.: Scholars Press, 1977), 389–400. Quotation on 392.

15. Bakan, *Duality of Human Existence*, 117.

16. Ibid.

17. Ibid., 212.

Chapter 6. The Child Jesus as Endangered Self

1. See Juliet Mitchell, ed., *The Selected Melanie Klein* (Harmondsworth, Middlesex: Penguin Books, 1986), 211–29. See also Alice Miller, *Banished Knowledge*, trans. Leila Vennewitz (New York: Doubleday, 1990), 44–46, where she challenges the Kleinian view of children.

2. Donald Capps, "Orestes Brownson: The Psychology of Religious Affiliation," *Journal for the Scientific Study of Religion* 7 (1968): 197–209; "John Henry Newman: A Study of Vocational Identity," *Journal for the Scientific Study of Religion* 9 (1970): 33–51; "The Death of Father Abraham: The Assassination of Lincoln and Its Effect on Frontier Mythology," in *Religious Encounters with Death*, ed. Frank E. Reynolds and Earle H. Waugh (University Park, Pa.: Pennsylvania State University Press, 1977), 233–44; "The Myth of Father Abraham: Psychosocial Influences in the Formation of Lincoln Biography," in *Encounter with Erikson*, ed. Donald Capps, Walter H. Capps, and M. Gerald Bradford (Missoula, Mont.: Scholars Press, 1977), 253–80; "Augustine's *Confessions*: The Scourge of Shame and the Silencing of Adeodatus," in *The Hunger of the Heart: Reflections on the Confessions of Augustine*, ed. Donald Capps and James E. Dittes (West Lafayette, Ind.: Society for the Scientific Study of Religion, 1990), 69–92.

3. The fact that John Henry Newman was "farmed out" to his grandmother's rural home while his parents pursued their professional and social lives in London gives particular poignancy to his claim that the modern world bears little evidence of God: "What shall be said to this heart-piercing, reason-bewildering fact? I can only answer, that either there is no Creator, or this living society of men is in a true sense discarded from His presence. Did I see a boy of good make and mind, with the tokens on him of a refined nature, cast upon the world without provision, unable to say whence he came, his birthplace or his family connections, I should conclude that there was some mystery connected with his history, and that he was one, of whom, from one cause or other, his parents were ashamed." *Apologia Pro Vita Sua* (New York: Image Books, 1956), 320.

4. Erik H. Erikson, *Young Man Luther* (New York: W. W. Norton & Co., 1958).

5. Alice Miller, *Thou Shalt Not Be Aware*, trans. Hildegarde and Hunter Hannum (New York: Meridian Books, 1984), 194–220.

6. Albert Schweitzer, *The Psychiatric Study of Jesus*, trans. Charles R. Joy (Boston: Beacon Press, 1948).

7. Ralph Waldo Emerson, "Self-Reliance," in *The Essays of Ralph Waldo Emerson* (Cambridge, Mass.: Belknap Press of Harvard University Press, 1987), 29.

8. Ibid.

9. See John W. Miller, "Jesus' 'Age Thirty Transition': A Psychohistorical Probe," *Journal of Psychology and Christianity* 6 (1987): 40–51. His position on the biblical understanding of God as Father is further elaborated in *Biblical Faith and Fathering: Why We Call God "Father"* (Mahwah, N.J.: Paulist Press, 1989).

10. Jane Schaberg, *The Illegitimacy of Jesus: A Feminist Theological Interpretation of the Infancy Narratives* (San Francisco: Harper & Row, 1987).

11. Ibid., xi.

12. Alice Miller, *The Untouched Key*, trans. Hildegard and Hunter Hannum (New York: Doubleday, 1990), 161.

13. See John Dominic Crossan, *Jesus: A Revolutionary Biography* (San Francisco: HarperSan Francisco, 1994), 18–24.

14. Ibid., 16.

15. See Schaberg, *Illegitimacy of Jesus*, 3, 201–2.

16. Ibid., 157–58.

17. Roland Bainton, "Luther: A Psychiatric Portrait," *Yale Review* 48 (1959): 405–10.

18. Joachim Jeremias, *New Testament Theology: The Proclamation of Jesus* (New York: Charles Scribner's Sons, 1971).

19. Burton L. Mack, *The Lost Gospel: The Book of Q and Christian Origins* (San Francisco: HarperSan Francisco, 1993), 76–77.

20. Paul W. Hollenbach, "Jesus, Demoniacs, and Public Authorities: A Socio-Historical Study," *Journal of the American Academy of Religion* 49 (1981): 567–88.

21. See David Bakan, "Reconsideration of the Problem of Introspection" and "Suicide and the Method of Introspection," in *On Method: Toward a Reconstruction of Psychological Investigation* (San Francisco: Jossey-Bass, 1967), 94–112, 113–21.

22. Sigmund Freud, *Psychopathology of Everyday Life*, trans A. A. Brill (New York: Mentor Books, 1951), 120.

23. See Hjalmar Sundén, *Die Religionen und Die Rollen: Ein Psychologische Untersuchen der Fromigkeit*, trans. from the Swedish by Herman Müller and Susanne Öhman (Berlin: Topelmann, 1959). For a summary of Sundén's biblical role theory, see Donald Capps, "Sundén's Role-Taking Theory: The Case of John Henry Newman and His Mentors," *Journal for the Scientific Study of Religion* 21 (1982): 58–70.

24. See D. MacKenzie Brown, ed., *Ultimate Concern: Tillich in Dialogue* (New York: Harper & Row, 1965), 156.

25. Crossan, *Jesus: A Revolutionary Biography*, pp. 66–70.

26. See René Girard, *Violence and the Sacred*, trans. Patrick Gregory (Baltimore: Johns Hopkins University Press, 1977), chs. 3 and 10; also his "Generative Scapegoating," in *Violent Origins*, ed. Robert G. Hamerton-Kelly (Stanford, Calif.: Stanford University Press, 1987), 73–105.

27. Crossan, *Jesus: A Revolutionary Biography*, 124–27.

28. Alice Miller, *Banished Knowledge*, 171–75, 193–94.

29. Rollo May, *My Quest for Beauty* (San Francisco: Saybrook Publishers, 1985), 63.

30. Ibid., 20–22.

31. Joan M. Erikson, *Wisdom and the Senses* (New York: W. W. Norton & Co., 1988).

32. Louise Glück, *The Wild Iris* (Hopewell, N.J.: Ecco Press, 1992). I am grateful to Jay Cooke for bringing Louise Glück's poetry to my attention.

33. Louise Glück, *Ararat* (Hopewell, N.J.: Ecco Press, 1990).

34. Glück, *Wild Iris*, 12.

35. Ibid., 43.

36. Ibid., 42.

37. Leander E. Keck, *The Church Confident* (Nashville: Abingdon Press, 1993), 61–62. The front cover of Keck's book has a quotation from Charles C. Morrison's Beecher Lectures at Yale Divinity School in 1939: "Christianity can repent, but it mut not whimper." This quotation is itself reflective of the childhood punishment scenario in which children first *repent* for disobeying their parents and then submit without *whimpering* to the ensuing punishment.

38. Luke Timothy Johnson, "Reshuffling the Gospels: Jesus According to Spong and Wilson," *Christian Century*, April 28, 1993, p. 457.

39. Mack, *The Lost Gospel*, p. 76.

40. Miller, *Biblical Faith and Fathering*, 94–95. Miller also argues that Jesus himself came to be viewed as a "spiritual father" to his followers: "He was a certain kind of father—perhaps the father that many of the alienated of his time had not had and were secretly longing for" (p. 92).

Chapter 7. A Garden of Childhood Verses

1. Martin E. Marty, *A Cry of Absence: Reflections for the Winter of the Heart* (San Francisco: Harper & Row, 1983), ch. 2.

2. Carl R. Rogers, *On Becoming a Person* (Boston: Houghton Mifflin Co. 1961), 26.

3. Gordon W. Allport struggled with the "general vs. particular" issue throughout his distinguished career as a social psychologist. See his "Personality: A Problem for Science or for Art," in *Personality & Social Encounter* (Boston: Beacon Press, 1960), 3–15; and his

"The General and the Unique in Psychological Science," in *The Person in Psychology* (Boston: Beacon Press, 1986), 81–102.

4. Maxim Gorky, *The Autobiography of Maxim Gorky* (New York: Collier Books, 1962), 23–37.

5. Thomas Merton, *The Seven Storey Mountain* (New York: Harcourt, Brace & Co., 1948), 13–16.

6. Dorothy Day, *The Long Loneliness* (New York: Harper & Brothers, 1952), 20–22.

7. Annie Dillard, *An American Childhood* (New York: Harper & Row, 1987), 20–23.

8. Lawrence Ferlinghetti, *Endless Life: Selected Poems* (New York: New Directions, 1981), 97–99.

9. William Stafford, *Stories That Could Be True* (New York: Harper & Row, 1977), 93.

10. William Stafford, *A Glass Face in the Rain* (New York: Harper & Row, 1982), 71.

11. Howard Nemerov, *The Collected Poems* (Chicago: University of Chicago Press, 1977), 230–31.

12. Galway Kinnell, *Mortal Acts, Mortal Words* (Boston: Houghton Mifflin Co., 1980), 57–58.

13. Sharon Olds, *The Gold Cell* (New York: Alfred A. Knopf, 1992), 34–35.

14. Thomas Carper, *Fiddle Lane* (Baltimore: Johns Hopkins University Press, 1991), 18.

15. Stafford, *A Glass Face in the Rain*, 91.

16. Louise Glück, *Ararat* (Hopewell, N.J.: Ecco Press, 1990), 47–49.

17. Stafford, *Stories That Could Be True*, 154.

18. Stafford, *A Glass Face in the Rain*, 106.

19. Galway Kinnell, *The Avenue Bearing the Initial of Christ into the New World* (Boston: Houghton Mifflin Co., 1974), 22.

20. William Stafford, *Passwords* (New York: HarperCollins, 1991), 78.

21. Stafford, *Stories That Could Be True*, 180.

22. William Stafford, *An Oregon Message* (New York: Harper & Row, 1987), 103.

23. Glück, *Ararat*, 36–37.

24. Ibid., 27. See also Alice Miller's essay on the artist, Käthe Kollwitz, whose mother was bereaved of three of her children, her first two and her last. "Käthe Kollwitz: A Mother's Dead Little Angels and Her Daughter's Activist Art," in *The Untouched Key*, trans. Hildegard and Hunter Hannum (New York: Doubleday, 1990), 19–35.

25. Olds, *Gold Cell*, 38–39.

26. Stephen Dunn, *Landscape at the End of the Century* (New York: W. W. Norton & Co., 1991), 33–34.

27. Stafford, *Stories That Could Be True*, 107.

28. Olds, *Gold Cell*, 43.

29. Carper, *Fiddle Lane*, 41.

30. Denise Levertov, *Evening Train* (New York: New Directions, 1992), 59.

31. Olds, *Gold Cell*, 40.

32. e. e. cummings, *Complete Poems, 1904–1962*, ed. George J. Firmage (New York: Liveright Publishing Corp., 1959), 39.

33. Stephen Dunn, *Between Angels* (New York: W. W. Norton & Co., 1989), 99–100.

34. Kinnell, *Mortal Acts, Mortal Words*, 11.

35. Stafford, *Stories That Could Be True*, 156.

36. Stafford, *An Oregon Message*, 108.

37. *The Confessions of Saint Augustine*, trans. R. S. Pine-Coffin (Baltimore: Penguin Books, 1961), 177.

38. Denise Levertov, *Oblique Prayers* (New York: New Directions, 1981), 85.

Chapter 8. The Soul Made Happy

1. Michael Lewis, *Shame: The Exposed Self* (New York: Free Press, 1992), 72–73.

2. Ibid., pp. 68–69. On the "transfer of blame" phenomenon, see also Gershen Kauf-

man, *Shame: The Power of Caring*, rev. ed. (Cambridge, Mass.: Schenkman Books, 1985), 81–85.

3. Ibid., 78.

4. Ibid., 79.

5. See Donald Capps, *The Depleted Self: Sin in a Narcissistic Age* (Minneapolis: Fortress Press, 1993), 12ff.

6. Lewis, *Shame: The Exposed Self*, 92–93.

7. Gershen Kaufman discusses the restoration of interpersonal bridges in "Restoring the Interpersonal Bridge: From Shame to a Self-Affirming Identity," in his *Shame: The Power of Caring*, 119–159.

8. Lewis, *Shame: The Exposed Self*, 76–77.

9. Erik H. Erikson, *Childhood and Society*, 2d rev. ed. (New York: W. W. Norton & Co., 1963), 252.

10. Donald Capps, "Parabolic Events in Augustine's Autobiography," *Theology Today* 40 (1983): 260–72. Quotation on 268.

11. Lewis, *Shame: The Exposed Self*, 128–37.

12. Carl R. Rogers, *On Becoming a Person* (Boston: Houghton Mifflin Co., 1961), 232ff.

13. William James, *The Varieties of Religious Experience* (New York: New American Library, 1958), 157.

14. See Donald Capps, "Sin, Narcissism, and the Changing Face of Conversion," *Journal of Religion and Health* 29 (1990): 233–51.

15. Bruno Bettelheim discusses this essay by Freud in his *Freud and Man's Soul* (New York: Vintage Books, 1984), 73–74.

16. Stafford, *Stories That Could Be True*, 64–65.

17. David Morgan, "Would Jesus Have Sat for a Portrait? The Likeness of Christ in the Popular Reception of Warner Sallman's Art," *Criterion* 33 (1994): 11–17.

18. In self-psychology terms, the internalized image of Jesus is a selfobject; i.e., an object in the external world that is experienced as part of the self and plays a vital role in the maintenance of self-cohesion and empowerment. Heinz Kohut provides an especially illuminating illustration of this phenomenon in *How Does Analysis Cure?*, ed. Arnold Goldberg (Chicago: University of Chicago Press, 1984), 19–20. In *Restoration of the Self*, Kohut asserts that "the psychologically healthy adult continues to need the mirroring of the self by selfobjects . . . and he continues to need targets for his idealization. No implication of immaturity or psychopathology must, therefore, be derived from the fact that another person is used as a selfobject—selfobject relations occur on all developmental levels and in psychological health as well as in psychological illness" (188). This suggests that the image of Jesus as selfobject need not be relinquished as we become mature adults.

19. Stafford, *An Oregon Message* (New York: HarperCollins, 1987), 41.

Index